Text Classics

JOAN LINDSAY was born in Melbourne in 1896, the daughter of a prominent barrister and a musician. She attended Clyde Girls Grammar—then situated in St Kilda East, later relocated to Mount Macedon—which was to inspire the Appleyard College of *Picnic at Hanging Rock*.

Originally trained as a visual artist, she turned to writing after her marriage to Sir Daryl Lindsay in London in 1922. The Lindsays travelled together in Europe and the United States, Daryl with his paints and Joan with her typewriter.

Her first novel, *Through Darkest Pondelayo* (1936), published under the pseudonym Serena Livingston-Stanley, was a parody of the travel books popular at the time. Her second, *Time without Clocks*—a semi-autobiographical account of the early years of her marriage—was published nearly thirty years later, in 1962.

Picnic at Hanging Rock, her most celebrated book, was published in 1967 and adapted into a feature film by Peter Weir in 1975. She wrote more books, essays and short stories, as well as several unpublished plays, novels and memoirs.

Sir Daryl died in 1976. Joan returned to the visual arts later in life, painting several works and supporting the local art community. She lived at their country home, Mulberry Hill, on the Mornington Peninsula, Victoria, until her death in December 1984.

PHILLIP ADAMS AO is a writer, broadcaster, filmmaker and farmer. He is a member of the Media Hall of Fame, and his writings have been appearing in local and international media for sixty-six years. Author of more than twenty books, he has received two Orders of Australia and was named by the National Trust as one of Australia's 100 Living National Treasures. He has presented ABC Radio National's *Late Night Live* for thirty years.

ALSO BY JOAN LINDSAY

Through Darkest Pondelayo
Facts Soft and Hard
Picnic at Hanging Rock
Syd Sixpence

Time without Clocks
Joan Lindsay

Text Publishing Melbourne Australia

textpublishing.com.au

The Text Publishing Company
Swann House
22 William Street
Melbourne Victoria 3000
Australia

First published in Australia by Cheshire Publishing Pty Ltd, 1962

This edition published in Australia and New Zealand by The Text Publishing Company, 2020

Cover design by Chong W.H.
Page design by Text
Typeset by Midland Typesetters

Printed and bound in Australia by Griffin Press, an accredited ISO/NZS 1401:2004 Environmental Management System printer

Primary print ISBN: 9781922268624 (paperback)
Ebook ISBN: 9781925923247 (ebook)

A catalogue record for this book is available from the National Library of Australia

CONTENTS

A Particularly Persuasive Illusion
by Phillip Adams AO

A NEW edition of *Time without Clocks*, an autobiography first published in 1962? The perfect time for me to recall a friendship with its author.

Barry Humphries unkindly describes my beloved accumulation of antiquities as 'Phillip's collection of broken rubble'. And the notoriously grumpy Sir Daryl Lindsay clearly shared his view—scowling in particular at my Egyptian sarcophagus. (When director of the National Gallery of Victoria he'd entombed Egyptian pieces in the basement.) But Lady Lindsay, darling Joan, was both enchanted and enchanting. They'd arrived at our Melbourne home on St Valentine's Day, and as she all but danced through the broken rubble she said, 'This is my day of days. I met Daryl on St Valentine's Day. We married on St Valentine's Day. And now we're here.'

We'd become friends under improbable circumstances. The ABC had hired young Adams for a long-forgotten program called *The Critics*, and sent me off to criticise a Norman Lindsay exhibition at Melbourne University. Looking at his great tub-thumping nude women I wasn't persuaded that Norman was the lascivious heterosexual of legend. And I expressed the opinion that, if I didn't know better, I'd suspect that the satyr was homosexual.

The next morning I was warned that a Lady Lindsay was on the phone, and prepared for the worst. Instead, a dainty, delicate voice that would become familiar said, 'Daryl and I always thought that.'

In the time before Peter Weir's film of *Picnic at Hanging Rock* (1967) Joan and I became quite close. And with the clues provided by St Valentine's Day I was able to decode much of the mystery of her most celebrated novel. I could detect other influences. Sir Daryl had a painting of a picnic at Hanging Rock hanging on the wall of his office at the NGV. Clearly E. M. Forster's *A Passage to India* had provided inspiration, with its centrepiece a harrowing description of a picnic at a monolith gone terribly wrong—set at the fictitious Marabar Caves. And then, quite by accident, I came upon a book that had become known as *The Ghosts of Versailles*. Two women from an Oxford College, Charlotte Anne Moberly and Eleanor Jourdain, had visited the famous gardens in 1911 and seemed, somehow, to have stepped back in time—and come across Marie Antoinette and her entourage.*

* It turned out that the women who had visited Versailles weren't entirely deluded, just sadly mistaken. Yes, they had encountered Marie Antoinette and her friends—or rather a group of gay men, friends of Oscar Wilde's, who'd dressed up as the ultimate drag queens. They'd do this once a year and drift around the Petit Trianon. I suspect this discovery would amuse Joan enormously. Among her attributes was a charming sense of humour.

I was intrigued by their book, the only account of 'paranormal phenomenon' I couldn't easily dismiss as fraud or delusion. When this confession appeared in a column in the *Age* Joan was on the phone again, very excited. 'That's why I wrote *Picnic*!'

And that's why I'm writing these few words of introduction to the new edition of *Time without Clocks*.

Picnic at Hanging Rock is science fiction in petticoats. The greatest clue? The coachman's watch stopping on the approach to the picnic venue. As Joan told me when I'd visit her home, 'I have no clocks in this house. I do not wear a watch. Clocks, watches, simply stop when I'm around. And, of course, my autobiography is called *Time without Clocks*.'

The girls at Hanging Rock did not disappear from the physical realm. They disappeared in time. To Joan, Miranda and her friends may return from the Rock today or tomorrow. Joan refused to believe in linear time. For her, times past present and future co-exist—a view shared by many a physicist, up to and including the sainted Einstein. (He'd tell people that linear time was an illusion, 'but a particularly persuasive one'.) Thus Joan, the antithesis of the scholar, let alone an academic or conventional intellectual, just happened to agree with some of the finest minds in the counterintuitive world of avant-garde science.

So, yes, it's timely to reprint *Time without Clocks*. For it's Joan's time again. I expect her to simply reappear, as bright as ever, as bubbly as Bollinger.

Time without Clocks

Time—whether you are burning it up by falling in love or spreading it out thin in a dentist's waiting room—is a commodity that cannot be weighed out and measured by clocks. The genius who first thought up a concoction of little cogwheels and pulleys and striking bells for the slicing of our days into twenty-four hours has considerably increased the muddle and confusion of the civilised world.

For most of the years of this book Daryl and I managed very happily without man-made time. Although on New Year's Eve we would hang up in the studio the gift calendar from the local store—a blonde with a sheaf of wattle blossom, a misty eyed spaniel with a hangover—neither the kitchen clock nor the figured squares of the calendar could measure our first golden summers at Mulberry Hill. They were the timeless clockless summers of a dream.

1

TAKE-OFF FROM ST KILDA

My Mother—a lively fact-skipping talker—was continually being pulled up and deflated in full cry by my time-conscious Father: 'Excuse me my dear but surely it was *Thursday* not *Friday* you lunched with Aunt Lizzie?'

My Mother was no more interested in dates than I am: she liked people and things and small exciting happenings: the pie they had for lunch, Aunt Lizzie's piano disgracefully out of tune, Aunt Lizzie herself with her little bead eyes that missed nothing and with more jet beads and bangles winking and tinkling with every barbed Weigallian thrust of her witty tongue. Aunt Lizzie doesn't appear in these pages and I have no idea when she died. But if like my Mother I had been obliged to check up on my Thursdays and Fridays, Junes and Julys, I would never have embarked on a book in which all the characters are—or have been—very much alive: loved, savoured and observed even if they are not all accurately pigeon-holed in Time.

Daryl and I were married in London on St Valentine's Day nineteen hundred and twenty-two—the only date I have ever remembered except 1066 and Waterloo. The reader is unlikely to encounter another. Enough then that at a particular moment in time I found myself in a somewhat dazed condition clutching a bridal bouquet of lily of the valley and driving down Bond Street in a too magnificent car lent for the occasion by a too rich friend. Outside the historic façade of Messrs P. and G. Colnaghi my new husband seized my reluctant arm still glued to the bouquet and sprang out. 'Come on Puss—I just want a few words with Harold Wright.' I had still to learn that the Lindsays rarely go direct to their destination without calling in somewhere else 'on the way'. Even to their own wedding.

Luckily no human creature was to be seen in the hushed velvet and morocco galleries—not even kind Mr Wright of the Print Department. We took a quick turn in the Park and arrived at the Hotel Cecil (immediately afterwards razed to the ground) in time to cut the wedding cake. It was a three-tiered cake rather like the Victoria and Albert Museum with sugar doves trembling on little wires and yellow sugar wattle blossom much admired by our English guests. We took it back with us to Australia nibbling it all the way like two starving rats. As we were steaming through the Sydney Heads I was ashamed to find there was hardly a slice each left for our respective families.

We entered the Harbour early in the morning, the sky pink and gold under a light haze of smoke from breakfast fires on shore. The sea was flat as a slab of blue glass reflecting the red roofed buildings above jade green shadowed coves. This was the Sydney for which I was often homesick on the other side of the world. The hotel where we sat drinking cup after cup of strong Australian tea was already shuttered against the glare of Castlereagh Street. Barred with sticky yellow sunlight the old-fashioned trams went bucketing along like fire engines and on the asphalt sidewalks the high heels of women stuck in the sizzling cracks. In Martin Place I knew there would be flowers—gay little stalls of dazzling garden flowers stiffly bunched in lolly pink paper. While I loaded myself up with phlox and zinnias Daryl bought a paper: the whole issue was filled with yesterday's racing in all States. The soft Sydney air growing ever warmer blew about our ears filling our eyes with dust, our nostrils with the Sydney smell of hot tar, petrol, coffee, and a faint salty whiff from Circular Quay.

We were to lunch with Daryl's three artist brothers: Norman, Percy and Lionel at their favourite Greek restaurant long since changed hands or disappeared. Like most painters the Lindsays all had a nose for the best places to eat and drink. Where was this one? I only remember my footsteps suddenly dragging as we walked up a sunny hill towards Macquarie Street. It was my first meeting with my three new brothers-in-law.

They were all there waiting for us over a glass of sherry, all talking at once and all addressing each other by the family name of 'Joe'. I remember Lionel embracing me warmly in his own delightful manner—a cool hand pressed on either cheek: I could feel my head being tilted backwards my hat slipping sideways. Then smack! the brisk downswooping Lindsay kiss! 'Delighted to meet you, old girl!'

'A dozen oysters to start off with Joe?'

'You know Joe you must admit old Joe here can *paint*. That was a damned good study, old man.'

'I say! Joe was telling me there's a cracking portrait by Tom Roberts kicking about at Gills in Melbourne...'

'A stumer!' puts in Lionel Joe, using a favourite word of his own coining.

'Joe you old bastard! give your poor wife some hock!' Daryl asked: 'Has anyone seen old Henry about lately? We heard in London he was pretty sick.' (A few days later, in Macquarie Street, we *did* see the poet Henry Lawson shuffling along with fever bright eyes in a shabby brown suit. Lionel slipped a coin into the half-opened hand as we passed but no word was spoken.)

The Joes were gregarious to a man and the meal was punctuated by a hundred alarums and excursions as one or other of the Lindsays sprang from the table to greet a friend lift a glass to someone on the other side of the room or examine a drawing pinned to the wall. I remember Lionel leaving his seat to throw both arms round the shoulders of a dignified individual in a tarboosh who willy-willy remained locked in a python embrace for several minutes while Lionel chatted of this and that. Finally he released the embarrassed manager with a hearty slap on the back and resumed his seat. 'That fellow makes the best Turkish coffee in Sydney. Superb!' The talk ranged over a vast international terrain that took in Proust and privvies and always, as a recurring theme song, painting. The brothers drew on a rich and inexhaustible store of shared experience family jokes wisdom and wit. There was much hilarious venom-spitting—the exclusive Lindsay brand of venom which I later came to recognise—laced with the milk of human kindness even as they tore their victims limb from limb. (Bores, public and private, any kind of pomposity in a top hat, the contemporary 'Wowser' in various guises.) Of an unpopular relative Daryl said: 'I've got nothing against the poor bastard but by God I could slit his throat!' Actually not one of the Joes would have willingly hurt a fly. During the oysters I had seen a strong family resemblance. By the time the lobster arrived—an item personally supervised by Percy as the expert—they had become four clear cut individuals alike only in the exuberant vitality that made everyone else in the room look like waxwork dummies. Percy the eldest could be tough when occasion demanded as when he quelled a quarrelsome drunk outside a Melbourne fish shop with a length of barracouta—an excellent substitute for a rubber truncheon. Today however he was gentle fresh-faced and shining as an elderly cherub, attired in spotless white and panama hat and carrying as he often did a string shopping bag. Dear happy-go-lucky Percy for all his casual ways was a very domesticated man and a good cook. Lionel in spite of the warm day was wearing his customary scarf about his neck, tossing it lightly over a shoulder as he talked with the graceful gesture of a matador with a cape. A passionate lover of Spain he might with his expressive eyes gracious manners and beautiful speaking voice easily have passed as a light complexioned Spaniard.

9

Although our table was a focus of attention I noticed that most of the patrons were unashamedly staring at Norman, already acclaimed a genius by the Australian public on account of his powerful cartoons in the Sydney *Bulletin*. While the man in the street gloated on the horned demons mealy-mouthed parsons and misunderstood prostitutes the more aesthetically minded admired the astounding mastery of technique. Norman Lindsay was a distinguished local celebrity—somebody to be pointed out strolling down George Street or lunching at the Hotel Australia with his strikingly handsome wife. I had expected him to be 'tall dark and handsome' something like the figure of Don Juan swaggering through hell in his own etching. One should never build up a mental image beforehand of a celebrity one is just about to meet. Mine of Norman was so wrong that it took several minutes to adjust myself to the reality of the frail-looking man across the table engaged on an impassioned analysis of Nietzsche's philosophy. As he talked a heavy lock of dark brown hair continually fell unnoticed across his forehead. The glass of wine at his elbow stood forgotten. The climate in which the dismal German thrived was far far away from Cytherea. As soon as he stopped talking it struck me as a sad over-sensitive face dominated by the too large nose and extraordinarily luminous eyes. With Nietzsche finally beaten and left for dead and the advent of the gorgonzola, the genius of *The Magic Pudding* and *Saturdee* took over and a wild internal gaiety shot up like a flame. Here was the great comic artist who like Phil May saw the cosmic humour of ordinary things that most people pass by...an amorous rooster in a back-yard...

an old sleepy dog woken by its own fleas...small-town little boys sniggering behind a fence...Prime Ministers, Prima Donnas, cockatoos...

The restaurant was beginning to empty, the waiters clearing away the glasses and shaking out the tablecloths. The four Lindsays were still talking. More wine was called for, more coffee. 'A brandy Joe...Waiter! A black coffee for the lady!' far into the sultry afternoon. All the Joes as they talked used their hands with the expressive gestures of painters who make more than ordinary play with the thumb. The air above our table seemed aflutter with hands as the air above a dovecote is aflutter with wings.

Now in the warm shuttered room the slats of sunlight are creeping across the litter of coffee cups and wine glasses. The tablecloths the menu a handkerchief and every other available surface is scribbled over with pencil notes and sketches. 'Wait a minute Joe...it was like this...and this.' A stub of pencil, a burnt match, a fountain pen, anything will do. The tired waiter who knows these customers of old folds his napkin over his arm opens a newspaper and sits down in a corner. At least they will tip him well when they remember to get up and go home. The wine the laughter most of all the talk—the sense of having suddenly landed on a new planet—has gone to my head. I long to tell these entrancing creatures that I love them all. Words fail me and I can only sit agape in admiring silence. Now and forever I know without any doubt (I was never quite certain at home) that the pen and brush are indeed mightier and ever so much more fun than the sword or even the cricket bat. In this illumined moment a web of tangled schoolgirl values

11

is swept away and I begin to live in the free Lindsay world of ideas and imagination.

All the Joes were happily married. Lionel's wife Jean was doubly related to the Lindsays as her brother Will Dyson the cartoonist had married the artist sister Ruby Lindsay, once described to me by Tonks of the Slade as the most beautiful woman in London. Brave gentle Jean was waging a lifelong battle against chronic asthma and rarely left home. We went out to see Lionel and Jean at Burns Road Wahroonga where they lived screened from the quiet little street by a tangle of tall camellias. The shady white house was filled to overflowing with pictures drawings and prints. Lionel had none of the preciousness of the expert and was amazingly unfussy about his collection which later became one of the most important in the Southern Hemisphere. Original Dürer engravings and Rembrandt etchings hung side by side with Meryons, D. Y. Camerons—perhaps one of his favourite woodcuts—wherever there happened to be room on a wall or lying hidden in portfolios while the crammed bookcases spilled their contents onto the floor and everywhere rare and valuable books stood about in piles on tables and chairs. At Burns Road the making of coffee, supervised by Lionel, was comparable to the tea ceremonies of Japan and how pleasant it was to sit drinking it on Lionel's favourite garden seat by the orange trees at the back of the house where the studio—a straightout craftsman's workshop—stood separate from the main building in a little space of unspoiled bush.

Nearby at Roseville Percy and his Jessie lived in a cottage as neat cheerful and shining as Percy himself and here we spent a night that followed the traditional Lindsay pattern of good food good conversation and good wine. I never met Jessie again but remembered her always for her hospitality to a new and shy relation.

Norman and his wife Rose asked us to stay at Springwood in the Blue Mountains where they lived in a long low wide verandahed house. The grounds sloping away into virgin forest were embellished with large cement or plaster figures of the artist's making—mostly fauns dryads and satyrs. He could do almost anything with his hands and was adept at the complicated craft of building miniature galleons and schooners exact in every detail. Rose who looked after his least personal want even to the buying of a railway ticket on one of his rare trips to the city had achieved a near miracle in remaining a forceful personality in her own right. Most people in close contact with Norman were almost unconsciously sucked into the whirlpool of his dynamic ego. Not so Rose. She was beautiful and kind and to my unsophisticated eye seemed the embodiment of worldly wisdom and the domestic arts. The weather was warm and we often ate out of doors under some spreading apple trees. Norman and Daryl would lie for hours stretched on the grass talking with unflagging zeal as they played absentmindedly with the two baby girls. Behind them on the shady verandah hovered an old-fashioned Nannie of the kind Norman called 'the barren custodians of other people's children'. His conversation was peppered with such aphorisms. Of all the Joes I think Norman had the most uninhibited and sparkling conversational flow—I remember cascades and cataracts of words falling on the sunny air against a background of cries of the children the yapping of terriers the calling of magpies! Restless hands—so like the hands of the famous Dürer engraving—evoking a strange magic of their own so that a listener was spellbound—drugged drained dry or merely exhausted—but never bored. And sometimes when the mantle of his missionary forebear Grandfather Thomas Williams fell upon him he would be filled with a burning desire to inspire reform convert flagellate expose and generally reshape humanity in the Lindsay mould of lusty paganism, denouncing with an almost evangelical fervour the Christian religion as the source of all earthly woes until the mood changed the air lightened and he was the Norman Lindsay of *The Magic Pudding* chasing Mr Goozle round the lawn. Mr Goozle was the pug, the two fox terriers were called Mr and Lady Stidger-Badger (presumably with a hyphen) and the little Australian terrier Wattle-whiskers Bungas. There was plenty of comic relief at Springwood where Norman revelled in the eccentricities of the locals as he had long ago at Creswick. He could imitate to perfection—and no doubt has drawn—Walter the handyman who prefaced every sentence with two ands: 'And and, Mrs Lindsay, shall I bring up some wood?...And and it's a fine day it is it is!'

When Norman went off to shut himself into the studio for a session of serious work Daryl would wander off into the gully at the end of the garden, making drawings and sketches of the lovely white limbed mountain trees. Both Rose and Norman had a genuine affection for Young Daryl and generously pressed us to stay on at Springwood as long as we liked. It was necessary for Daryl to begin earning a

14

living without further delay. Reluctantly we said goodbye to the Joes and set sail for our home state of Victoria.

We arrived at Port Melbourne on a Sunday morning. My Father whom we later learned had shown no marked enthusiasm at the prospect of an artist son-in-law had bicycled down to the wharf to meet us while my Mother fluttered about in her little St Kilda drawing-room. A firm believer in stabilised marriage, the Church of England, Debentures and the Melbourne Club, in small matters my Father had small regard for the conventions. This morning for instance he had arrived at the Pier bolt upright on his old-fashioned push bike across whose handlebars was strapped a long-handled tennis racquet shaped like an egg-spoon. He wore much washed white and grey striped flannel pants and for reasons best known to himself an almost threadbare sports jacket of Harris tweed. His handmade buckskin shoes were dazzlingly white. His tweed cap several sizes too large was pulled hard down over bright blue eyes half hidden by tufts of greying eyebrows. Daryl on the watch for a taxi disgorging an elderly gentleman in dark Sunday clothes as befitted a K.C. and a Judge of the Supreme Court, was delighted when a slightly raffish bicyclist shook him cordially by the hand. As for my Father, who knows what he had been expecting in the way of long hair and flowing cape—perhaps even sandals!—one never knew with these arty chaps—his concept of the art world being based like so many of his generation on du Maurier's *Trilby* a popular novel of his youth. Thank Heaven this tall young man in the grey flannel London suit was no fancy dress Bohemian! With mutual respect and undisguised relief the two men

15

looked each other straight in the eye. Within minutes they were talking about cricket and the ship's run from Sydney.

My English Mother who approved of nearly all young men—especially those who had nice manners and were free of what she called the Australian 'twang'—took one quick feminine look at mine and decided she was going to like him. He began teasing her on the very first day—over her deplorable carving of the Sunday joint. A few Sundays later he was expertly wielding the carving knife himself. Very soon she was showing him her little niggling watercolours which he was too honest to praise. He re-hung the few good pictures in the little yellow drawing-room, admired the ornaments she despised and forcibly removed from its place of honour in the cabinet the Dresden china shoe made of rosebuds. Henceforth the word of 'my artist son-in-law' on all things aesthetic became law. As they came to know each other better and in her distracted loneliness after my Father's death, he helped her over innumerable—often invisible—stiles. I see now that he was a young man possessed of an uncanny insight into the minds and hearts of middle-aged Edwardian ladies whom he often understood much better than they did themselves. For these and many other reasons she loved him dearly until the day of her death.

With about as much practical experience of house hunting as a canary my Mother set out one afternoon to find us a flat. She returned an hour later having paid a week's rent in advance and a handsome deposit on a small flat in St Kilda which she pronounced exactly what we wanted. This was partly because she had only the sketchiest knowledge of housekeeping and partly I now suspect because the crazy two-level apartment was in easy walking distance of my old home in St Kilda. As soon as Daryl and I set eyes on it we realised it was the kind of flat on which most people would have gladly paid a deposit to be rid of forever. Only a newly married couple completely undomesticated and pretty far gone in love would have put up with it after the first week. My Mother was overjoyed at having secured such a prize single handed. We moved in at once and remained there quite happily for nearly a year.

My Mother had failed to observe that about ninety per cent of our living space was taken up by two steep flights of very dark stairs leading to the one room in which we ate slept and worked. We wrote and painted squatting on the uncarpeted floor in a sea of shoes paintboxes drawing boards suitcases rolls of drawing paper and canvas and always at any hour of the day or night, cups of tea. All our shoes had drawing pins embedded in the soles. In those days I was untidy not by conviction or even laziness—I just didn't notice whether a room was tidy or not. When it began to dawn on me that an unemptied teapot on the floor or a vase of dead flowers would stay there for all eternity unless I did something about it I began to mend my ways. Apart from the toasting of crumpets and frying of eggs at students' camps my knowledge of cooking was nil. For our first roast it was Daryl who miraculously knew how to prod the beef to see if it was the required shade of pink while I shamefacedly buried a sodden apple tart under our landlady's rose bush. Apparently we hadn't thought of a cookery book or of a garbage can for the burial of dead pies. Having no domestic yardstick by which to measure my first kitchen—a dark little hole off the bathroom—I cheerfully set about learning to cook in semi-darkness and a strong smell of escaping gas. We had no telephone and if either of us was forced to write a letter we bought a stamp at the sweet shop round the corner. Daryl was working hard and visitors were few. Amongst them was George Bell, already an established painter, just returned from England with his English bride lovely in the style of du Maurier. Another was Freddie, a friend of my student days, a slim eager young man foaming at the mouth with original ideas on every subject under the sun which later sorted themselves out when Frederick Ward became a vital force in Australian industrial design. Now and then we were visited by a thin—very thin—sprinkling of our respective relations including an uncle who made no bones about his disapproval of Norman's etchings and drawings on our walls.

One afternoon at the ever-sinister hour of four o'clock I had a formal call from an old friend of the family Mrs Fanning—an elegant little lady who may well have been the last of her generation in Melbourne to sally forth card-case in hand. Certainly she was the last person I ever saw with an ostrich feather boa wound tightly round the neck. I was alone in the flat and watched with a sinking heart from the upstairs window as two little kid gloved hands searched in a beaded purse for the 'visiting cards' in case I was 'not at home'. There was no cake for tea but I did my best with the Queen Anne silver teapot, suddenly aware of the dark un-carpeted stairs and pile of unwashed dishes beside the kitchen sink. When I innocently thanked Mrs Fanning for taking the trouble to come and see me her eyebrows flew up:

'But my dear child I should never *dream* of *not* calling on your mother's daughter!' The ritual call on a young married woman was a purely social gesture. Although the 'calling' era with its rigid 'At Home' days was virtually over even in conventional Melbourne I did receive another this time from Lady Miller (mother of Studley of the Miller Bequest to our National Gallery). I was terrified of Lady Miller who wore an immense pompadour of snowy hair with the dignity of a crown and straight as a ramrod arrived one day at our gate in a car like a plum coloured hansom cab very high off the ground with a plum coloured chauffeur to match who furtively pushed a sheaf of visiting cards under our door and hurried away. Another Toorak lady who went on paying formal calls until the effort became too great even for people with chauffeurs and coachmen was beautiful statuesque Mrs Payne of 'Leura' who drove about delivering her cards in a spanking varnished brougham. My Mother who hated the whole business got through it somehow in a hansom reluctantly hired for the afternoon. Such were the last flickerings of Edwardian social life in Melbourne, soon to be extinguished for ever.

The second-hand shops in Chapel Street provided an endless source of free entertainment, especially on Friday nights when they remained open till nine o'clock or later if you were on gossiping terms with the proprietor. In those days a second-hand shop had nothing 'arty' about it—even one selling really good antiques was not called a 'gallery'. The Chapel Street shops were for the most part an unashamed straightout jumble of white elephants where glorious hours could be passed hunting for buried treasure amongst rusty stoves discarded radiators tools without handles pots without lids cedar washstands hat racks enormous sideboards iron bedsteads kerosene lamps dinner sets fashioned for geese and sucking pigs—sometimes beautiful; horsehair sofas sea shells ornaments—mostly bad. A few fleas beetles or borers and sometimes an odd bug. These were the bower birds' nests in which a regular prowler with a flair for quality could now and then dig up an object that made the hunt worthwhile. Nearly all our friends in the trade were genuine characters, collecting old stuff and turning it over for hard cash. Some of these astute men and women had a natural good taste in everything they handled, training themselves to become real experts in various fields.

Mr Chant for instance had started his professional career at a country sale when he bid his last seven and sixpence for a small shabby box. When he opened it at home it contained a few odds and ends which he sold for a few shillings and on this meagre capital and a wheelbarrow had built up the basis of his collection. When we first knew him he was conducting his business in a bluestone cottage tucked away behind the A.J.C. jam factory in Prahran. He was a big gentle free-sweating man with the hairy chest of a labourer visible winter and summer but one had only to watch the thick fingers handling a rare piece of glass or pewter to understand the secret of his success.

The Chants' cottage was wedged between the towering brick wall of the factory and the railway embankment, so close that passing trains set the china and glass rattling on the shelves. It was hidden from Chapel Street by an immense hoarding in which a hole had been cut for a little

20

gate opening onto a small secluded yard. But for the reek of boiling jam and tomato sauce and the roar of the railway it might have been a cottage in the country, the long grass sprinkled with self-sown marigolds and two straggling fig trees that bore delicious fruit. On a summer evening the children would come running down the path at the click of the gate and the whole family gave us an exuberant welcome out of all proportion to the few shillings which occasionally changed hands. They were a cheerful united family though money was often tight. When trade slackened and the domestic pot showed signs of going off the boil, Mr Chant would resume his old profession of crumpet making. We once came upon him busy with a professional batch of crumpets but as far as I know his expert knowledge of old pewter silver and glass was entirely self-taught.

There was no shop window at the cottage but everything in it was for sale at a price, even the beds they slept in. The dark and cheerful disorder of the little front room lit by a kerosene lamp would have been a perfect subject for an engraving by Cruikshank who would have revelled in Mr Chant's rounded belly woollen cap and carpet slippers. While the little mother sat nursing the latest baby in a rocking chair the silent bright-eyed children scampered about like mice amongst the mahogany chairs and tables. We arrived one evening when the children had just sat down to tea at a round Victorian table—evidently a new acquisition. When their father whisked off the cloth to show us the grain of the cedar underneath they unconcernedly picked up their mugs and plates and retreated to finish their bread and jam as best they could in the candlelit bedroom. Mrs Chant

21

went on calmly feeding the baby at her breast but her chair was soon up-ended by her husband in search of the price tag underneath, almost before she could pick up the infant and move to another seat. We have this little rocking chair still and no doubt could have bought the baby's cradle and shawl as well. The more valuable pieces of china and glass were stored in the same cedar chest of drawers where Mrs Chant kept her few clothes and more intimate personal effects along with the silver spoons Staffordshire figures pewter mugs and anything else likely to be wanted in a hurry to show a customer. There could have been no secrets and certainly no privacy in the Chant ménage where every drawer was liable to be ransacked under the eagle eye of a fellow dealer, every cupboard turned inside out at a customer's lightest wish. It was a perpetual Mad Hatter's Party in which everybody and everything was forever moving on one with the utmost good humour, exchanging not only places at table but the beds they slept in, the chairs they sat on, hats coats boots mugs plates and spoons. Nothing belonged to anybody and I can still see the little skinny Cruikshank arms and legs of the children emerging from a fantastic variety of garments put on at random each morning from the communal store.

When we first knew them the business was limited to a few dealers and private clients like ourselves. Mr Chant deserved to make a success of it. Finally he did, moving from Prahran to a more sophisticated suburb where he made more money and lost something of the simplicity that had first endeared him to us in Chapel Street.

A rather sinister figure in the antique trade was old Mr Enderby from England. Invariably in a hard black hat, he liked to invite his lady clients upstairs to his tiny bedroom above the shop in lower Malvern Road, where he had some really fine Georgian pieces. Another colourful character in the same district was Naylor Gill who believed himself with some justification the living reincarnation of his hero Napoleon Bonaparte. When I remarked on the resemblance he said: 'Ah! but you should see me in profile— with my teeth in!' Amongst other foibles he had a genuine horror of the owl which he considered a bird of ill omen whose likeness in any form he never allowed in the shop. In the perpetual dusty twilight the rays of the late afternoon sun would fall sometimes on the rainbow glint of a crystal chandelier on dolphins and fishes of Venetian glass on Boule and Sèvres timepieces. Gilded eagles (never owls of course) were flanked by large framed oil paintings of the Victorian bush by the Australian Napoleon's own hand. Of these he was childishly proud. Not far off—sole ruler of a small dark shop crammed with sideboards cupboards tables and chairs in Chapel Street—was Miss Gill, I think a sister. Emerging from behind the barricades of old cedar and mahogany in which she specialised, Miss Gill seemed to her customers disarmingly vague as though her thoughts were still on higher things somewhere in the mysterious back premises of the shop. Actually the rather wild coiffure of greying reddish hair belied an excellent business head beneath. Miss Gill was about as vague and easily fooled as a Wall Street stockbroker.

Not far away a brother of the artist Christine Baker had collected a stock of unusual and interesting stuff at modest prices (including one of the finest Georgian bookcases in

Australia later bought by Sir Keith Murdoch). We soon came to know all these interesting people and spent many rewarding hours in their company, examining the latest special purchases and comparing notes of our own modest 'finds'—often long after closing time when Chapel Street was deserted except for an occasional passerby peering into the shop window lit by a single lamp. At last hunger would drive us back to the flat with a parcel of fish and chips from the Prahran Market and perhaps a Staffordshire dog or a bit of Waterford glass picked up for a few shillings. Once on the 'dummy' of the old cable tram we found ourselves sitting next a little man in a raincoat clutching a parcel of unusual shape. After riding a couple of blocks in silence Daryl leant across me to ask: 'Have you by any chance a Regency mirror in that parcel?' He had. (As Lionel would have said: A stumer of a mirror) and the owner recognising a blood brother opened it up then and there for inspection. It wasn't for sale but provided food for conversation for the rest of the journey.

Daryl was subconsciously memorising and appraising all that he saw—good or bad, fake or genuine antique— gaining knowledge and experience that was later to prove so valuable at the National Gallery. At the moment it was nothing more than fun—like the fish and chips on Friday nights and playing with the Chant children under the fig tree. And so the first year of married life flew by.

2

LOVE AND HARD WORK
IN A COTTAGE

The lease of the St Kilda flat was just running out when we came upon a little old cottage at 16 Bruce Street Toorak. A studio living room opened onto a tangle of stunted fruit trees a flowering pittosporum and uncut grass strewn with little red poppies. There were camellias at the trellised porch and an oak tree sheltered a small sunny kitchen whose stove was actually visible to the naked eye of the cook. A charming little marble mantelpiece in the bedroom had been replaced by a monstrosity of cheap varnished wood and bevelled glass mirrors. On our first night at Number Sixteen we had just gone to bed exhausted with the day's move when up went the light: 'It's no good Puss I can't get to sleep with that damned thing in the room!' and off he went in his pyjamas in search of a hammer and chisel to prise it from the wall.

In the secluded garden shut away from the street by a paling fence light filtered through the dark shining leaves of the pittosporum round which Daryl had soon built a circular seat and laid a circle of paving stones on the grass. Sitting in the garden on a summer evening with the cicadas shrilling in the bushes and possums stealthily swinging from branch to branch overhead we could almost think ourselves in the country.

At the foot of the street lay the unspoiled reaches of the Yarra. Wandering along the riverbank through clumps of wild parsley and ever-stirring river grasses we would sometimes see the alert little figure of our neighbour Professor Chisholm, usually in a long overcoat, hurrying briskly along with a pile of books under his arm. Or perhaps Sir Arthur Streeton—somewhat ungainly but always well turned out—a painter who loved the river as much as we did and lived in a pleasant old house round the corner. Not far from the Streetons our milkman occupied a vine-covered wooden cottage overlooking the river flats where he grazed his cows. Coming home from a late party one morning we found ourselves faced with a three-mile walk and were thankful to be picked up by our friendly young milkman already jogging along on his rounds in a low two-wheeled cart. In my chiffon party dress and high heeled shoes how glad I was to sit dangling my legs over the tailboard amongst the cans to be delivered along with the milk at our own front door!

There were few motor cars to disturb the peace of the back streets—only now and then the distant ping ping of the bell of a cable tram grinding its leisurely way along

Toorak Road. We often travelled on this tram where the friendly trammies would allow us to pay the fare in stamps or 'some other day' if we were out of ready cash. In the Toorak tram we often travelled with Studley Miller making his solitary bachelor way to the city in a heavy dark suit and brown boots, clutching to his bosom a flat black despatch case. Poor Studley hated draughts and as the tram terminus was practically at his mother's gate he was usually able to secure a coveted corner seat which had the added advantage of precluding casual conversation. He was a shy joyless man for all his wealth. Although we knew that he had an academic appreciation of the Old Masters and regularly attended classical concerts, few of his friends were aware of what must surely have been a major preoccupation in his later years—the magnificent bequest to the National Gallery of Victoria.

Certain human beings need a dog or cat about the place, just as my Mother needed a piano even when she had no time to play it. Daryl, I soon discovered, needed at least one horse—not only to ride on when we lived in the country but to lean against in silent communion, to brush down and feed and have its saddle and bridle laboriously polished, its faults and virtues discussed with equally horse-minded friends. In Alma Road even Daryl had been unable to conjure up equine accommodation in a three-roomed flat. We had only been a few weeks at Number Sixteen when he arranged to rent for a few shillings a week a large paddock a few blocks away towards the river and by some mysterious process known only to hard-up devotees of the horse had possessed himself of a handsome thoroughbred

27

hack to graze in it. A good deal of his—the horse's—time was spent cropping the grass on our front lawn where he was almost as frequent—but much more welcome—a visitor as the tabby cat from next door, an uninhibited gate-crasher with a passion for chasing torturing and finally devouring our carefully tamed birds. Nothing could wipe the smug mystic smile off its face not even a powerful jet of water from our garden hose aimed by Daryl between its insolent lime green eyes. Our continuous warfare against the intruder became so marked we were almost afraid to look its owner—a pleasant elderly solicitor—in the face for fear of legal proceedings. One morning he called on Daryl 'for a few words'—ominous phrase! To our relief the cat was not even mentioned as all our neighbour wanted was advice on a family miniature—the first, though we didn't recognise it, of a series of lifelong cries for professional help from laymen in distress such as the elderly clergyman who rang at 7.30 a.m. urgently demanding the value of a watercolour. ('Oh just a scene, with some trees...no, I'm afraid I can't remember the name of the artist.')

Marnie Bassett later to achieve world recognition as the scholarly author of *The Hentys* was newly married and living round the corner in Douglas Street. Both Marnie and I were determined to become efficient cooks and long and deadly earnest were our consultations on scone making and the 'stock pot' recommended to every young housewife by Mrs Beeton and Marnie's capable little Scotch mother Lady Masson. When Marnie actually came out one day with a fruit pie there was almost as much excitement as over the publication of her first book.

My Father enjoyed an occasional change of menu and climate at the cottage so different to his own well-ordered domestic routine at home at St Kilda where breakfast appeared on the stroke of eight and dinner at seven. Meals at Number Sixteen were at no stated times—on a day when both of us were at work in the studio a visitor arriving in obvious expectation of four o'clock tea might easily find us sitting down to a well-earned kipper.

The first time my Father came by formal invitation to dinner at Bruce Street he gazed in simple wonder at our roast lamb as if I had suddenly performed the mango trick at the table. Finally he asked: 'Where did you get it?'

'The butcher of course!'

'I mean—where did you get it *cooked*? The pastry-cook's?' When it was explained that the joint had been roasted by his own daughter in her own gas oven he was deeply impressed. It didn't occur to me at the time that his 'pastrycook' was probably the equivalent in his youth of the delicatessen of today. He was a man of very simple tastes but completely undomesticated and belonged to a period and way of life when the head of the household hardly ever entered his own kitchen. Once a year he would put his head round the kitchen door to wish the cook a Merry Christmas and slip her a sovereign. On her day off he would eat with a slightly martyred air cold meat and sweets left over from the night before or perhaps a little something warmed up by the parlourmaid. Nowadays when anyone can go to the delicatessen round the corner for the makings of a pleasant meal it seems incredible that my Mother who much preferred her Steinway Grand to the kitchen stove would have fasted all day rather than attempt the intricate business of boiling an egg or even making a cup of tea.

Skilled in every domestic art including the making of luscious sausage rolls was Lottie, our first experience of Hired Help. Knowing Daryl's contempt for the commercial variety which is nearly all flabby pastry and hardly any meat she would sometimes bring them to work on Monday mornings still hot from her own oven. A creature of pale sombre beauty, ink black hair and heavy lidded eyes like Parma violets, she looked like an early Italian saint as she stood at our kitchen sink washing our dishes with long sensitive hands. Lottie's religion gave her a matter of fact acceptance of all earthly trials and tribulations as it did of all earthly joys—hers was a red-blooded philosophy that embraced everything with a sort of joyous calm: funerals and weddings newborn babies pigs' trotters with onion sauce a ticket in a lottery a drop of something in her strong milkless tea a flutter on the racecourse with Bert on Saturday afternoons. Lottie was a fountain of entertaining gossip and racy anecdote drawn from an enormous following of relatives, friends and lame dogs of both sexes all apparently in need of her personal help and advice. She was for ever performing acts of superhuman generosity: arranging a wedding party in her own home for a shiftless niece, baking birthday and Christmas cakes for friends bereft of butter and eggs, bailing a difficult brother-in-law out of a tight corner, dressing other people's children's dolls, drawing the innards of a neighbour's Sunday rooster, finding work for a friend in the country. Cheerful and fearless she shouldered other people's burdens as lightly as she did her own which included chronic ill health and an insanely jealous husband, a travelling photographer called Bert. They had been married for fifteen years without producing children. Lottie once told me without a trace of self-pity: 'Just as well, I say! Bert would always be that suspicious they wasn't his!' He was suspicious of every breath she drew and could hardly bear her out of his sight. Most women doomed to a life sentence under the watchful eye of Sultan Bert would have made at least one attempt to walk out on him. As far as I know Lottie never did. Perhaps contrary to popular opinion it was their mutual enjoyment of gambling that kept the home together. Every Saturday afternoon they cheerfully punted a certain percentage of their joint weekly earnings at the Races—the Trots—the Dogs. The photographer's job took him all over the countryside during the working week and whenever he could he insisted on taking Lottie perched beside him on the high seat of his jinker with the photographic gear stowed in the boot. His wife was not enthusiastic about these excursions but she made the best of them and we can be sure the harness on the ginger mare shone like the sun, as did our wood and copper brass and silver and anything that could be polished to shining cleanliness at Number Sixteen. What a sense of calm wellbeing Lottie brought with her on Monday mornings! Walking into the studio in a clean print overall matching her violet eyes with a characteristic little drag of 'Me Leg'.

Lottie belonged to that indomitable company of frail women who prolong their earthly span by sheer force of character and spiritual strength through years of continuous ill health, mentioned only in the most offhand manner:

31

'Me Ulcer…Me Kidneys…Me Leg…' The pallor of the fine boned face was probably caused by chronic overwork, those delicious shadows under the violet eyes by kidney trouble. In the end of course she *did* die of one of her numerous physical ills, leaving poor Bert with no further cause for jealousy as a solitary lift attendant in the city.

We were getting caught up and involved with too many people: I don't mean hardworking friends like George Bell and Bill Dyson, or Doctor Clive Stephen whose vast practice in Prahran kept him busy with medical and human problems twenty-four hours a day. There is a sort of freemasonry amongst the working fraternity that makes it worth while sitting up all night to finish an article or a drawing. I am thinking of the time-devouring bores the telephone-chatterers the casual acquaintance who only wanted 'a peep at your husband's studio' and stayed peeping and gossiping for a precious hour. These were the people who all unconsciously produced the headaches bilious attacks crossings out and minor frustrations that were making it almost impossible for Daryl to get down to the serious business of painting. Few people will call uninvited on a business man during professional working hours but the artist is considered fair game for people who have nothing better to do on a week-day afternoon. How astonished some of these innocently exasperating visitors would have been to have heard themselves described by Norman Lindsay as 'Social Vampires! Blood Suckers! Leeches who think nothing of robbing a creative artist of his most precious possession—his time'. Poor Norman suffered from these social leeches in the heyday of Springwood where his Irish charm and natural good manners made it impossible for him to be rude to anyone on his own doormat and no doubt many an unfinished drawing was thereby ruined.

Few young artists can afford to live on their earnings from 'straight' art. The studio at the cottage was often inches deep in the surgical drawings that Daryl was making for Dr (later Sir Hugh) Devine. It was rewarding work in which he found real interest and even pleasure. Hughie was a hard worker himself, an enthusiast who inspired hard work and enthusiasm in other people. Sometimes he would turn up straight from a special operation that he wanted drawn up as a working diagram, bringing with him photographs, medical books and sometimes weird-looking surgical gadgets invented by himself, many of which were adopted in America and elsewhere. It was the artist's job to translate these operations into lineal terms easily understood by Devine's students and fellow surgeons. Sometimes he would be hastily summoned to stand by in the theatre while Devine was performing a major abdominal operation with a new surgical technique when every detail had to be observed and noted with unfailing accuracy. Because of haemorrhages and other practical disadvantages the camera is of little use in the making of exact surgical records. The writhing Blake-like colons and intestines, the bladders and stomachs in watercolour, boldly splashed for greater clarity in blues and pinks and decisively outlined in black, were often works of art in their own field. Some years later the Lindsay drawings, greatly magnified, were thrown on the screen at the famous Mayo Clinic in America where Devine was a guest lecturer and were afterwards reproduced in his book on abdominal surgery.

An unexpected windfall was a commission from a Melbourne newspaper to cover Melba's Farewell Gala Performance of *La Bohème*. Her Majesty's Theatre gay with flags greenery and souvenir programmes was packed from floor to ceiling. An audience tense with the pent-up emotion of years of Melba-worship released at the final curtain an orgy of foot stamping tears bravas cooees kisses streamers and the jungle drumming of moist kid-gloved hands. It was a night of madness and magic and as the curtain came down for the last time none of us would have been much surprised if the Diva had topped off a superb performance by sailing off the stage on a golden cloud. Back at Number Sixteen we cooked bacon and eggs and sat up all night writing and drawing in a frantic effort to produce our copy on time for the evening splash on the front page. Never was a handsome pay cheque more welcome or more excitingly come by! However such heady interludes were rare and the main source of our bread and butter was so called 'commercial art'.

Art—particularly the commercial variety—was at a low ebb, not only in Australia but all over the world. In Melbourne aesthetic standards depended mainly on the personal taste of the business man in charge of the job. It was shockingly paid and if the artist's gum trees cigarette cartons and silk stockinged blondes failed to please he was given the sack. For Daryl struggling with life-like teapots for Mr Thompson of Robur Tea, commercial art was a pot-boiling necessity and in the Bourke Street Advertising Studio in the Sun Buildings which he was then sharing with his old friend Cyril Dillon all was grist to the Dillon-Lindsay mill. Actually old Mr Thompson rather fancied himself as a patron of the arts and his taste ran towards letters made of forget-me-nots and giant neatly steaming teacups. He was a kindly man who treated his artists generously according to the standards of the day, and there was great rejoicing when Cyril who knew exactly how to handle the all-powerful Thompson nailed down a long-range contract for a series of large (full colour) posters advertising his famous brew. The key figure of the young Ceylon teaplanter in tropical suit and sun helmet who decorated the Melbourne hoardings for so many years was actually a self-portrait by Daryl, laboriously executed in full regalia, twisting and turning in front of the studio mirror.

Now and again in an emergency I helped them out as a model. Calling in at Bourke Street one morning I was asked to 'take off your hat lie down on the floor and try and look as if a lot of rabbits are running all over you!' I was getting used to such requests and obediently lay down on the dusty boards in a conscientious attempt to impersonate a heroic female figure of Australia being overrun by the rabbit pest. This of course was long before the days of myxomatosis. We all thought the man who had ordered the drawing for propaganda purposes was a lunatic: probably he was simply ahead of his time. The money for this job was good and I later posed again for the same client, this time being overrun by rats. When the rats—or rabbits—had been superimposed by the artist on my prostrate form the result was truly blood curdling and when the snappy pamphlet finally came into circulation I was not sorry that my face was as unrecognisable as the handsome young tea-planter's.

35

I was also roped in as a model for Eliza of *Uncle Tom's Cabin* being chased by bloodhounds over the ice.

Daryl was earning a regular weekly cheque doing illustrations for a boys' magazine long since defunct. I wonder how many people still remember *Pals* with its dashing black and white drawings of death and disaster, many of them signed D. L.? In times of crisis I was sometimes a stand-in for a *Pals* boy in a specially difficult attitude—gripping a branch over a precipice or riding a bolting horse, when I would hang onto a chair so that the artist could check up on the anatomical angles of arms and legs. We used to get a lot of fun out of these drawings. How I wish I could see one of them now! They were regarded by the artist as a job to be done as rapidly as possible with no nonsense of wasting time reading the accompanying text once he had grasped the main idea of the plot and the age group of the schoolboy hero. He must have made hundreds of these innocent drawings of boys riding bicycles boys shooting tigers boys playing cricket and football boys leaping from railway trains and motor cars, being tossed by bulls, falling out of aeroplanes—invariably in half-mast trousers and striped cricketing caps. One day we had a frantic ring from the Editorial Office: Captain So and So, hero of the current *Pals* serial, had been drawn this week without his beard! The magazine was just going to press as a messenger arrived in the studio where the artist hurriedly applied the Captain's flowing inky beard according to last week's formula and the situation was saved.

Daryl was finding it almost impossible to get together enough watercolours for a small show even when he could snatch a few days out of town. A favourite painting ground

36

was Sunbury a few miles out of Melbourne with its yellow hills wide skies old bluestone houses and barns and its deep brown creeks laced with little foaming falls. George Bell was fond of Sunbury too and sometimes miraculously provided transport for three as well as all our luggage and painting gear on an old-fashioned motor bike and side car. On this we went merrily bumping over the trackless paddocks armed with a billy can and sandwiches to turn up ravenous for high tea at Gus Ford's Ball Court Hotel where we woke in the morning to the gobbling of turkeys in the clean yard off the kitchen the smell of frying and wood smoke from the one-fire stove where Mrs Ford was cooking a sumptuous country breakfast for the half dozen regular boarders. We became so friendly with the Fords that we were put in sole charge of the hotel one Saturday night when they attended a local ball leaving detailed instructions as to who could be safely served with an after-hours beer. And once, at Easter, I helped Mrs Ford to peel the potatoes and dish up the enormous goose. Daryl always hated leaving Sunbury to go back to town where the drawing board groaned under arrears of routine commercial work.

Before taking leave of Number Sixteen let me remember some of the people who were givers, not takers, of time; whose presence enlarged the horizon, expanded the hour. Friends who left behind them in the empty rooms a sense of exhilaration unaccountable by ordinary standards of tea and talk. Some were neighbours like Sir Baldwin Spencer who often walked round from his house in Tintern Avenue. Some were birds of passage alighting for a brief exchange on our doorstep. One hour or twenty-four! How little it matters now when the clock no longer ticks and only the quality remains, with General Bridges for ever settling down amongst a sea of watercolours on the studio floor... Lionel Lindsay pink faced and pyjamaed still standing at the foot of our bed quoting Flaubert before breakfast against a background of crimson camellias flattened at the window...Melba cross-legged on a low beaded stool... Lilian Borsdorff tall elegant and gay walking up the path on the highest heels out of Paris to taste my first casserole steak. How unbelievably simple it all was! Under the shade of the pittosporum we used to eat and drink talk argue and laugh, bring out the old wind-up gramophone with the first Sophie Tucker records or the box of dominoes. The little paved circle was our club and cost us nothing. Sometimes the horse would be peaceably eating the grass on the front lawn or the two little Morrison boys from round the corner collecting our snails from the daisies at 3d. a hundred, while the cat-monster from next door smirked down at us from the top of the lemon tree safely out of reach of Daryl's hose. There were plenty of lemons but knowing nothing of calories or vitamins we preferred the joyous indulgence of mid-day flagons of creamy chocolate and endless cups of tea and Daryl suddenly calling for the odd sardine—why not? Always sardines under the flowering pittosporum sliding about on saucers on our knees as we sat back in the sagging green and white striped canvas deck chairs.

Hubert Wilkins, even seated in an arm-chair in our little drawing-room, gave me the impression of a bird poised for instant flight. As I remember him he was always on the wing, a mysterious creature just setting out to spend a year or two under an iceberg or to wrestle with some abstruse scientific problem on top of the frozen world. At the studio party in Chelsea where I had first met him he had seemed only half with us in the hot noisy room. The ill-fated ship in which he was to sail next day was waiting in the Thames, his spirit already traversing the icy wastes ahead.

Wilkins and Daryl had savoured each other's company sporadically over the years but the pattern of their lives was so different they had few chances of meeting. When they did their conversation was apt to begin again exactly where it had left off regardless of such births deaths marriages as might have intervened in their personal lives. When the explorer spent an evening with us at Bruce Street—I think en route for the South Pole—their talk was not of people and things but ideas and the adventures of the mind. Wilkins was fascinated by the now scientifically acceptable theory of musical notes having their exact tonal counterpart in the colours of the spectrum (incidentally a favourite subject of Daryl's brother Norman). A thin golden thread of mysticism rather surprisingly wound in and out amongst the explorer's facts and figures and hard-won scientific data. After this night I never saw him again. Charming, elusive, to most people unknowable. Like one of his icebergs seven-eighths below the surface and only a fraction of the whole on view to the world. Wilkins' bravery and powers of physical endurance must have been almost superhuman. Yet there were little humanising cracks and fissures in the ice. What did he look like? I can only remember oddly luminous eyes and a small dark and not entirely successful beard.

General Sir Tom Bridges when we met him in Melbourne was the much publicised hero of Mons who had led his men into battle to the strains of a penny whistle. He was such an essentially modest person we felt he must have hated the penny whistle tag that invariably went with his name when he later became the Governor of South Australia. On a short visit to Melbourne he came to tea with us at the cottage. I wasn't used to entertaining generals and wished I knew more about polo or whatever it was a general was likely to chat about. For me a professional soldier was mentally and physically always in uniform—just as a bishop—not that I had ever met one face to face—was always in gaiters talking about God. I had visions of a teacup balanced on a knife-creased khaki knee.

The very tall broad-shouldered man wasn't of course in khaki but unbelievably handsome in grey flannel. A soldier, obviously! But what gentle non-military eyes! taking in at one swift glance the studio walls hung with the usual mixture of this and that, mainly watercolours and drawings. The next minute he had plunged headlong into the art of watercolour painting—particularly the Norwich School—a subject which lasted us for the rest of the afternoon. No polo. De Wint Cox Cotman: our General knew them all intimately as a painter knows them by individual works. Greta Bridge. Norwich Cathedral. How the devil did he get that dark *behind* that light patch? Soon we were all squatting on the floor with Sir Tom examining prints and drawings with such a discerning eye that we were not surprised to hear later—he didn't tell us himself—that he was a watercolourist of more than 'gifted amateur' status

40

and would have liked to have taken up art professionally. He seemed glad to be off the Vice-Regal chain and as there was no hovering A.D.C. with urgent murmurs of the next engagement I hope he was very late indeed. Picking up a loosely washed-in sketch of Daryl's he asked: 'How long did it take you to do that?' Daryl said: 'After a day of failures I suppose about twenty minutes. A watercolour's not worth a tinker's curse unless it's spontaneous!' The General took this sketch with him when he went back to England.

A good deal of what Melba herself would have called 'damn nonsense' has already been written about that remarkable woman—a complex personality who on paper has so far failed to come to life as a human being for thousands of Australians born too late to have seen and heard her for themselves. It isn't easy of course to draw a convincing posthumous portrait of a person who looked sometimes like a Roman Emperor sometimes a frail feminine Mimi. Actually this dual role calling for masculine horse sense and feminine charm might be said to have run through Melba's whole personality whether on or off stage. It helps I think to explain why she was loved hated and often misunderstood. Melba could swear like a bullock driver, was courteous and truly kind to people she liked, and enjoyed being rude to people she didn't like when she felt they deserved it. She called Royalty by their first names and detested snobs. As a serious artist she had a contempt for popular judgment and popular taste. How few serious artists like Melba have had the courage to say so! Actually it was their aesthetic standards she deplored; the public themselves—the people who stood in queues outside the box office to buy a seat for one of her concerts—she loved.

41

Listening to Melba for the first time was an emotional experience beyond everyday living like getting religion or falling in love. The first pure notes of 'Chanson Hindoue' as she stood looking straight before her with loosely folded hands—she appeared to have no special concert mannerisms—stilled a vast audience to frozen attention as at the call of a far-off magic bird. And as she sang to them 'Home Sweet Home' magnificent in a jewelled tiara, transforming the hackneyed air into a thing of delicate beauty, a genuine love for these her very own people welled up in her heart. A few minutes later Melba down to earth in a fur jacket was driving out to Lilydale where George and Edie a whisky and soda and a log fire were awaiting her at Coombe.

As Nellie Mitchell the young Australian who had battled her way to stardom she had always remembered and loved the little township of Lilydale and it was here within a few miles of her father's limestone quarry that she had built her Australian home. At Coombe she was relaxed, houseproud, fond of her cockatoo and the dogs, enjoyed the good country food and talking to her Italian gardener about the asparagus which she taught us to cut and cook green as they do in Italy. When Daryl and I first knew Dame Nellie she was already an almost legendary figure. In her own lifetime she seemed to have joined the Immortals, as much a part of History as Queen Victoria or the Pope. I have no idea how old she was when she died and it is significant that nobody wanted to know her age when she was alive as long as she went on singing—which she did, very nearly to the end. The glorious voice was no casual gift from Heaven. Its ultimate perfection was developed by will-power self-sacrifice and gruelling years of hard work. When she was no longer young the lines of that desperate struggle for perfection and even for recognition could sometimes be seen in her face. It was a strong clear-cut face dominated by the large luminous eyes—too strong I suppose by feminine standards of beauty. Longstaff in his portrait in the Melbourne Gallery has missed the strength—I can't imagine that Melba in real life was ever starry-eyed. They were eyes that recognised quality wherever they saw it—in hats food jewels antique silver and glass. She knew instinctively when to buy and sell shares whether a business was sound or a human being a humbug and could appreciate a frothy musical comedy far removed from her own line of country so long as it was good theatre.

With personal friends Melba's relations were direct and honest. She was fond of Daryl and without any special knowledge of painting had faith in him as a young man of character likely to make good. Like herself too he was inclined to say exactly what he thought. At Coombe Cottage one night when our hostess was to sing for a local charity after dinner he asked her to excuse him from coming to the concert: 'If you don't mind Dame Nellie I'd rather stay here by the fire and talk to George' (George Armstrong, Melba's son). I saw her throw Daryl a quick incredulous look. Then she burst out laughing and playfully slapped his cheek. 'Do exactly as you like! George, give him some whisky. He's the only person who has ever told me to my face he doesn't want to hear me sing!'

A quickly roused temper was saved by a sense of humour. To the young and shy she was charming. She once asked Daryl to bring a young architect called Cheetham to lunch at Coombe. The poor fellow was so nervous at the thought of meeting Melba face to face in her own home that he insisted on stopping for frequent stabilising nips at the country pubs en route. When they arrived at lunch time Melba who was playing with a cockatoo on the front lawn greeted the white faced Cheetham with: 'How do you do young man—you have a most unfortunate name for one of your profession.' Then quickly sensing his shyness took them inside for a stiff whisky. After this they got on famously. Sometimes she invited us to her box at the opera. As soon as she entered the dim lit alcove through the little door at the rear her personal magnetism was felt all through the theatre and every eye in the house watched the shadowy figure of Melba take her seat. I was thankful for the concealing shadows on the night Daryl tore the seat of his dress trousers on a nail on the staircase. Unable to leave the box during the performance, he finally crept out as the lights were being turned off. Melba thought it was a huge joke. (She couldn't know that replacing his best trousers was a serious financial problem for us.)

Melba was the kind of woman who looks her best in a tiara. She dressed smartly in her own style and her rather heavy figure still had a certain grace. When we last saw her on the stage she moved with the free disciplined ease of a dancer. At Bruce Street I remember her choosing a very low beaded footstool on which she sat like a girl cross-legged in a slim tight skirt: 'Don't get a chair, I always like sitting on stools.'

One afternoon Melba called at Number Sixteen accompanied by a silent young Englishman in suede shoes whose mission in life appeared to be holding her crocodile handbag while she flitted about the studio looking at this and that like an eager child. She was interested in everything. The silent young man was Beverley Nichols who later wrote a life of his benefactor and friend which did little to endear him to Melba's admirers or his own.

Professor Sir Baldwin Spencer's brilliant research work on the Australian Aboriginals had made him a celebrity beyond the scientific confines of the anthropological world. We loved to see him walking briskly down the path to the studio with his curly white hair tossing about his ears and eyes. He was a man of simple tastes and at Bruce Street needed no entertainment apart from being allowed to rummage in the studio like a blue-eyed magpie amongst the sketches and drawings that covered every inch of available space including the floor, picking out a pencil note here, a drawing there, whistling softly to himself at an old sketch by Daryl's sister Ruby, peering into a Will Dyson cartoon, Daryl's latest watercolour by the river, *Pals* boys at a tiger hunt, Hughie Devine's intestines…Next to anthropology art was his great love. He was one of the first Gallery Trustees to be appointed to the Felton Bequest and one of the first informed and serious private collectors of Australian art. When I was a schoolgirl he sometimes took me to the National Gallery before it was opened to the public for the day. With a sense of high adventure I would follow him down the long silent rooms where maybe an attendant in shirt sleeves would be polishing the parquet floor—for the rest we had the place to ourselves. It was the ideal way of looking at pictures. Sir Baldwin knew exactly how much

45

to say or leave unsaid about his favourites to an impressionable schoolgirl. Every word that fell from his lips was silently treasured and ever afterwards remembered. I can hear him now standing before a special landscape bending down so close to the picture that his head nearly touched the frame, a lock of hair falling over one blue eye, a tobacco stained finger tracing the lines of the composition in the air. He was the first person I ever heard using the word 'quality' about a painting in the sense that painters use it. 'Just look at the quality of the shadow in that foreground... whewww...! it takes a great master to put in a foreground. Lots of people can paint the distance.' Many of the things I go to the Gallery to look at today were first revealed to me by Sir Baldwin—the Courbet *Forest*, the Blakes, the early Streeton's, the Phillips Fox. I don't suppose he ever realised what those first intoxicating glimpses of a magic world had meant to me as I stood shyly beside him, inarticulate with a strange and secret joy.

Sir Baldwin had a natural understanding of young people and all his life had many friends of different generations. He grew very fond of Daryl and invited him to accompany him on his last scientific expedition into the Interior—an invitation which Daryl most reluctantly had to refuse. By nature he was reserved even shy and was probably at his best and happiest and most truly at ease far away from civilisation camping out under the stars with his beloved Aboriginals. His direct uncomplicated approach to the blacks made him understood by the Aboriginal mind so that he was able to observe and record from the human as well as the purely scientific angle, being finally accepted as one of themselves by some of the shyest and wildest tribes in the outback. Back in Melbourne he sought the company of artists. George Lambert Billy McInnes Arthur Streeton John Longstaff Norman and Lionel Lindsay were all personal friends. At least two fine portraits were painted of the Professor during his lifetime. Lambert's shows him as I like best to remember him—vitally alive hatless under a boisterous sky the white curls tossing in the wind. Artists liked and respected Sir Baldwin who never made even the informed layman's mistake of valuing his own judgment too highly in matters of art. In the company of professional painters he looked on himself as an amateur and was free of the arrogance of many a self-styled connoisseur. A drawing that suddenly caught his eye hanging on the wall of his own or anyone else's house could so excite him even if he had seen it a thousand times before that I have seen him spring from his chair at a meal, take a sort of tripping run to the focal point and stand there rooted to the spot in rapt inspection. If it came up to expectations as a find or an old favourite suddenly seen with a fresh eye a strange hissing sound as of gas escaping from a pipe would presently emerge from under the ragged moustache. Amongst the art dealers this characteristic hissing or whistle was eagerly awaited as a mark of approval. I once asked Willie Gill of the Fine Arts how a certain exhibition by one of the Lindsay family was going. 'Fine,' said Willie. 'Sir Baldwin's been here whistling all round the room.'

Though never a rich man he bought generously and was often forced to house the latest acquisitions under his bed or pile them on tables and shelves for lack of room.

A good Scottish housewife, Lady Spencer was in despair when more and more and more drawings portfolios of prints and etchings and oil paintings in large gold frames arrived at the already over-filled immaculate house in Tintern Avenue. Australian painters should respect the courage and enthusiasm of Sir Baldwin who bought Australian art and built up a worthwhile local collection at a time when the few Australians who bought pictures preferred usually to buy them in Europe as a souvenir of the Grand Tour. Many Melbourne drawing-rooms are still decorated with luscious Swiss and Italian scenes by Professor This and That...The fact that he didn't invariably back the right artistic horse is of no moment today and Time the only really reliable sifter out and assessor is already singling out some of his purchases as major works. When he died he had done an invaluable service to Australian painting in having raised the whole standard and prestige of Australian art in the public mind.

The Countess of Stradbroke was a sparkler: a beautiful wayward creature who looked her best in diamonds preferably long earrings and a tiara. Everything about her flashed and sparkled even when she was wearing no jewellery at all. When the Hungarian artist De Lazlo painted her portrait he missed the diamond look and made her a soulful wearer of pearls. In spite of numerous sons and daughters as tall as herself she had kept her willowy figure and youthful carriage. Large deep shadowed eyes and a cloud of raven black hair gave her the semi-tragic air of a Duse. In actual fact she adored childish practical jokes and was bored to death with the small formalities of life at Stonnington— a boom-time mansion then serving as Victoria's state

Government House. As the wife of the Governor of Victoria her sense of humour and the low gurgling laugh often heard at the wrong moment must have got her into some tight Vice-Regal corners. A few society diehards in Melbourne thought her too unconventional for the job. By the rank and file of Australians she was accepted as one of ourselves which from an Australian is the subtlest compliment a visitor can be paid. She enjoyed meeting all kinds of people in all walks of life. She was one of the first Vice-Regal ladies to make an uncomfortable camping trip into the outback and in the Territory she was always remembered as a good mixer beautiful and witty.

Although Stonnington was only a few miles away from Bruce Street it was the focal point of quite a different world to ours. Lady Stradbroke knew that with us she could safely let off a certain amount of social steam. Of some of Melbourne's social climbers she told us with the characteristic gurgle: 'Oh yes! the So and So's were asked to a formal dinner, don't you know, but not to *tea*.' (*Tea* at Stonnington meant a cosy chat in her private sitting-room over hot buttered toast.) The gentle easy-going Earl adored his wife. He once came to call for her at Bruce Street in a shabby Ford car. At home in England a man of simple country tastes, in Victoria with due regard for Vice-Regal procedure he sneaked in with a sheepish expression of conscious guilt at our side door. Lord Stradbroke's term of office in Australia was cruelly saddened by the death of Christopher, the youngest son, of a wasting disease which twenty years later could probably have been cured. On the delicate little boy his mother lavished an excess of maternal love sadly lacking in her relationships with the girls. It is common knowledge that beautiful 'sparklers' are not always the best mothers of adolescent daughters. Brought up very strictly in the country and now suddenly exposed to the full blaze of their mother's personality the Stradbroke girls wilted visibly like pale candles before a fire. In Melbourne she failed to dress them adequately for social occasions and was resentful of their dowdy appearance at balls and garden parties. It is not everyone who can look exquisitely regal in last year's tea gown at a dinner party as she could herself. By County standards the Stradbrokes were hard up although the Victorian appointment had helped Lord Stradbroke to effect some economies by closing down Henham Hall—the family seat in Suffolk. Hard up or not the Earl who at home was Master of Hounds and a keen lover of horses managed to race The Night Patrol in Australia—a handsome horse whose portrait Daryl was later commissioned to paint for the Henham collection. A few years later Lady Stradbroke told us in England that she had come into a considerable fortune owing to the unexpected deaths of a long string of distant relatives. By this time one of the girls had married and another was doing social work in the London slums.

An ever welcome friend was Nevin (Jim) Tait of J. C. Williamson fame—a theatrical impresario who enjoyed most of the good things of life for nearly eighty years. When Jim turned up in Melbourne from the other side of the world it was always an excuse for a really good party. Nobody enjoyed a party more. He was naturally gregarious and it was no effort for him to be as kind courteous and gay as he invariably appeared.

One evening he brought to the cottage what appeared to us to be the entire cast of the Italian Grand Opera Theatre then playing in Melbourne. For this unaccustomed feast Mrs Lindsay had sent from Creswick the largest turkey I have ever seen. With loving care she had herself tightly packed the bird's cavernous inside with vine leaves and charcoal to keep it fresh on its long iceless journey by train. In my ignorance I cooked the lot! But as most of our guests were hungry after the show and unable to speak a word of English (including Toti dal Monte the star) we heard no complaints.

Most of our artist friends were good company and like nearly all painters stimulating and often brilliant talkers. Specially remembered at the cottage are George Bell and Arthur Streeton, both neighbours and the watercolourists Blamire Young and Harold Herbert. Harold who adored any kind of a party in his bachelor days was a confirmed goer-out-and-sitter-up-late. Prodigiously talented in his own sphere he could dash off a watercolour in about the same time as it would take Daryl to get his paints out. His paintings sold so readily that he was able to make a good living with the minimum of hard work. He had a studio somewhere off the top of Bourke Street and always took a taxi no matter how short the distance and often left it ticking over on the kerb for hours while he chatted to a friend over a few beers or went about his business inside. Everyone liked Harold for his easy-going gregarious charm and sense of humour. Once seriously ill in a private hospital, he wearied for a little night life and artfully dressing up a pillow with a painted paper face laid it on his bed and retired by way of the window for a few hours' respite from hospital routine. On the day of his funeral a notice went up on the board at his club asking members to have a drink at his expense in memory of an old friend. Daryl's brother-in-law the cartoonist Bill Dyson who had been living in London since before the war was temporarily in Melbourne and living a few doors away. Bill was on a newspaper assignment bitterly regretted owing to the deplorable policy of a handful of editorial sparrows meeting in the board room each Monday morning and plotting the course of Dyson's weekly cartoons. Bill, a near genius high flying as a lone eagle, was unused in London to being told what to draw. He never gave a damn for local politics anyway and was concerned mainly with social and ethical problems in a wide field. A frustrated philosopher of the brush and pen he was miserably unhappy in Melbourne and as soon as his contract expired returned to London where he could express himself as he liked. Of a very different temperament was Louis McCubbin, more or less contentedly manacled to a government contract as a post-war artist for the Australian War Museum. On his release he became the happy and successful Director of the National Gallery of South Australia. Two perfect guests at a small dinner were Sir John Longstaff the portrait painter and Syd Ure Smith, then making art history with his quarterly journal *Art in Australia*.

All these people were men of established reputation in their respective fields and I listened with awe to their casual talk of such sacred subjects as Sydney's coveted Archibald Prize and Melbourne's Felton Bequest. An Archibald prize-winner and Trustee of the Melbourne Gallery Longstaff was painting a portrait of me (in a top-heavy velvet turban) 'for fun', which it certainly was for the sitter. In his big Collins Street studio the artist worked in a series of little tripping runs from the easel and back, sometimes the whole length of the room, talking animatedly the whole time. When I last saw this vigorous sketch a few years ago it was disfigured by a swipe of indigo paint right across the nose, impossible to remove without repainting the whole face. Even so it recalled some delightful hours with our charming old friend. George Bell had meanwhile embarked on a three-quarter portrait of Daryl youthful and blue-eyed in a canary yellow sweater. He never alas! quite completed it because the subject became unruly and refused to sit any longer.

Amongst non-painting friends was Keith Murdoch— still a bachelor—good looking always beautifully turned out and rather shy. Young as he was, Keith was already a power in the newspaper world. A few years later he and his youthful bride were to become our near neighbours at Cruden Farm. Three brothers all remarkable for gracious manners and good looks set off by London tailoring were Clive Jack and 'Prince' Baillieu. Apart from the extraordinary financial flair which runs right through the family the Baillieus have always been attracted to the Arts. The 'Uncles' as they were known in their family circle became our lifelong friends. For Prince all his long life unmarried—warmhearted and perhaps a little lonely—both of us felt the kind of special affection one feels for a favourite uncle. He was a keen racing man and what fun it was when he invited us to drive out with him to Flemington. Immaculate in a grey top hat he made a notable figure in the Members' Reserve. In the little old committee room under the bluestone grand stand shaded in Cup Week by spring green elms we would lunch on cold turkey oysters and champagne. Although he often had a horse running his bets were almost as modest as our half-crowns. Prince truly loved racing rather than gambling and was the first person who ever commissioned Daryl to paint a horse. Always elegant courteous and wholly at ease, if ever a man could truly be called a gentleman it was surely 'Uncle Prince'. The younger brother Jack was a family man, already an informed and perceptive collector of fine furniture for his big house in Toorak, assisted by its architect Desbrowe Annear. Keith Murdoch too was getting bitten with the collecting bug that finally blossomed into connoisseurship and the fine collection at Heathfield. A visitor apt to come drifting down our little front path like a dead leaf, always without warning, was the surgeon Hamilton Russell, old then and incredibly vague but surprisingly on the ball when his interest was roused. He loved the company of painters and musicians particularly if they were young hard up and aspiring. 'Hammie' as he was known to his young friends was strong on the need for a creative artist to make certain material sacrifices for Art's sake. He himself was a curious mixture of puritanical self-discipline and sensuous appreciation of all things beautiful. Rumour was persistent that in his youth Hammie had been crossed in love.

Another visitor was Theodore Fink of the Melbourne *Herald* who looked even more like a teddy bear than the real thing and could talk non-stop for an hour so brilliantly that he was seldom a bore. For all his tough business training he had a genuine love for art and artists. His robust taste was less sophisticated than Dr Felix Meyer's who sometimes dropped in at Number Sixteen and with whom it was always a delight to look at and talk about painting. His wife Mary daughter of Professor Nanson of Melbourne was a gifted painter of rare sensibility. An always welcome guest was our old friend Professor Sir Archibald Strong, then at the Melbourne University, who would talk to us in his charming scholarly way about *Beowulf* and Rimbaud and Marcel Proust—usually in our little pink drawing-room because Archie hated the Australian sun that fell through the pittosporum leaves onto his fine closely cropped head and thick round glasses.

These were some of the people who came and went at Number Sixteen, enriching our young lives and giving life and colour to our cool shabby rooms.

3
GOOD-BYE TO NUMBER SIXTEEN

From the beginning we had been working towards the ultimate goal of a house of our own in the country where Daryl
could settle down to serious painting. We must have been
at Bruce Street nearly three years when thanks to *Pals* boys
and tigers, teapots and teaplanters, rats and rabbits and
the sale of an occasional watercolour, we reached the stage
of scribbling endless wildly impractical plans for dream
houses on the backs of envelopes and writing pads. All of
them were large enough for a family of twelve and ranged
in design from an Italian palazzo (designed by me regardless
of expense) with plenty of marble and a balustraded sun
roof to Leicester McAulay's dashing conception of a giant
log cabin with built-in wooden bunks. Daryl who had lived
for long stretches in England favoured fairly consistently a
Georgian mansion of warm red brick about the size of the

White House with columns and pineapples and of course a handsome set of Georgian stables to match. We had no land to build on and very little money but at least it made us feel that something was going to happen.

When something *did* happen and the house of our dreams suddenly materialised under our eyes—or rather its roof did and one chimney—it happened so quickly we hardly knew it had happened at all, at the exact moment in time and space when the corrugated iron roof of a four-roomed weatherboard cottage at Baxter, Victoria, Australia, caught and held for a moment the last pale light of a winter afternoon. In that moment the lines of our destiny were laid down as surely as the steel tracks of the railway running alongside the country road on which our old friend Jack Mann was taking us for a ride in his buggy and pair. We had just turned off from the post office and store on the Baxter Road and were trotting along past Fulton's farm when Jack leaned across us to point with his whip. 'See the roof of a cottage on the hill opposite? I heard the old couple want to sell out and live in town.'

Behind a clump of pine trees, black against the evening sky, the flash of an iron roof was spotlighted for a moment through a hole of late sunlight in a passing cloud.

Daryl said casually: 'Nice position isn't it Puss? How much do they want for it Jack?'

Jack didn't know or very much care, being more concerned with his own immediate present in getting us back to the railway station on time for the evening train and his ponies to their stable on Mount Eliza. He couldn't know that the ponies had achieved their purpose in carrying us into an unguessed-at future that lay hidden somewhere below that light patch of sky, sealed over by a passing cloud that didn't lift again although we continued to look back over our shoulders for quite a long time...

A few days later we were back on the same road hanging over the gate of a neglected drive. The house itself lay almost hidden behind the tall pines, navy blue in the morning light. The air sparkled, smelling of eucalyptus and the sea. The thinly grassed paddocks were watered by one muddy waterhole in which a little red cow was standing apparently turned to stone at the sight of two strangers from town. From an ugly little wooden state school in a paddock next door came the singsong drone of children's voices floating out of the prison-like windows to mingle with the gurgling of magpies high in the school pines. Suddenly Daryl said: 'Would you mind very much having a school at our front gate?'

I don't remember ever discussing whether or why we wanted to live at Mulberry Hill as it was afterwards called. The thing that did need urgent and agonising discussion was the yet unknown price the owners were asking and how much we could afford to pay. Back at Number Sixteen Daryl began doing hundreds of elaborate little sums. I kept on coming across them on old letters, on the fly leaves of books, on scraps of paper in the W.C. When at last the elusive figures were trapped and written down in a notebook we took the mid-day Saturday train to Baxter. We brought sandwiches and ate them sitting under a gorse hedge opposite the railway station—old Mr Fulton's hedge—in the short sweet-smelling grass. This time the owners were waiting for us, by appointment, and we could see the smoke from the one chimney curling up against the crests of the pines.

As soon as we turned the bend in the unmade drive we saw the enormous mulberry tree spreading its leafless branches over the yard—somehow I had known there would be a mulberry tree—and White Leghorn fowls pecking in the dust under the straggling cherry plums. Like nearly all Australian cottages in the country the back door was the only one in regular use—you could tell by the well-worn track leading across the yard past the wood shed and a Coolgardie safe (a safe made of wet sacking) in which a pair of unskinned rabbits was hanging. At the door was a corrugated iron water tank on four wooden legs and underneath the tap a few tins of geraniums and asparagus fern. A splendid grape vine draped itself along the whole length of the house.

The old couple were sitting one on each side of the stove in the whitewashed kitchen on little wooden chairs. Perched between them on the back of another chair a white cockatoo was bobbing up and down in a kind of early Victorian curtsey in time to a continuous refrain which grew louder and louder as we talked: 'I'm the best old cocky in Baxter! Baxter! Baxter!'

'The bird belongs to my son who works on the railways,' Mrs McCubbin said. 'He's always very excited of a Saturday afternoon because he knows my son comes home for the weekend.'

'Wonderful how a bird can know these things,' said her husband, a small bright-eyed old man who was looking at us very hard with his head on one side, exactly as he would have looked at a pair of fowls in the Frankston Market. Summing us up. (Only this time the fowls were the prospective buyers.)

The day was colourless—a frame for tremendous happenings. Neither cold nor warm, sunny nor grey. Just a day. Perhaps the most significant of our lives. Was this really the way a house was bought and finally lived in forever? Were we buying the Future too, to the sound of the iron fountain hissing on the stove, the big round kitchen clock tick-tocking away on the mantelpiece? It was the sort of family clock I could understand and appreciate—we had one in the dining-room at home—which everyone knew was either fifteen minutes fast or seventeen slow and when it struck three it really meant nine. We asked the McCubbins to remind us when we should leave to catch the train back to Melbourne—so far not much progress had been made from the business angle. We had tea and home-made scones and talked about everything under the sun except the price and terms of sale. We talked about the great age of the mulberry tree, of the way Baxter had looked when the McCubbins had settled there thirty years ago, about the cockatoo-owning son, about their nextdoor neighbour Alec Vince whose unpruned orchard could be seen through the kitchen window.

'A fine fella, Alec,' said the old man, 'and a good neighbour.'

At the word neighbour his wife, a spry little woman rather like one of her own hens, looked up quickly as if he had said too much and rising from the rocking chair suggested we might like to take a look at the rest of the house. Somewhere at the side was a wash-house with an enormous bricked-in copper two wooden troughs almost as high as her armpits a tin bath and an enormous mangle. It was hard to imagine the diminutive Mrs McCubbin operating any one of these articles single handed but her simple pride in her domestic arrangements was sincere and touching. Two small spotless rooms faced onto a narrow passage leading to the closed front door. There was little to distinguish the cottage from a hundred others in the Victorian country but to Mrs McCubbin it was Home. And as the chain rattled off the hook and the seldom used door groaned itself open onto a shimmer of pale grass that stretched away to treetops and a silver band of distant Westernport Bay, I knew that for her this was the day that old people fear and dread—the day of final separation from the living past. This was the view of field and orchard she had lived with for over thirty years—when she dropped the cat out her bedroom window under the stars, when she brought in the little red cow we had seen tethered in the paddock onto the road, when she helped her husband stooping and straightening to gather the apples in front of the house in the short autumn afternoons...The McCubbins were old and somehow suddenly it was terrible to be old with a neat little bun of grey hair and black felt slippers.

I heard Daryl asking: 'How many acres have you here?' And the strangely reluctant answer from the old man 'Twenty-nine. Used to be thirty before the Government went and bought an acre for the schoolhouse down at our gate.'

In the kitchen there fell a long silence broken only by the clock and the curtseying cockatoo. It was nearly time to leave for the train.

'We heard you wanted to sell this property? Is that right?'

The old man threw a quick almost guilty look at his wife: 'That's right...If I can get My Price.' It was the eternal voice of the peasant echoing down the centuries. The old lady said a propos of nothing: 'My married daughter lives in Brunswick.'

'I'm the best old cocky in Baxter,' screamed the cockatoo.

We only just caught the train with Mr McCubbin's price still undisclosed. Both of us felt it was a dark secret locked forever beneath that little black waistcoat and never in his lifetime to be divulged. Finally we made what is called in Real Estate circles a Firm Offer for the cottage and twenty-nine acres of land. It was Firm all right. We couldn't have raised another penny piece...

A few weeks later the contract was signed and Mulberry Hill was ours. The derelict fences and scrubby gums, the swamp tea-tree she-oak and wild cherry the bracken fern the brown water-hole the wildflowers hiding in the thin sand-rooted grass the patches of greenhood orchids, heath, pink and white, and lime green native fuchsia. Ours the narrow creek that gushed ostentatiously with small fussy waterfalls all winter and, we rightly guessed, would run dry on the first hot day in summer. Ours the clouds sailing over Mount Eliza, the gurgle of magpies in the pines, the gentle rasp of dry grass on a summer afternoon, the hot fragrance of over-ripe mulberries on the lawn. There *would* be a lawn some day under the grand old tree and a little walled-in courtyard with camellias...

One thing we wanted badly and were unable to buy—the Best Old Cocky in Baxter. He was so much a part of the whitewashed old kitchen and his one and only sentence, at Baxter a triumphant testament, would be quite wasted on visitors to the Brunswick cottage. However we did succeed in buying the iron fountain on the kitchen stove and the two wooden chairs on which the old couple had been sitting on our first visit.

When we told my Father we had bought a small property at Baxter he said rather acidly: 'I confess I don't see why you young people want to settle in the swamps of Langwarrin.' Langwarrin was the next station to Baxter. He must have passed through it by train and noticed the low-lying tea-tree skirting the line. An admirably discreet father-in-law he never criticised our domestic affairs. Always shy where his own private feelings were concerned, it was probably his way of expressing his disappointment that we were to leave Melbourne so soon.

Daryl was spending hours at his drawing board working out the plans for a simple wooden house to be incorporated with the existing four rooms of the McCubbin cottage. First priorities for the new Mulberry Hill were two items that most people can do without: somewhere to paint and somewhere to stable at least one horse. Tearing off the flimsy McCubbin verandah and knocking out the walls of the narrow passage gave us light and air and a fair sized studio facing out over the orchard. The stables, wooden to match the house, had a roomy loft with a little iron horse from Normandy nailed on the door. (An extra loose box was later built from the packing cases in which our furniture had travelled from England and for years our meadow hay was labelled NOT WANTED ON THE VOYAGE in large black letters.) The kitchen was left in its original whitewashed simplicity with its one big window looking into Vince's orchard next door. A semi-circular porch with slender white columns and long wooden shutters gave character to the front elevation and facing onto a small courtyard at the back was the little green door that everyone used in the end, shadowed by the mulberry tree.

Building a house in the country where there is no gas water or electric light is beset with unforeseen hazards that never appear on paper. We soon discovered that plans and elevations were hardly more than the first step before plunging into the uncharted seas of lighting and heating road making and sewerage fencing and timber cutting pole erecting pipe laying dam blasting and if you have reached that sheep-like stage of social conformity—the telephone. Feeling the need of some professional advice on these and other knotty points we called in our friend Desbrowe Annear, at this time the most expensive and much sought after architect in Melbourne—probably in Australia. There were all sorts of stories of Annear's deliberate eccentricities quips quirks and exuberant flights of architectural fancy, particularly with well-heeled lady clients who usually ended by loving or hating their architect in about equal proportions. An architectural attention-getter he would load his houses with as much ornament as he felt his client could stand. He argued that well off people in Melbourne or the wealthy Western District squatters could afford to live in elaborately decorated houses—few of them had much taste anyway—so why not? At least he was giving them something infinitely better than terracotta griffins on the roof-tree and fancy leadlights with tulips in the drawing-room.

Desbrowe Annear had once been poor himself and now lived in comparative luxury. He had worked hard to attain it. With us he came right down to earth, as we had known he would, to the fact that we had little money to spend on fancy-work at Baxter. After suggesting a few minor altera-tions in Daryl's plans he offered to personally superintend the building. He was already middle-aged when we first knew him. As Annear has long since passed into Australia's architectural history as a vital force in the swingover in public taste after the First World War, it may be of interest to recall him from a purely personal angle. He was what is known as a 'character' and gloried in it, so much so that his personal mannerisms were as consciously elaborated as the Adams mantelpieces he delighted in. A devotee of good living he loved to play host in his studio cottage in South Yarra where he dispensed hospitality in true eighteenth century style. I can see now that he belonged far more to the eighteenth century than his own. He had collected some beautiful table appointments and when a shy artist at one of his dinner parties smashed one of the best Georgian glasses, the host brushed it off with 'My dear fellow—don't give it another thought.' He had trouble with his false teeth and at another party either as an act of bravado or practical convenience took them out and laid them beside his plate rather than spoil his enjoyment of the next course. In spite of chronically ill-fitting dentures unruly half-grey hair florid complexion protruding stomach and sagging often food-stained suits he had a personal charm that transcended such minor discrepancies with an almost royal aplomb. He was so witty so indiscreet and so truly loved beautiful things that only the most strait-laced clients objected to his eccentricities and occasional full-blooded lapses into vulgarity. To his credit he was the same with everyone and like his friend George Lambert he could behave perfectly if he was in the mood. In all things he was rococo, standing for a touch of fantasy in suburbia. When he had finished a job for a female client he would present her with an enormous volume of his favourite cookery book—unless they had already parted in anger. Annear liked getting his own way not only in architectural matters but everything else, and usually did. This in no way detracted from his kindness of heart and he was truly mourned by his friends when he died a few years after the time of which I am writing.

From 'Whelan the Wrecker' we bought slates the colour of over-ripe grapes for our roof, slender balustrades for the balcony porch and somebody's old cedar staircase. These and an exciting variety of odds and ends all found a suitable home at Mulberry Hill. But our frequent calls made it necessary to buy our first car. Annear offered us the use of his own while we were learning to drive and threw in his English chauffeur Muggeridge to give us lessons. A husband and wife taking simultaneous instruction from the same teacher in the same car gives limitless scope for back seat driving by all concerned. Annear's car was a heavily built old-fashioned model whose shining brass and iron grey paint-work suggested a naval launch with Muggeridge in a peaked cap shouting orders at the helm. It had a complicated gear change called double declutching that called for split second perfection of timing. An excellent driver himself and a whale for discipline Muggeridge must have been near despair as we fluked gaily in and out of the gear box in turns, the hideous scrapings and grindings accompanied by streams of mutual criticism and advice.

'Look out there Puss...Didn't you *see* that chap on the bicycle? Muggeridge, should my wife have changed into third on that last hill? Oh by jove, Puss, you nearly got that old lady's umbrella with the mudguard...!'

'Muggeridge, should my husband pass a stationary tram or *not*?...Anyway I'm sure it's my turn...'

How glad poor Muggeridge must have been when the Lindsays finally got their licences—mine by a nerve-racking ordeal that included stalling on the cable tram track in crowded Bourke Street and Daryl, characteristically, in the little old Home Town of Creswick where the dispenser of driving licences turned out to be an old school friend enchanted to be taken for a drive down the long straight country road from the police station. It ended with a hearty handshake and:

'Well Daryl, it's been nice to have a yarn about old times after all that long...by the way, didn't you say something about wanting a driving licence? O.K. just wait there and I'll bring it out for you to sign...'

When Muggeridge drove us down to Baxter with Annear to inspect the job in progress it was the occasion for an eighteenth century al fresco luncheon. The architect, no lover of a snatched sandwich, provided a generous hamper containing a luscious pie a bottle or two of claret fruit coffee and something exotic in the way of cheese. The feast was set out with some formality by the chauffeur on a folding table in the fragrant sawdusty shade of the pines and consumed to the ring of hammers and sawing of wood from the steadily rising house. Now and again the harsh cries as of a rooster in mortal agony would issue from the bewhiskered lips of Jim Haggart the rosy cheeked martinet builder in charge. Old Haggart squawked and spluttered shouted and barked but seldom bit and had got together a splendid team of artisans as honest and capable as he was himself. Amongst them was a wiry ginger-headed youth called Syd arbitrarily rechristened Albert for the duration of the job as there was already a senior carpenter of the same name. We took a great fancy to Syd who was later promoted to the responsible position of caretaker. He slept in the studio and incidentally made some clever and spirited drawings by the light of his kerosene hurricane lamp. Although old Jim enjoyed roaring at the workmen he was gentleness itself with his large woolly dog and a wonderful hand with bees, the only living creatures for whom he would willingly lower his foghorn voice to a gentle murmur. I once watched him wooing an angry swarm into a kerosene tin in our courtyard attired like a bewhiskered surrealist bride in floating veils of mosquito netting and big leather gloves. A devout Methodist he had a rather unexpected taste in embarrassing practical jokes—such as the day when my Mother picking her timid way over some loose planks was terrified by a roaring red-faced Jack-in-the-box popping up over a wall: 'Now then! what do you think you're doing trespassing on my foundations!' My highly nervous Mother nearly lost her balance and sprained her ankle so presumably the joke was a success. ('Nice lady your mother,' said Jim afterwards. 'You can tell her from me, she'll always be welcome if she likes to come and take a look at the job!') A true practical joker is of a race apart.

How why and where Daryl had somehow got hold of a horse and jinker in which one Sunday we drove the thirty miles to Baxter from Toorak, only horse lovers will know. We made an early start with sandwiches and two bottles of cider which rolled out onto the road before we left the suburbs and had to be retrieved by me under the noses of Sunday church goers in Williams Road. The Point Nepean Road skirting the Bay was already crowded with two-way traffic that made manoeuvring the high-spirited horse—no hired and weary nag—a skilled professional job. Daryl was in his element and we bowled along at a good bat my feet firmly pressed down onto the cider until the horse lost a shoe somewhere near Cheltenham with about half way to go. It took nearly two hours tracking down the local blacksmith who was spending Sunday morning in bed but got up and there and then in pyjamas and raincoat followed us to the forge. We arrived at Baxter late in the afternoon and ate our belated lunch under the pine trees with our eyes glued to the miracle of the almost finished house. The tall window with the rounded top—my treasure from Whelan the Wrecker—was in place at last in the studio where it remained for years with the word BAR written in gold letters a foot high. The rounded balcony was neatly railed with its little white banisters—also from Whelan's—which gave it a cheerful faintly nautical air like the Captain's Bridge. The shutters were already hung and to me the house was practically finished ready for us to move in except for the paint. I had forgotten that supremely important item in a country house—the septic tank.

We made our next inspection with Mr Goodman the sanitary expert who had expressed a wish to see the actual site where the tank was to be installed. Mr Goodman was an exotic type with a diamond tiepin and thick black curls. Like all true experts he was a creative artist after his fashion and as we drove along the Nepean Road he became quite lyrical over various sanitary instalments made by him for his firm. Passing a certain convent he waved a beringed hand over his shoulder with a gesture of genuine pride: 'If I may say so, we did a beautiful job for those nuns...'

'I'm sure you did,' I shouted from the back seat. (We were passengers in Mr Goodman's black open Chev.)

'Wonderful women!' he added thoughtfully, though whether his thoughts were of a professional or religious nature I couldn't tell.

'Did your firm do that school over there?' Daryl asked. Mr Goodman looked glum: 'We did. Put in a two seater as a matter of fact—not nearly large enough to do the job—but some people will never listen to expert advice before it's too late.'

As we were nearing Mulberry Hill and had got to know each other better the talk took a more technical turn. 'How many people in your household on an average would you say?' We told him—ourselves possibly a cook occasional guests and an outdoors man. 'Right,' said Mr Goodman. 'Now how many times a day would you and your wife be using the inside lavatory?' It was no use beating about the bush with Mr Goodman and we answered to the best of our ability. Arrived at the actual location of the proposed tank he had become quite starry eyed with the joy of creation and after some serious figuring with a gold pencil came out with one of the most undemocratic statements I have yet to hear in this glorious democracy: 'S Tank A. Size 2 will be large enough for your household. That allows for twice a day for yourselves and once for the staff!'

My Father drove down with us to Baxter to have his first sight of the house in the 'swamps of Langwarrin'. He hated motor cars and would have preferred to have gone almost any distance on his old-fashioned push bike which he still rode to tennis every Sunday. I think he was secretly anxious to see for himself what sort of a job an artist had made of planning and building a house. Unable himself to nail two pieces of wood together he was deeply impressed, walking through the light airy rooms admiring everything and asking no questions. The leg of lamb at Bruce Street was nothing to this—a house, with real plumbing and a staircase brought in pieces from Whelan the Wrecker in the boot of the car. Wonderful! He looked, I fancied, at Daryl with a new respect as a practical man of affairs. With his old tweed cap pulled well down over his blue eyes he lay full length under the apple trees at the studio door munching sandwiches. He sincerely loved the Australian countryside and was amazed at the extent and beauty of our view. Looking out over Fulton's paddocks he said—suddenly a lawyer not a father-in-law: 'I suppose you are aware that those flats opposite have been earmarked some years ago as a racecourse.' He was harking back as elderly people do to his youth when the Baxter Flats had indeed been seriously considered as a suitable site for a new racecourse. This was a happy day for all three. In a few months we would be well settled in and he promised to come down soon for a golfing week-end. It was chilly driving home but he insisted on riding alone in the open seat at the back wrapped in a tartan travelling rug. We teased him and called him the Gypsy Queen. I suppose I remember these foolish trifles so clearly because it was the only time he ever came to Mulberry Hill. Within a few weeks he had died of pneumonia...

Mulberry Hill was at last a liveable reality ready to be occupied as soon as we could cut the last threads that held us in town. Melbourne people about this time were becoming collectors of 'antiques' which included practically any domestic object that had once belonged to somebody's grandmother. We decided to have a small sale of our more citified 'furniture and effects' as they were later described in the auctioneer's catalogue, such as the little French suite covered in pink brocade which by no amount of wishful thinking could be envisaged in a weatherboard house in the bush. We hated parting with some of the things we had so excitedly tracked down in England. A sale can be as unpredictable as a sea voyage—so many cross currents can temper the financial breeze. At an auction in the country we once watched two local viragoes frenziedly outbidding each other in sixpenny bids for a bedroom jug of the commonest kind which as everyone in the crowd including the contestants could see had a large hole in the bottom. Hair flying, faces scarlet, eyes fixed in a maniacal state on the auctioneer, their hoarse cries rent the still air of the summer morning as the prices soared to incredible heights of lunacy and the delighted audience applauded from the shade of the gums. Leonard Joel of a well-known Melbourne firm was a trusted friend and adviser from the old Chapel Street days when we thought a day well spent lunching on stale buns in a marquee and bidding in breathless half crowns for a bit of glass or a brass candlestick. Joel had always looked after our interests with tender care and now agreed to take on the Bruce Street sale which he advised us to hold in its cottage setting, adding a few pieces from his own collection to supplement our rather meagre showing.

We had planned to slip away from the cottage directly after breakfast on the day of the sale and drive direct to Mulberry Hill. However we were hardly out of bed when the house was seething with strangers waving catalogues at each other and men in hard black hats whispering and pointing and making pencil notes. Amongst them were many of our old Chapel Street friends in the trade who had rolled up in force. Feeling as embarrassed as onlookers at our own funeral, we had a hasty cup of tea in the locked kitchen and made a dash for the ancient Buick which had been standing all night in the lane piled high with the 'effects' that had been crowded out of the main furniture van, already on the road—my fur coat—an ankle length garment of which I was sinfully proud—Webster's unabridged *Dictionary* weighing at least twenty pounds, the garden hose a maidenhair fern in a Chinese jar, a broken majolica cupid whose arm I had been meaning to mend for years, a wooden bucket churn for the making of ice-cream, a plaster cast of my mother's hand taken in Naples, a broom a kettle dozens of suitcases and paper parcels. When at last we had fitted ourselves in amongst all these objects, with a meat safe and frying pan lashed together and clashing like cymbals in the boot, the only thing missing was a pet seal and Groucho Marx in the driver's seat.

I come from a family of train catchers clock winders conscientious followers of road maps and railway guides. After a day with the Wallaby Club in the country my Father would give a ball-to-ball description of his itinerary to his admiring family. 'Well I caught the nine forty in nice time by taking a bus to Balaclava Station—picked up Fred Mann at Beaumaris and joined the main party at eleven fifteen just as they were passing the Cheltenham Post Office.'

'Splendid!' put in my Mother: incapable of looking up a timetable herself she had a proper respect for those who could.

'Then, coming home—you remember my dear I left my bicycle at the railway station this morning—I found that by coming straight along Dandenong Road instead of my usual route through the Reserve I cut at least ten minutes off the travelling time...a most satisfactory day!'

It took me a good many years to become accustomed to the Lindsay method of reaching our destination not by the shortest and most practical route as they did at home but by a series of unpredictable leaps and bounds into the outer space of unknown suburbs short cuts detours and stopovers to see

74

a man about a horse an old lady about a piece of tapestry someone else about a chair or a cask of wine. All these people by a happy dispensation of Fate invariably lived 'on the way' to wherever we happened to be going, like the owner of a small vineyard twelve miles out of Geelong or the ex-jockey who knew a lady who knew a gentleman who was considering parting with a perfect hack at Croydon—just nicely up to your weight sir—on the back of an envelope…And so, on the morning of the sale I wasn't unduly surprised to find that we were expected for a farewell coffee at 'Stonnington' 'on the way' to Mulberry Hill. The Stradbroke family gave us a spirited send off. Lady Stradbroke was delighted with our gypsy transport and as we drove very slowly down the drive for fear of dropping anything off before we got safely past the sentry at the Vice-Regal gates, heads were popping out of upstairs windows and suddenly the portico was full of waving handkerchiefs and we were out on the tramlines and heading for the Nepean Road and the little white house waiting for us under the mulberry tree.

The carrier's vans had arrived before us. They were already unloading under the pines and up-ended wooden crates were exuding torrents of objects wrapped in newspaper onto the dusty grass. There is something vaguely obscene about one's intimate household goods exposed to the relentless light of heaven, like Salvador Dali's clocks and pianos forlorn on an ocean beach. A large gold mirror destined for the studio mantelpiece looked incredibly vulgar leaning against a lilac bush while the round cedar table criss-crossed with scratches—in the tree-shaded cottage invisible—lay legless and glittering in the sun. Various unrelated objects—a saddle a carpet sweeper a set of fire-irons—stood about in isolated groups like guests at a party who refuse to mix. On the old-fashioned sofa where my Father used to take his nightly forty winks sat a bust of Carlyle embarrassingly larger than life, his plaster shoulders swathed in a dirty sack and sneering as well he might at the predatory instincts of mankind here exemplified. Had he not himself damnably suffered from ownership of a house in London with its attendant tortures of leaking roofs and crowing cocks? Originally modelled from life by an uncle of my Father, the thin lipped philosopher never really settled down at Mulberry Hill and finally left to take up residence at the Rowden White Library in Melbourne.

As Carlyle knew only too well, human beings are mostly incapable of learning from the experiences of other human beings. Whoever heard of a drunkard profiting from the sight of another with D.T's? Or a gambler renouncing cards because another shoots himself at Monte Carlo? I had yet to learn that personal possession whether of children dogs houses furniture or anything else means personal responsibility much trouble and much joy. At last we had a place of our very own in which to put more and more *things*!—including of course the majolica cupid with the broken wing. It seemed very important in those first years that nothing was lost or broken and when very soon my favourite piece of Waterford glass was smashed in an orgy of dusting I actually cried.

At last the dark cavern mouths of the vans were closing and the rooms no longer rang with echoes. The afternoon sunlight waned and a shadow lay over Mount Eliza.

Now from paintings imprisoned in gold frames and

sheets of glass, from delicate goblets lying shoulder to shoulder in their wooden crates, from Lionel's Chinese jar and Isobel's Worcester plate whose painted roses seemed to live and breathe, invisible filaments were reaching out towards a new area of attachment, trembling in the warm swimming twilight like the faintly stirring antennae of sea anemones in some fifth dimensional sea. This was the end of a long long journey and Mulberry Hill the rock to which they would hereafter cling as they had clung to the walls of temples farmhouse kitchens and prim Georgian side-boards. Some of them would be here at Baxter still clinging long after we ourselves had become part of the elements to which everything returns in the end: copper and brass, Sèvres china and juicy human flesh, even the piano, laboriously manoeuvred through the windows of the sitting-room by two sweating men, whose keyboard started off as an elephant tusk, whose varnished case a forest tree.

In my student days at the National Gallery the walls of the working studios were painted with lifelike bleeding hearts a giant spider casting its shadow on the ceiling snippets of philosophy and adolescent wit. Above the door facing the easels was written in bold red letters ARS LONGA—VITA BREVIS. For months I looked at it every day. When Daryl and I began a new life together at Mulberry Hill I knew as everyone knows that our earthly stay is short but it was not yet a truth engraved on my heart as it is today. Vita brevis...just words written up on a wall. Watch your step. No smoking. Life is short. Life at this moment seemed as infinite as the quiet evening sky and I was filled with a sense of continuity of all beautiful things.

4

A HOUSE ON A HILL

Our windows stood open all night and strange new country scents and sounds drifted into our big white attic room upstairs, beginning with the bedtime gossip and occasional nightmares of starlings and sparrows and followed by the wheezing of possums already drunk and disorderly in preparation for a late party on the tank stand which often lasted till 4 a.m. On a moonlight night the cry of a wakeful magpie, the monotonous two syllable mopoke in our little park and always the distant barking of Fulton's chained dogs. Sometimes a prowling fox yelped from the tall bracken in Vince's tangled orchard and our row of Black Orpington matrons pressed together for warmth in their respectable black dresses and drugged in the deep sleep of godfearing hens, would hear it too, and from the stuffy darkness of the henhouse cry out on a thin high note of fear, aware of danger lurking under the moon. In the morning we woke—in a faintly ridiculous fourposter bed (heaved upstairs by four sweating men) to the skittering of birds in the mulberry tree. Sometimes a bird sillier or more adventurous than the rest flew right into the room and out again and this we knew was lucky in a new house.

The kitchen was still a shambles of empty crates and canisters unsorted china and lidless saucepans. I hadn't learned yet how to cope with Mrs McCubbin's beautifully blacked and polished one-fire stove and was doing the cooking in the studio over an open fire—mainly with a frying pan and a few odd cups and plates. In the studio all was cheerful confusion. A certain number of routine drawings still had to be posted off to town each week and the drawing table had been set up under the window while *Pals* boys and an occasional set of intestines combined with the smell of oil and whitelead Indian ink and turpentine gave it a homely air.

The main furniture had been quite easy to place in the various rooms. It was several years before we had a major reshuffle at Mulberry Hill and then only when we had become tired of an individual piece—the fourposter bed, the grandfather clock with suns and moons and big golden hands on which Russell Grimwade had worked with such patient skill to keep it tick-tocking all night on the landing, and the poor old Bengal tiger burning far too bright one long hot summer on the drawing-room floor. The trouble really began when the last crate and newspaper parcel had been unpacked and little groups of miscellaneous objects stood about on the floor waiting to be 'placed' like refugees at a clearing station. Here was the beaded fender stool, Mrs Chant's rocking chair, lamps, dessert plates ornaments, like a game of chess played on the bare boards: move one piece and the whole pattern changes. To get at the Chelsea shepherdess the Staffordshire dogs have to be lifted and stood up in the fireplace. The set of German goblets then moves up one and we can get a track to the door into the hall where the shepherdess lies beside her shepherd on a meat dish. The largest Windsor chair with spreading arms looks right nowhere: more like a hen taking a dustbath than a chair. The alabaster lamp so elegant in the little drawing-room at Bruce Street is downright vulgar at Mulberry Hill, while the tall gilt mirror of the marble-topped console table scrapes the ceiling of the little country hall with its gilded crest, like an outsize bird of paradise crammed into a neat white cage. The Sèvres and ormolu clock—a charming wedding present from a French nun—that had ceased to function the moment it arrived and ever after, perched on the drawing-room mantelpiece, looking as out of place as a person in fancy dress at a board meeting. Then suddenly one morning all these things fell into place of themselves as they usually do if you can be strong minded enough to leave them to settle down.

The pictures fitted exactly into the positions long ago worked out in Daryl's plans. The Wilson Steer watercolour (a wedding present given us by the artist in London) went up in the drawing-room the first night and stayed there ever after. So did the pastel portrait by Henry Tonks, always referred to by my Mother as 'My Poor Little Daughter'! At Bruce Street we had got so tired of unsolicited criticism of this distinguished drawing that we had ended by taking it off the wall—such bitter hostility can a serious work of art arouse in the lay breast! It used to astonish us— it wouldn't today—when normally well-mannered and reasonably tolerant friends would pounce on the Tonks drawing like terriers onto a rat. Most of them I suppose were only concerned with what they called a 'likeness' and would have secretly preferred a photograph.

As soon as the house was in some kind of order my Mother's Irish cook arrived from St Kilda to lend us a hand for a few months. Plump rosy-cheeked smiling Kate would have delighted the heart of Mrs Beeton with an iron stock pot on the one-fire stove and snow white washing on the lines. No detergent or washing machines—just a good old-fashioned yellow soap and the giant McCubbin copper, wonderful for the boiling of lobsters, heated underneath by household rubbish and stirred by hand with an old broom handle. Primitive of course but for years our sheets smelled of lavender and sunshine. Kate a big strapping girl on strong pink marble legs never complained of anything and even seemed to like working in the country kitchen—no mixmasters milk-masters juice-extractors cream extortion- ists that pass for necessities today. For years we had no gas or electric power. A big kerosene lamp with a tin shade hung on a chain from the wooden ceiling and two smaller lamps with shining tin reflectors stood on either side of the stove for the convenience of the cook. On the mantelpiece stood the copper preserving pan from my old home and the two red and white Staffordshire dogs from Bruce Street who had perched there like homing doves on the very first day. The male dog was a handsome fellow we called Keith Murdoch because of the rather solemn and kindly expression of its big eyes. The smaller female with a locket round her neck was Mrs Davis, a very different character and absurdly like somebody's fussy little aunt of that name.

The kitchen was the core and centre of the house where something was always going on quite apart from the serious business of cooking. The man who came to fix the tank or to see the Boss about the sawbench or the dog tax ended up with tea at the large wooden table. The iron kettle was always on the boil. Coats boots and hats in wet weather were dried out in front of the stove and day-old ducklings preparing to face the world wrapped in flannel in a cardboard shoe-box. Kate taught me the rudiments of jam making. Sometimes I made jam at midnight when everyone was in bed: the lamplight and hot sweet smell of fruit bubbling in the copper pan made a perfect accompaniment to reading or writing at the kitchen table interrupted only by an occasional stir of the wooden spoon.

As well as jam making I was learning a great many other things that it is right and proper to know something about when you live in the country. At Baxter I learned how to lift and store the onion crop so that the onion in the end became my favourite vegetable, just as the hen and the magpie became my favourite birds, simply because I grew to understand something of their habits and way of life. You can probably get fond of anything—cockroaches or watching other people playing cricket—if you get to understand them well enough. At Baxter both of us learned to tell the time as accurately as we found necessary in the country by the angle of shade on the courtyard bricks the light falling on the stable roof the 8.5 train whistling at the crossroads—a sound I would recognise in Heaven. In the country the weather is all important. 'Is it or isn't it going to rain?' has nothing to do with taxis and umbrellas as it has in town. We had a barometer just inside the door at Mulberry Hill, not quite as infallible as that time-tested portent in these parts: a Shooting in the Big Toe. We studied the changes in our own particular patch of sky, the shape and texture of the clouds, the way the prudent ants made endless food-laden processions against a coming deluge, the way the tarantulas appeared spreadeagled on the inside walls of the house. The bees knew better than we did when rain was imminent and stayed at home. We were often wrong in our forecasts but so, more often than not, were the Official Weather Reports. Daryl taught me how to light a fire in the open with one match and how to make billy tea without touching the redhot smoke-blackened lid. He also taught me the joy and value of wine—not as something kept for weddings or some special occasion as it had been in my Father's house but as an adjunct to everyday living. There was a small cellar under the house deep enough to stand up straight in and here we laid down some good but inexpensive Australian wines. Daryl said: 'If times get bad at least we'll have a bottle or two!' Bad times did come, very soon, for the Depression was just ahead and how thankful we were that many a simple dinner of eggs salad and cheese was transformed by a modest pint of claret into a civilised meal.

While Kate and I were setting the house to rights Daryl was making new gates mending the dilapidated fences carting wood planting hedges supervising the excavation of a big new dam without which it would have been impossible to grow flowers and vegetables in our sandy soil. Already he had acquired a couple of dogs, a magpie called 'Grip the Raven' who ate his breakfast with us on the table, trailing honey from his sharp beak, a horse-of-all-work for the jinker and cart and by his usual horse magic a hack for himself to ride. Also, by straightout commercial purchase at the Dandenong Market, a pig. I had always wanted a fowl-yard of my own and as well as a mixed bag of McCubbin left-over cats (non-mousers to a man who only appeared for meals at the kitchen door) we had taken over the few remaining McCubbin hens. With the dejected rooster in charge they had soon petered out on a sadly unbalanced diet of windfall plums, somebody having once told us that fruit whitened the flesh of table poultry. After this disastrous beginning we had bought on sound local advice some pedigree Black Orpingtons, and a setting of Sussex Lights, lovely birds that look like Balkan maidens in festive muslin speckled black and white and brilliant scarlet headdresses, who laid enormous speckled eggs. The penned commercial hen is a miserable egg-producing slave who never knows the joy of laying amongst dusty ivy or on the seat of an old jinker in the cartshed where the eggs can safely accumulate without fear of detection. Our free-moving hens spent half their day strolling and gossiping on the drying green. They were happy as larks and happy hens lay eggs with yolks yellow as buttercups. There were ducks soon, plain and fancy, and exquisitely useless little bantam roosters solely for the pleasure of looking at them—especially Charlie,

84

an aristocrat from Cambodia who enchanted Daryl by waddling around the drying green with the lurching gait of a drunken sailor, continually hitching up long golden feather trousers.

When we showed my Mother Daryl's beautifully drawn plans for the garden she at once offered to lend us Thomas for a few days to help with the practical business of laying down the new lawns. It was a noble gesture as Thomas was the apple of her eye—a lantern-jawed Irishman who looked much more like a daguerreotype of Abraham Lincoln than a gardener until he bared a set of broken yellow teeth in an Irish grin. Thomas had been the custodian of our old-fashioned garden at St Kilda ever since the day he had stepped off the immigrant ship from Liverpool with his wife and young children, boarded a St Kilda tram knocked on our front door and asked for a job. Any sort of job. It was a Saturday afternoon. My Father was at home and in want of a gardener and Thomas sharp-witted and coura-geous had moved in next day. By a combination of Irish cunning and unceasing labours he had somehow contrived to keep the well-established old garden of hardy shrubs lawns and trees in reasonable order for twenty years. My Father was deeply impressed with his expert polishing of boots with old-fashioned blacking and my Mother liked to chat with the new gardener as she snipped away at the dead rose heads enjoying his Irish wit and unexpected taste for classical music. Sweeping the drive under the drawing-room windows to the strains of Bach and Beethoven from her Steinway Grand he would stop, leaning on his broom, to whistle an accompaniment in perfect harmony. The fact that he had never learned to read or write had probably sharpened his eyes and ears. Of an inventive turn of mind, he was expert at salvaging from apparently useless junk a rimless wheel, a piece of rusty iron likely to 'come in handy' such as the old tin bath which I saw him (mounted on a derelict ladies' bike) balancing on his head and one uplifted arm. Later he transformed it into 'a bit of a hoose for the hens'. And once during my Mother's absence in England he had constructed by way of a surprise a sort of nightmare folly of old bottles and broken bricks crowned on top with a jam tin holding a sickly plant—this was too much even for my Mother, for whom Thomas by this time could do no wrong. Actually his talents apart from gardening were considerable and over the years my parents' unconcealed admiration had gone to his head so that when he mounted my sister's long discarded bicycle and pedalled to Baxter from St Kilda he would brook no criticism in the garden or anywhere else.

Having dismounted under our mulberry tree removed his bicycle clips rolled up his shirt sleeves and handed round a bag of peppermints he carried in the pocket of a greasy vest worn winter and summer with an immense silver watch and chain, he got immediately to work on the new lawns. It was obvious even to amateurs like ourselves that Thomas knew even less about laying down a lawn in the Australian country than we did. After all, how should he, born and bred in a back street in Liverpool! The real miracle was that he had managed to bluff his way through life as a professional gardener. There were no fancy preparations of digging and trenching, no careful selection of the most

86

suitable seed for our dry grey sand and limited water supply. Soon pound after pound of Best English Lawn Mixture which would have done very nicely in the mists of Killarney, was pouring out of paper bags thick as caraway seeds on top of a cake. Thomas was in his glory, eyes gleaming long yellow teeth bared, whistling sucking his peppermints and ordering more and yet more seed. The weather was warm and rivulets of sweat stiffened his grey flannel shirt. None of us—least of all the expert—knew or cared if it was the right time of the year to lay down a new lawn. In the course of time a scum of palest green appeared under the mulberry whose thick thirsty roots encouraged by the unaccustomed watering soon humped themselves like the coils of the sea-serpent above the surface of Loch Ness. The two front lawns which we were unable to water at all made a brave attempt for a few weeks every spring—for the rest of the year they looked like two semi-circular mats of the brown tufted matting made by convicts in gaol.

As soon as Thomas, his mission proudly accomplished, had bicycled back to St Kilda, we began on an orgy of planning and planting. My idea of what a flower garden should look like was crazily based on childish memories of an illustrated calendar called Gardens of England sent us every year by an English aunt. All of them had emerald turf and glowing herbaceous borders spiked with ten-foot delphiniums. According to the seedsmen's illustrated catalogues it appeared that most of the flowers I knew were greatly changed—even their names. Thus the humble larkspur (now 'Thompson's Giant Princess') had not only gone up in the social scale but was twice the size, the shy whitey-brown mignonette had a new bottle green boldness, while a flaming orange cartwheel of a dahlia was rather alarmingly said to bloom 'all the year round'. We drove into Frankston in the newly painted black and yellow jinker and came home with so many packets of seeds so many seedlings shrubs in pots and tins tubers and bulbs and, of course, delphiniums, that I feared the beds would hardly hold them all. Everything went in together, camellias and pansies mignonette and sunflowers, sink or swim.

My brother-in-law Lionel was a gardener of long experience and a passionate believer in the virtues of stable manure. At the height of his carnation growing period he was walking with a friend in Wahroonga one day and suddenly stopped in his tracks, transfixed as a horse-drawn cart trundled down the street, and radiant with uplifted arm exclaimed: 'Oh what a glorious sight!...No no old man! Not the acacias. The *manure*! Practically unprocurable in Sydney since the war!' (Like the last bottle of Napoleon brandy, the last quire of Whatman's watercolour paper, the last available pen drawing by Vierge Meryon or Keane. An amiable obsession leading to a jackdaw accumulation in the Lindsay home.)

With Lionel in mind we piled stable manure on top of everything and waited for the seeds to come up and plants to grow. Like most amateurs we made the fatal mistake of accepting anything offered us for the garden by well-meaning friends, such as the two sinister pieces of cactus—grey leather cubes, strongly rooted and already spiked like porcupines which we planted in two prim tubs on either side of the porch in the courtyard. What they really needed of course was a sizeable slice of Mexican desert. When the toughest began thrusting an arm through the upstairs window there was nothing for it but death or transportation for life to the Botany Bay of the Melbourne University.

Cousin Edie (Lady Harrison Moore) was a generous donor of garden stuff. Brought up at Karbarook, the old àBeckett home in Melbourne with its flower and vegetable gardens tennis courts hay field and even a fern gully at the front gate, Edie was all her long life unconcerned with questions of space. When she married room could always be found in her various houses and gardens for one more lilac another dinner service a new set of shelves for Cousin Willie's law books. She had once offered a live goat to a mutual friend with an ailing child, then living in a small flat in Toorak. (When the gift was not unnaturally declined, Cousin Edie was a little hurt and genuinely puzzled. Surely room could have been found, somewhere, for such a minor addition to the household as a goat?) At Arolla, the spacious old house where the Harrison Moores were living when we were married, the deliberately untamed garden was a riot of unpruned fruit trees, their suckers forcing their way through long very green grass scattered with white and blue violets and English snowdrops with tiny green spots. Here for many happy years lived brilliant unpredictable Edie and her brilliant legal and ever logical husband, known in our family circle by the hopelessly inappropriate name of Cousin Willie. Sir William Harrison Moore was a small fine-boned man of commanding presence infinite learning warm kindly wisdom and sardonic wit. The neatly tucked-in little mouth—a sort of legal rosebud—that in precise and measured accents said exactly the right things to fascinate the small relations playing in his garden, uttered at Geneva weighty pronouncements on International Law that were to echo round the world.

On the evening we had been asked to call in at Arolla and collect 'a few plants' which Edie thought we would like for the garden at Mulberry Hill, Daryl was sickening for influenza and as it was raining and bitterly cold we decided to make our excuses and collect the plants next time we were in town. We arrived at dusk to find Edie waiting for us under the dripping creepers on the porch whose little blue and red glass lozenges I had always admired as a child. The pale banded hair and pale oval face gave her the air of a slightly raffish Madonna, supported by an ominous long handled spade. As we had feared the 'plants' were several poplars in full leaf, some at least fifteen feet long as they lay in the wet grass, the mud still clinging to their roots. Before Daryl could open his mouth in protest, Edie, for whom no material obstacle ever had much significance, was already dragging the biggest towards the front gate. 'Nonsense Daryl! You can easily tie them onto the boot of your car. The lilacs are over there. How about a few clumps of white violets?...Will! Where are you? Daryl wants some string.' At this point the dapper little figure of Cousin Willie emerged from the house and at sight of Daryl's flushed and desperate face said briskly, 'My dear Edie, can't you see the man doesn't want plants. He wants a stiff whisky!'

We planted a few of the poplars beside the dam and the lilacs round about the house in the dry sandy soil where thanks surely to Edie's green fingers they lived and flourished to remind us of one of my relations whom I truly loved. Another was Uncle Ted àBeckett who gave us not plants for our new garden but his old sundial which was specially engraved for practical use in the Southern Hemisphere. When it came into our possession however it was a far from accurate time-piece. The plate had worked loose on the pedestal and could be spun round like a roulette wheel. It was exactly the right kind of sundial for Mulberry Hill and we found it strangely satisfying to establish our own points of the compass and our own private time. Our friend and neighbour Russell Grimwade, an expert who called trees affectionately by their Latin names, presented us with fifty young Lambertiana cypresses for a formal hedge to cut off the coir mats from the little bit of natural bush we called the Park, and a lemon scented gum three inches high in a jam tin which he planted with loving care at the end of the path leading to Uncle Ted's sundial. Russell, whose scientific mind demanded accuracy in all things, swooped on the sundial like a hawk when it was first set up at Mulberry Hill. 'Most interesting Daryl! I had no idea this house faced so far south!'

'It probably doesn't,' I said, giving the dial a spin as an infuriated spider ran out from under the VII. Sadly Russell shook his head. It was beyond his comprehension that two otherwise rational beings could thus flippantly flout the laws of time science and geography.

Daryl, who had left me in sole command of the flower garden that first year, was attacking the vegetable patch with the same passionate concentration he brought to frying an egg mending a fence schooling a horse or painting a lily. All these things he understood very well. The growing of vegetables was a black art full of traps and pitfalls. He was in despair when his carrots at first so promising in lacy rows ended up with fur coats and antlers like stags, and his cauliflowers turned to solid wood. And what in Hell were the invisible creatures who hollowed out every ripe tomato overnight and left them hanging like rosy Chinese lanterns amongst the leaves? Our neighbour Alec Vince sometimes wandered across the orchard to lean over the dividing fence and shake his head in sympathy at these disasters though he had plenty of troubles of his own. Alec who could never bring himself to trap or shoot a living creature—including snakes—accepted every cataclysm of Nature, every pest and plague, with an almost godlike resignation, seldom rousing himself to constructive action with spray-pump and hoe. For all the years we knew him his fruit trees were ravaged by something he called 'The Himalaya'. I pictured The Himalaya as a kind of winged rat and was disappointed to learn from Alec a few years before he died that it was almost too small to be seen by the naked eye. Whether it was an animal or a fungus we never discovered.

When we first knew him Alec was a gentle elderly bachelor with thick greying hair fresh pink complexion and baby blue eyes that looked out on the always inexplicable world in simple honest wonder from under thick bushy eyebrows and in all seasons a battered felt hat. As he appeared to exist on a diet of stale bread—he usually walked five miles into Frankston for his stores—strong black tea brewed in a smoky iron pot and his own fruits in season, I suggested he should make himself some plum jam by way of a change, but after a day of stirring and boiling according to instructions it had failed to set and he had thrown it out. When I asked how much sugar he had used his face fell. 'Sugar, Missus? By cripes I do believe I forgot the sugar!' As well expect a scrub wren to make jam! He was as undomesticated as a wild bird and as naturally clean, rising with the sun and tucking his head under his wing as soon as it grew dark. In all weathers he slept in a little unlined room off the stable and packing shed, where a large placid Chinese-looking draught mare—known to her owner and everyone else as The Horse—and a few fowls, were rather more luxuriously housed in clean straw. As far as we knew The Horse had no name of its own any more than the nameless sexless Sphinx. The large brown animal probably had Chinese blood in its veins—perhaps from an ancestor brought to Australia by a Chinese market gardener. The generous arch of its great neck was reminiscent of the stone horses dug up in old Chinese tombs. Nobody had ever seen it with a burden on the concave swoop of its broad back. Alec was devoted to The Horse and only rarely gave it some trifling task. Mostly it just stood in the orchard meditating and waiting for Alec to appear with a bag of chaff, an expensive luxury it never was denied even when times were bad. Sometimes from the orchard Alec's toneless monologue could be heard drifting away amongst the apple trees while The Horse stood still, pretending to listen and obey. Now and then it did some light harrowing when the cries of 'Come on you! Get a move on! Keep outer my potatoes! Woa! Woa!' were soporific as a lullaby to both horse and man, soon leading to forty winks for Alec lying full length in the bracken fern in the old felt hat with a hole in the crown through which a solitary curl of hair waved like a plume, while tiny darting wrens played hide and seek over The Horse's sunken back. For a few weeks in spring it became slightly more active, resentful of the heavy collar and performing miracles of wriggling its huge head through the fence of our vegetable garden where it had once polished off seven of Daryl's young cauliflowers at a blow. Alec was as much distressed as if it had been caught robbing a bank.

By the end of that first summer we had learned the bitter truth known to every gardener but never divulged in the seedsmen's catalogues—Nature is totally unreliable in the matter of seeds. Millions never come up at all. Most of ours that season were eaten by birds cutworms ants crickets and mice. Those that did actually appear above ground and withstood the onslaughts of ravenous spring slugs and snails later keeled over and died under the scorching summer sun. In the end the sole survivors of the herbaceous border were the original McCubbin marguerites. A few hardy shrubs battled on to ultimate health and beauty—the humble laurustinus whose creamy pink-budded trusses Daryl liked to paint in a mixed bunch, the handsome looking-glass bush with its stiff shining foliage too often degraded to the camouflage of suburban railway platforms.

Ye Olde English Garden had sunk without a trace. Now all I wanted was flowers—any sort of flowers that would look as happy with us as they did in Mrs Swanson's garden on Golf Links Road, where asparagus fern and nasturtiums rambled in lovely confusion and daisies wallflowers and geraniums grew as they liked, in and out of the tea-tree scrub at the back of the cottage. Mrs Swanson was a born gardener and the whole Swanson family seemed to know by instinct when to plant and sow, strike a cutting, lift a temperamental shrub. Jim the eldest boy became a distinguished professional grower and authority on Australian flowers and trees, with a clientele all over the world, while Syd (the 'young Albert' of Jim Haggart's building team) had already given up bricklaying to train as a gardener under the Grimwade expert Mr Bully. No name could have been a better fit for the diminutive Cornishman who strutted like a sergeant-major amongst the Grimwade roses at Westerfield, regimenting and sternly disciplining the flowers and humans under his rule. For Bully the prizewinning rose at the Flower Show was the goal.

Soon after the disastrous start of our new garden certain changes were afoot in the gardens of the Grimwade town and country houses. It was arranged with Bully's approval that young Syd should come to us as temporary gardener at Mulberry Hill. The laconic ginger-haired youth was wise beyond his years and soon taught us the basic rules of home gardening. He loved flowers for themselves and understood my wanting mignonette all the year round as other people want roses, and Daryl's scorn of stiffnecked gladioli whose spiritual home is a vase on a hotel mantelpiece. For Daryl the first vegetable garden had become a graveyard of blighted hopes. It seemed that vegetables like flowers had a way of simply disappearing. What had happened to all those hopefully planted Early Wonders Prolific Podders Chalk's Early Jewels and Yorkshire Heroes? With the coming of Syd we were soon in full production. We learned the best way of watering in dry weather and were initiated into a mysterious process known to professional gardeners as Keeping the Vegetables Moving. 'You want to keep those caulies moving or they won't come to no good,' Syd would say screwing up an expert blue eye at a row of young seedlings—motionless, certainly, but apparently in perfect health—and out would come the Dutch hoe, an instrument I had secretly despised as a tool fit only for ladies in gardening gloves. Under the skilled instructions of Syd we scratched away at the soil like a couple of bandicoots. Daryl who had always understood something of farming was planting his vegetables in rotation and trenching and manuring the starved soil with spectacular results. When Syd finally left us to take over the Grimwade garden at Westerfield there were always flowers for me to pick and Daryl to paint. As for vegetables, the Boss had become a skilled grower in his own right. As George Lambert had once told him: 'Daryl painting is so bloody difficult if you can learn to paint you can learn to do anything.'

5

UNDER THE MULBERRY TREE

In the sort of country house that before the war possessed that almost ritual article of furniture a Hall Table as well as a Hall Door and a parlourmaid to open it there was often set out an ink bottle and newly nibbed pen beside a handsome volume, usually of morocco leather, called the Visitors' Book; its ruled pages filled with the neatly-inscribed names and addresses of male and female ghosts. There used to be one of those books at Greystones—a country house where I often stayed as a child. It lay open on the mahogany table in the square dark hall between the bronze figure of the Dancing Faun and a silver vase which Miss Cora always kept filled with roses. In it lay buried innumerable ghostly house parties featuring Professor Tucker Sir Archibald Strong 'Sir Sammy' (Chief justice Griffith) my Mother and the Allardyce girls...Once on a certain hall table in

Victoria's Western District, Daryl and I came unexpectedly across our own names that leaped with a skeleton rattle from the open page of the Visitors' Book. Apparently my young husband and I had arrived at this very house on the seventeenth day of some forgotten month and year and left again on the nineteenth—a visit pinpointed in eternity by our scratching pens. Of it I could recall nothing at all except a vague impression of too much rich food and of somehow being mental misfits in an atmosphere of sapping physical comfort. Fascinated by this macabre volume we began leafing through its neat musty pages. Nearly all the names were unknown to us except for a few people already dead. Some had defied the passage of time between the morocco boards with bold signatures inches high, others in pale spidery scrawls trailed despairingly across the page as if the writers knew themselves doomed to oblivion from the moment they tipped the cook and stepped into the dog cart waiting at the front door to take them to the train.

Although we must have belonged to the period of the Visitors' Book it never occurred to us at Mulberry Hill to enter up the names of our visitors for future reference— even if we had owned a hall table on which to put one. A visitor could never find a spot to lay anything down in our little hall unless he took the desperate step of removing an enormous green glass jar which always stood on the oak chest, in summer filled with foxgloves lilies and canterbury bells, in winter with beetroot leaves, bracken fern, the flowering tops of parsnips. Nowadays I have learnt that the first requirement of a female guest in a strange house is a mirror in the hall. In spite of these and other domestic shortcomings—the Niagara roar from the upstairs lavatory, the nightly orgies of possums on the spareroom roof, the sinister cat called the Wyvern which used to flatten itself like a vampire bat against the spareroom window in the dead of night—we enjoyed a succession of guests at Mulberry Hill. The order and sequence of their comings and goings is no longer important nor the small domestic plannings and contrivings for their comfort—a train to be met at Langwarrin station with Syd and the trap, a bed to be made up for Saturday night, a day-long roaring fire in the sitting-room for the Professor, a pair of ducks to be killed and dressed for the joyous arrival of Mr Rinder or my mother-in-law...the washings and polishings, the special excursion to the cellar for a long-hoarded bottle of Burgundy for Lionel or Basil Burdett, the baking of Hilda's towering sponge cake that necessitated nine fresh eggs. Hilda, the gay little English red-head who succeeded Kate in the kitchen was a creative artist whose inspired cheese soufflé is still remembered.

Some of our best loved visitors stayed only an hour, a day; others for weeks or months returning year after year like the swallows that nested above the columns of the front porch. Short or long, how little it matters now! By some happy flick of Fate their lives were linked with ours at Mulberry Hill for the duration of a spring, a sunset, the sharing of a bottle.

One of the first people to occupy our spare bedroom was Frank Rinder, then acting as London adviser to the wealthy Australian Felton Bequest. Through his far-sighted buying policy the Melbourne Gallery was already on the world map and Rinder was much in the public eye. Best known to Australians as the man who secured for Melbourne the famous Van Eyck Madonna it may be of interest here to recall that trim little figure as it entered our private lives. Sir Baldwin Spencer who remained throughout a staunch supporter of Rinder's much discussed Melbourne purchases had several years previously given me a letter of introduction to Mrs Rinder. She had at once asked me to dinner at St John's Wood explaining that the only other dinner guest would be 'a young Australian painter, Daryl Lindsay'.

In the cosy little three storied house the drawing-room curtains were drawn across the French windows looking into a secluded back garden, lightly powdered with snow. The flames of a coal fire leaped on polished brasses and everywhere the eye fell upon rare and valuable prints—etchings and drawings looking so much at home that the Rinders' house had none of the sterile formality of a museum and one might easily come across a Rembrandt etching in the bathroom, a Blake drawing on the back stairs. Mrs Rinder, as we so often saw her over the years to come, was sitting on a low chair by the fire in a flowing velvet gown, sheltered from the heat by a little needlework screen. She greeted her two Australian guests with a sweet cordiality I shall never forget, as did her husband who came trotting in from some inner sanctum—small, dapper, eyes sparkling behind gold-rimmed spectacles, the smooth pink face of an intelligent baby fresh from a scalding bath. Both the Rinders radiated a quality which really has no other name but old-fashioned 'goodness'. Simply to look at them

100

was to love and trust them on sight. At dinner there were hothouse pears French wines fine old Georgian silver and glass. The talk in which the young Australian painter joined with easy assurance soared far and away beyond my limited understanding of such Bond Street mysteries as 'first and second states' a drypoint 'coming up at Sotheby's next week' the 'provenance' of a certain portrait now at Something or other Castle. ('Perhaps you'd like to take a run down to Dorset and take a look at it with me my dear boy?') Then, too, the holy name of Rembrandt was here tossed lightly into the conversation as if the master were about to hold an exhibition of his own works in Brussels—or was it in Paris? It was all rather confusing and I was even a little shocked. I remember all this so clearly because it was the first time I had ever been conscious of an Old Master as a human being—a person who had once laughed and drunk wine and peeled a pear with a silver knife as we were doing now. After dinner Mr Rinder gave us a jubilant account with much gleeful rubbing of hands and little spurts of bubbling delight of his recent buy for the Felton—the Van Eyck Madonna and Child. Reluctant to let this exquisite small painting out of his hands he had carried it off in a horse-drawn cab—I think to the vaults of the British Museum—for safe keeping, supported as ever by his wife whom he always referred to with old world punctilio as 'Mrs Rinder'. Never shall I forget his description of that momentous drive— it really *was* momentous for our Melbourne Gallery—with the Madonna sitting on Mrs Rinder's lap. Even the memory of it made his colour rise. 'In a cab, my dear Lambie! in a cab! with Mrs Rinder...' How we warmed to him for hating to see the last of this little masterpiece, so soon to shine out like a jewel on the other side of the world! That evening was the first of many meetings with the Rinders who became our lifelong friends. When we married and left for Australia they told us: 'Perhaps some day Frank will come out to Melbourne for the Bequest.' And so, after a few years he did. Which brings me back to Mulberry Hill.

Sad to say this eagerly awaited visit to Australia was anything but unmitigated happiness. It was Frank Rinder's first experience of dealing in the flesh with his Australian Trustees—there were then about sixteen on the National Gallery alone—and when we first saw him in Melbourne the gaiety and enthusiasm so characteristic in London had evaporated. He was like a vintage champagne gone flat, though the sparkle came back when we had him to ourselves in the country peace of Mulberry Hill. If he had imagined that sweet reason would prevail amongst his various critics when they fully understood all that he had to tell of the complications at the London end, he must have been cruelly disillusioned. The endless arguments decisions and counter-decisions were anathema to his own direct and simple approach to Felton problems. This is not the place to enter into the rights and wrongs of the unfortunate Rinder affair. Let us remember the joy with which he would escape now and then from the battle round the Trustees' table to an environment where he knew himself loved and trusted and could wriggle his toes in comfort as he did at home in St John's Wood.

He arrived to stay with us for the first time when we had no help at all in the house—perhaps Hilda was on holiday—while outside, a Pickwickian plum pudding of a boy called Bert reluctantly fed the fowls and swept the courtyard when not otherwise engaged eating boiled sweets out of paper bags. However after the first few minutes in front of the drawing-room fire it was apparent that the domestic set-up was as far removed from our guest's conscious thought as a racecourse is from an angel newly descended from Heaven. When Daryl brought him his early cup of tea next morning, in a dressing gown, he may or may not have observed that this was no parlourmaid who drew back his curtains and raised the blind! I am sure he never knew that his hostess folded his little pyjamas made his bed and filled his hot water bottle as well as acting as cook. Like my Father, to whose generation he must have roughly belonged, Mr Rinder was gloriously unaware of the mechanics of domesticity. From a female point of view this made him an ideal house guest. The gracious comfort of St John's Wood thanks to Mrs Rinder's capable organisation backstage seemed achieved without effort, and meticulous attention to the choice and service of the appropriate wine was probably the extent of the host's participation in household affairs. Although we warned him we were to dine informally that night in the studio I was not really surprised when our guest emerged at eight o'clock in his usual evening clothes. 'But my dear Lambie, this is delightful! delightful!' (Nobody except Mr Rinder has ever called me 'My dear Lambie' and how those words bring back the pleasant timbre of his warm Scottish voice!) As I went in and out of the kitchen and studio preparing the meal he trotted backwards and forwards after me, talking of his beloved William Blake. 'Tiger tiger burning bright, in the forest of the night' he quoted, unaware that either of us was doing anything but having a fascinating tête-à-tête conversation, as indeed we were, 'Could anything be simpler than those words? Genius...!'

'Genius!' I agreed, wondering whether to throw away the burned potatoes and settle for a dinner of boiled eggs or to battle on with new potatoes and peas, with ninety per cent of my mind on that fabulous tiger...At last everything was ready to begin grilling our chops over the wood fire. Daryl went off to the cellar to produce the right bottle and Mr Rinder and I, now well away on the *Paradiso*, crouched together over the glowing logs. At this moment I knew that I was about to be very very sick—there was no time for explanations—and thrusting the griller neatly stacked with six chops into poor Mr Rinder's unresponsive hand, I fled blindly from the room. A few minutes later Daryl returned to the studio to find our guest in dinner jacket and shiny pumps still crouching over the fire, still clutching the griller exactly as he had received it from my hand. The chops were done to a cinder and there was a look of innocent wonderment on the earnest pink face. Why had Lambie suddenly rushed away in the middle of that very interesting conversation? and what, oh what, was the strange implement he was holding? 'What on earth are you doing and what are you trying to cook?' asked Daryl seizing the griller. 'I don't know my dear boy but they *seem* to have the forms of *fish*!' This I feel sure was the first and last appearance of Frank Rinder in the role of cook!

Although he lived largely for art and the vision of the inner eye Mr Rinder was no coldblooded highbrow, and feeling it our duty to show a visitor from England something of the Australian countryside we set out one drizzling afternoon for a short walk through the bush paddocks behind the dam. Here the trees were strange and grey, dry strips of bark crackled underfoot and birds camouflaged by the dun coloured foliage called to each other unseen in the sweet harsh bird language of the Australian bush. Although I agree with Max Beerbohm that coherent conversation is impossible during the act of walking, Mr Rinder and Daryl, striding through the soaked bracken fern and long damp grey green grass, were in no way inhibited by the exercise. In fine conversational fig they talked animatedly of the Scotch painter D. Y. Cameron (Rinder bought a magnificent example for Melbourne), Blake again, his daughter Esther, his friend George Clausen, a rare Rembrandt etching lately seen in Brussels...When I picked one of our bush orchids and showed it to him lying like a little shell in the palm of my hand he looked at it intently like a person suddenly transported from one astral plane to another, before returning to the broken thread of the conversation. We might have been out for a walk in St John's Wood.

We returned to a huge log fire in the sitting-room where he kicked off his shoes—sure sign he was feeling happy and relaxed—and stood there warming his neat little feet. Over tea and hot buttered toast we got to talking of religion by way of the Van Eyck Madonna of which he had a coloured reproduction in his pocket. A chance remark of mine had distressed him I think. He felt I was missing the spiritual implications of the lovely mother and child and characteristically began curling and uncurling and undulating his

105

grey woollen toes (Mr Rinder's feet were as expressive as his hands). 'But my dear Lambie, dear Lambie...surely you can understand...' I was pigheaded, hated compromising with Rinder's clear-cut intelligence and wouldn't retract. 'But dammit my dear dear Lambie...' His voice fades away into the past. It is a long long time since Frank Rinder joined his beloved Blake and the Angels on the Lawn.

We have always preferred our special vintage guests undiluted at Mulberry Hill. You can put the very best ingredients into a Christmas pudding and still produce a sodden failure. Daryl's mother and the painter George Lambert were individually two very special vintage guests. Collectively my mother-in-law and the fashionable portrait painter were about the last two people we would have voluntarily thrown together for a cosy week-end.

Lambert just arrived in Australia after a long absence overseas had expressed a wish to make a drawing of 'the Mother of the Lindsays' whom he had never met, and hearing that Mrs Lindsay was expected for a long arranged holiday at Mulberry Hill: 'What could be nicer,' said George, 'than to draw the old lady in her son's home in the country?' The fact that the old lady had an iron will equal to his own, was not at all anxious to be immortalised by Lambert or anyone else and would need the most tactful persuasion to make her agree to his proposal, simply didn't enter George's head.

At this point of his career the artist was saturated with success, artistic and social, and everything came easily—sometimes too easily—to his hand. His impact on the Australian social scene was spectacular. The tall broad-shouldered graceful figure set off by Bond Street tailoring, the slender hands in yellow washleather gloves, the bold lively blue eyes, the neat fire-gold beard—everything about him was eye-catching, including much of his painting, although as an artist he actually had far more than the surface brilliance for which he was first publicly acclaimed in this country. He was a brilliant draughtsman with pencil or pen: a brilliant colourist. Everything he touched seemed to have a sort of firework brilliance exploding fizzing and somehow spotlighting the drabness of contemporary local art then largely dominated by the far from fizzy practitioners of the Meldrum School. He made women look beautiful and exciting yet recognisably themselves. Rich husbands had their wives painted by Lambert for sums hitherto undreamed of in the annals of Australian portraiture. Not only the paintings and drawings of society women, thoroughbred horses, the artist in a fancy dressing gown and the ringleted children of the rich, but the man himself carried this peculiar quality of excitement. Lambert was the kind of man who made strangers turn round for another look as he came swinging down Collins Street on a fine afternoon, often with a carefully selected lady on his arm—perhaps the Hon. Mrs Pitt Rivers, daughter of Australia's Governor-General Lord Forster, perhaps Miss Gladys Collins immortalised in one of the most accomplished portraits he ever painted—the White Glove. Or perhaps in animated conversation with Sir Baldwin Spencer (one of the first collectors to recognise his quality as a painter) Sir Arthur Streeton or the architect Desbrowe Annear. For women, except those few who disliked him on sight, Lambert had a tantalising attraction—probably because they sensed that for George, even at his most romantic, art was the motive force of his life. He would break any social engagement if he was engaged on an important painting. A superb mimic and story teller possessed of a charming tenor voice—he was liable to break into bursts of grand opera at unexpected moments—a devotee of ballroom dancing and the then fashionable tango, horse-riding, good food and good wine—no wonder Australian hostesses fought like tiger cats to secure this prize guest for their dinner parties! He was spoiled of course; could be arrogant and sometimes unnecessarily rude. To an insignificant little stranger who introduced himself to the artist in Kings Road Chelsea with 'I know you very well by sight Mr Lambert,' he replied: 'And I know *you*—but hitherto I have managed to avoid you.' Now and then he was taken with moody spells when he drank gloomily and to excess, disappearing from the social scene for weeks on end. Partly because of ill health and partly because of the strains and stresses of the creative inner life George Lambert preferred to work out his personal problems alone behind the closed doors of his studio. Something of a larrikin, something of the *grand seigneur*—to the end he was unpredictable. Even in death—a sudden collapse after dismounting from his horse after a morning ride in the country.

And so, when my mother-in-law was asked to sit to George for her portrait her reactions were just as we had feared. Actually it was rather like proposing to the modest and dignified old lady that she should put on her best black dress and perform a tap dance before Royalty. She was well used of course to the temperamental vagaries of her artist sons and daughters, as well she might be—she had produced five professional painters—but it was rarely now that she exerted herself socially or left the old home in Creswick. The many friends who wanted to see her came to talk with her quietly in her own little drawing-room with the long silk curtains where she was completely happy and at ease. George Lambert was a celebrity in Australia— blown from one side of the world to the other on a heady gust of publicity—most of it untrue. Mrs Lindsay was no prude but Lambert as she probably visualised him—the worldly society portrait painter and much hunted lion— was hardly her cup of tea. Janey Lindsay, the daughter of a well-known missionary Thomas Williams and the first white child to be born in Fiji, had none of the intolerance sometimes associated with a missionary background. Like her spirited father she was absolutely fearless of physical danger. A devout member of the Wesleyan Church (and a life-long admirer of Melbourne's Dr Irving Benson) her religion was the invigorating kind that feeds and supports the human spirit and to the end of her long life she never became desiccated in body or mind.

She had married very young and as there was never much money in the country doctor's busy household social pleasures were few and Janey though possessed of a perfect natural dignity remained always a little shy. The mother of ten high powered boys and girls all madly individual— several of them streaked with genius—to say nothing of a charming Irish husband who washed his hands of prac- tical affairs with a courteous 'My dear Janey—I leave it to you,' Dr Lindsay's wife had need of infinite humour infinite understanding. Janey had both. She was probably the most selfless woman I have ever met, without losing one iota of her individuality. When she ticked off the Creswick grocer or admonished an hysterical female about to have a baby they liked her all the better for it. Few situations were beyond her powers of coping. I once saw her on the shore of the Ballarat Lake dealing most effectively with an assault by an angry black swan. The big bird had already taken a peck at the old lady's handbag when he was pulled up by a smart rap on his head from a silk umbrella and a clear cut command of 'Cease sir!' that sent him hurrying shamefacedly back to the reeds.

When I first knew my mother-in-law she was already widowed. A compact little figure still sweetly rounded in the appropriate feminine places; dainty though not in the fussy Dresden china manner. Hers was rather the firm delicate beauty of a furled lily bud or a smooth pink shell. There were few lines on her face and her skin was still almost babyish pink and white although the hair, once golden and long enough for Janey to sit on it out riding, now lay in thick snow-white waves of natural ordered elegance on either side of the fine-drawn parting. The eyes seemed to give out a clear blue light behind gold-rimmed glasses. The strong deceptively soft little hands were exquisitely shaped—seldom idle for eighty years they were never restless on her lap as women's hands are suffered to be restless today. But then Janey was the product of the disciplined strength combined with femininity of the Victorian age. I never heard her complain of anything as it affected herself—of loneliness (she must often have been lonely in her old

110

age) of lack of money or of anything else. In her simple philosophy everything was accepted as God's Will.

On the day I first came upon her sitting in her favourite low chair in the Creswick drawing-room she was wearing a simple black silk dress with a single piece of old-fashioned jewellery at the throat. Probably she had been busy with her favourite tatting and as another new daughter-in-law walked into the house she came towards me arms outstretched in full and loving acceptance of her Daryl's choice.

When Mrs Lindsay finally consented, thanks to the diplomacy of her youngest son, to pose for Lambert as 'the Mother of the Lindsays' she did so with her customary grace and common sense. If dear modest Janey must endure the limelight for the sake of posterity then let it be in the role of matriarch! She was intensely quietly proud of her children.

As my mother-in-law was to spend some time at Baxter and needed a few hours to settle in she arrived first, in a splendid little bonnet, carrying a pot of strawberry jam for me and in her handbag the gold locket and chain which later appeared in the portrait. Now that she had made her decision she was obviously excited about the whole thing; asking us what Lambert was like and how long the sittings were likely to take—both questions impossible to answer. Hilda Reynolds was engaged on a special duck for lunch— it was a Sunday I remember—Daryl had a tray of drinks ready in the drawing-room and we sat down to wait for the artist to arrive. The moment he came into the room—almost blowing in, his step was so light and springy—we knew that things were going to work out all right. It was easy enough of course for George to be gallant and charming to a delightful old lady but within a few seconds of their meeting he must have sensed that this matriarchal old lady was anything but Lavender and Old Lace in spite of the charming piece she wore at her throat, and that the Lambertian charm alone would cut very little ice with 'the Mother of the Lindsays'. With her he was immediately unaffected and natural—George at his very best—and two pairs of bright blue eyes summed each other up in mutual satisfaction. Lambert was so witty courteous and gay, above all so natural, that by the time lunch was served his model had completely relaxed and if she had been armed with a little fan as she sometimes was, she would have been tapping him playfully on the wrist. Lambert told a lot of good stories at lunch all deliriously funny and every one of them fit for the ears of John Wesley himself. Janey even joined us in a glass of light wine and went off to her room in high good humour to fix the lace collar of the drawing. My dear mother-in-law had fallen for George with the simplicity of a child. As for George he was obviously enslaved from the beginning by the sweetness, humour and down to earth common sense that had made the wife of Dr Robert Charles the uncrowned queen of Creswick ever since she first took her seat beside him in the buggy.

Without an undercurrent of mutual understanding between artist and sitter a portrait is doomed to failure unless it is a purely abstract expression. Lambert, a realistic painter who held that a portrait should be a great many things including a recognisable likeness, was always very much aware of the subject's personality. In the masterly drawing of 'the Mother of the Lindsays' he has gone beyond the delicate features and rippling white hair that were an easy bait for the photographers. This is not the wife of a country doctor dressed up for a sitting: it is the Janey I knew and loved looking out on the world with a Buddha-like serenity. By Lambertian standards it was completed in record time, I think two quite short sittings at which both artist and sitter enjoyed themselves enormously. For years it graced the sitting-room at Mulberry Hill and later the drawing-room at Melbourne Mansions as a treasured possession of Mr John Connell of the National Gallery's Connell Collection. Mr Connell was an old friend of the Lindsay family with a respect and affection verging on adoration for the subject of our drawing whom he had first known as a young bride. The Lambert portrait gave him such pleasure in his old age when he was confined to the flat through failing health that we parted with it willingly knowing that he would honour his promise to bequeath it to her youngest son in whose possession it is today.

In the National Gallery of Victoria hangs a small oil painting entitled *The Sitting Room at Mulberry Hill* that brings back to mind two of our earliest visitors: George and Edith Bell. George had not yet joined the ranks of 'contemporary' art in which he was so soon to be an Australian pioneer, while the female figure clamped self-consciously to the moss-roses of the chintz sofa cover had only vaguely heard tell of Cézanne whose European reputation took an astonishing number of years to reach these shores. While George worked diligently at his easel at the window, my eye rested on a round Victorian table, flowers in a curly

Worcester vase, the elegant Sèvres clock on the mantelpiece, the beaded fender stool where Mr Rinder kicked off his shoes, the green silk lampshade on the oil lamp, the window curtains with their elaborate pelmets. A pleasant room easily dated as somewhere in the early thirties, as the painting itself is dated by the style and vision of the painter. In our studio hangs another painting of much the same period—a lifesize three-quarter length portrait of Daryl with large sad blue eyes. No wonder he looks sad! As far as I remember he had fifteen sittings!

George was one of the most adaptable of all our guests, arriving armed with vast quantities of paints and canvas, ready to sleep anywhere and perfectly content to live on anything from garlic sausage to strong black tea. As the Baxter landscape was not entirely to his painting taste his visits were usually stopovers on the way to Flinders Tooradin or Wonthaggi sometimes with Daryl wedged into the side-car of the old red 'Indian' or perhaps in the vintage Bell car, long as a tram, that sucked up petrol like a sponge. Unlike Wilson Steer who would concentrate on what he called his 'pitch' where he was content to huddle in comfort in a doorway or other shelter and make the best of painting what he could see—and what a best it was!—George and Daryl would spend hours striding over the paddocks in search of a suitable subject. Both were fettered in those days by a more or less literal approach to nature and weather was of paramount importance—the north wind that changes colours and forms, the sudden rain that fuzzes over the contours of a hill. The fishing village of Tooradin with its open boats moored on a tidal creek was a favourite sketching ground, loved especially by George who knew everything about boats, including how to build and expertly sail them. With sure knowledge he set down their rhythmic curves and delicate verticals. At Tooradin there was a comfortable old wooden hotel, fishermen to chat with and occasionally a run out into the Bay for fish. After one of these excursions I was presented with ninety freshly caught whiting—uncleaned! (The only time I can remember wishing we had a few more near neighbours.) Tooradin was a fisherman's paradise: its only disadvantage—when the fish were biting so were the giant mosquitoes that bred in its reedy swamps.

Like a good many people who live in town my Mother loved not so much the country as the idea of it. Born in England, her imagination ran to bluebells and lush green woods rather than the harsh realities of our little stretch of grey green bush. Yet in her own way she was sensitive to natural beauty and even painted tight little watercolour sketches of scenes that had taken her fancy. Not long ago I came across one of her five-by-nine inch sketching blocks. Almost all the tiny painstaking drawings were gallant attempts at vast panoramas of mountains plains and the sea. How clearly they recalled our school holidays at Sorrento a week-end at Healesville or Macedon or Bacchus Marsh—not only the subject, always recognisable, but the artist herself whose pale eyes seemed always seeking something half-understood and just out of reach.

A few days at Mulberry Hill was the perfect compromise between town and country life for a guest who was never expected to put her nice little nose out of doors or even pat a dog—an animal of which she went in genuine terror all her life. Nor was she troubled with picnics which she dreaded—except the kind that take place in a closed car. On a warm—but not too warm—day (perhaps a breeze—but not too windy) armed with emergency wraps (like Steer, an alarmist about the slightest draught) she would make a tentative sortie into the sheltered courtyard soon to return with her conscience satisfied that she had been breathing the pure country air. My Mother's natural domain at Baxter, and instinctively she knew it was not the harsh dry and rather terrifying Australian bush beyond our courtyard wall and across the snake inhabited paddocks of long grass where seeds invariably got into her stockings and the flies fought their way under the fly veil pinned to her hat. It was the big airy sitting-room where stood her former treasured Bechstein in its new home with the lid open, waiting to be played—no flies, snakes or draughts, no troublesome callers—just herself and her dear old friend the piano. During her stay music flowed through the usually silent house, sometimes before breakfast and sometimes long after we had gone upstairs to bed.

At dusk I have seen Cliff our garden boy slip into the darkening drawing-room unbidden and light the lamp that stood ready beside the piano and the two wax candles in their brass sconces on either side of the keyboard while the shadows lengthened in the courtyard and the birds who had been chirping away all afternoon in an ecstasy of competition fell silent for the night. And next morning, through the open window (only the top please darling—it's just a *teeny* bit draughty) resounding chords of Beethoven and

116

Brahms, lacy trills of Bach and Chopin would follow me into the garden and the green light under the mulberry tree was filled with music and moving leaves and shadows and singing of birds.

No sooner was my Mother installed for a few days at Mulberry Hill than the boy Cliff developed a passionate desire to clean the long drawing-room windows when the top step of the ladder became a reserved seat in the front row of the stalls. Conscious of the rapt round boy face pressed against the glass the pianist would vary the programme to include a Chopin valse, a luscious excerpt from *Madame Butterfly*. At which the window would be pushed wide open and after some conversational exchanges further pretence of window cleaning would be abandoned and the two would settle down to enjoy a recital of assorted music.

'Don't go much on that sort of thing myself,' said Cliff of a stiff classical number, 'but gee! your mother's hot stuff on the piano.'

He was naturally musical with a good ear and memory. The two became firm friends and on an evening when we were obliged to leave my Mother alone in the house, Cliff insisted on staying after work to serve her evening meal which he did most expertly on a tray. A few years ago I came across Cliff happily married at Sorrento. I was touched to find that he had never forgotten my Mother or her music.

Oddly enough neither her first nor her second husband had the smallest appreciation of her musical gifts except at second hand and as a matter of personal pride. I can imagine my Father telling a friend at the Melbourne Club:

'My wife is considered a very able pianist,' as he would say of his son-in-law: 'People who know about these things tell me Daryl is quite a promising artist.' The poor man was almost belligerently allergic to the sound of the piano and would sometimes put his head round the door while his wife was filling the little yellow drawing-room with her music to inquire plaintively: 'My dear if you will please tell me when you leave off playing I shall come in and sit down...' On this point they understood each other perfectly and my mother never felt affronted. She was accustomed to playing alone, for her own pleasure, lost in a roseate cloud of Heaven knows what joys and sorrows that we her children never knew. When I try to remember her at Baxter she becomes nebulous and uncertain as she often was in real life. At the piano her personality underwent a curious transformation. In practical matters so timid, at the piano she knew exactly where she was going; exactly what she had set out to do—with the intricate pattern of music taking shape under firm white fingers that found it so difficult to thread a needle, find a shilling in a handbag, fit a key into a lock...

As related in an earlier chapter, my Father died before we came to live at Baxter. A few years later my Mother married Professor T. G. Tucker, a long standing friend of the family and a fairly frequent visitor to Mulberry Hill.

Tommy Tucker as he was known to his cronies was one of the great teachers and scholars of his generation who did much to build up an international reputation for the University of Melbourne. Sir Baldwin Spencer, Sir Thomas Lyle, Sir Orme Masson, Horace (Barney) Allen, Sir Archibald

Strong...as children we were fortunate in knowing such illustrious academic figures in their less alarming role of family friends who came to our house in St Kilda to partake of roast beef, perhaps a little music or a game of croquet on Sunday afternoons. As I remember them they were all men of simple tastes and subtle humour—a great deal of laughter and a great deal of tea. All were outstanding personalities in their own right. In those days individual idiosyncrasies and personal mannerisms were rather encouraged than deplored. We would have been disappointed if Archie Strong who always wore his hair *en brosse* had allowed it to grow or Barney Allen given up eating quantities of pink iced cake. The University of my youth was indeed a seat of learning in the medieval sense that it all seemed remote from the hurly-burly of everyday living—a place where people went to think about all manner of things as well as passing examinations. Stepping off the old Carlton cable tram on one of the rare treats when we children were taken to tea at one of the professors' houses—the Allens perhaps or the Massons, cosily hidden behind its private garden of shrubs and trees—the air as we passed through the big gates in Grattan Street seemed somehow rarefied, the sweeping lawns silent as a dream. In the centre of the grounds a shallow lake mirrored the University swans against a background of many trees and few buildings dominated by the 'Melbourne Gothic' Wilson Hall.

My stepfather detested being photographed and as the excellent portrait by Phillips Fox was burned in the now historic Wilson Hall it may be of interest to describe his appearance as I remember him at Mulberry Hill shortly after his retirement from his professorial post. I think of him as a full length figure rather than a portrait head. He was the kind of person who is pointed out in the distance in a crowd and ever afterwards recognised and remembered. Tall slim surprisingly upright even in extreme old age and always something of a dandy, gloves and a light cane, a broad-brimmed fedora hat, patent leather shoes, large pearl tiepin and an unusually high white collar completely hiding the thin neck were typical accessories of his wardrobe. The lean craggy face with its gingery grey moustache and bright blue eyes was so vivacious and when he cared to exert himself so full of personal charm—particularly when warmed up to a feast of conversation—that the individual features were swallowed up in the general effect, like the details in a portrait by Goya. Women were prone to fall for him on sight and I have no doubt that a great many people, including my Mother, forgetting the rather ill-shaped nose and remembering only the pervading charm wisdom and wit would have pronounced Professor Tucker a handsome man.

Essentially an urban type, he is more easily recalled sauntering in Kensington Gardens or along the pleasant streets of Cambridge (not long before his death I revisited with him his former college of sixty years past) than cranking up his old-fashioned motor car for a run to the Dandenongs. Although the Australian bush had appealed to him as a young man fresh from England with a sense of beauty stimulated by the poetry of his adored Homer Sappho and the ancient Greeks, the Professor's reactions to country life at Mulberry Hill were much the same as my mother's, only perhaps a little more venturesome.

Occasionally he would take a short stroll or saunter into the stable yard to take a look at the horses or the pigsty. As a former Trustee of the National Gallery of Victoria he had a sincere if limited interest in painting—a subject on which he was never dogmatic—and liked to potter about in the studio. While his wife retreated to the piano he liked best to stretch out on a long chair in the courtyard always with a book at his elbow—Longinus, the sonnets of Shakespeare or, strangely, the American humorist O. Henry. He was the best reader-aloud I have ever listened to—though being-read-aloud-to can be sheer unmitigated torture only a shade less embarrassing than being forced to listen to a recitation. My stepfather was so natural when he read aloud a favourite sonnet in his beautifully modulated voice that I never thought of it as a performance. He must have been an inspiring lecturer, lighting up by a few words the hidden meaning of a single line. Generations of Australian school children were brought up on his famous and highly original *Latin Grammar*. In my youth children regarded the authors of school textbooks as unseen monsters goading us on to further feats of memory sweat and toil. I had an almost personal hate for the unknown Green of *Green's History of England* and for Professor Meiklejohn, whom I always saw as an old gentleman in a pepper and salt suit with a scraggy grey beard, author of the fussy pre-war maps we were obliged to copy with hateful scratchy instruments called 'mapping pens'. Doing a crossword puzzle in the courtyard at Mulberry Hill one day we began talking about T. G.'s Grammar. I asked the reason behind some of the very odd English wording of the lessons and quoted at random

121

the enigmatic phrase: 'With a fork, at Marseilles.' Nothing could have pleased the old man better. 'But you see? My dear girl, you have never forgotten that fork! It was the fork that made you remember. When I wrote that bit about the fork I always hoped it would make the children think.' He was delighted when I recalled another of his sentences my brother and I had always enjoyed. 'You did not try to catch a herd of trembling mice in a net, did you?' An example if I remember rightly after all these years of the ablative absolute. So much for the sane teaching of the classics to the young! All his life T. G. Tucker preached the gospel of common sense. He used to say: 'Try and remember the Greeks and Romans were men and women just like ourselves although they lived so long ago. Don't think of them as living statues walking about in white draperies.'

As a guest in our house the Professor's wants were few. He liked his comforts but they were comforts easily supplied—simple well-cooked food, in practically any weather a blazing fire, and *Webster's Dictionary* within easy reach of the slender hand of which he was pardonably a trifle vain. If possible *Roget's Thesaurus* as well. (Luckily we possessed both books.) Like my mother he had managed all his life to unload with perfect good manners the burden of practical domestic affairs onto other people. ('My dear, I assure you there are a number of excellent people who *like* that kind of thing...') Thus in wartime England he would request their devoted housekeeper for a sole, or a fresh peach or two, with the naïveté of a child. He was not a greedy man but food—even during a war—was surely something more or less palatable that appeared at stated

122

intervals on one's plate. And besides he didn't really care for so many kippers and powdered eggs...

T. G. and my Mother were indefatigable travellers under the leisurely guidance of Thomas Cook. Now and then we would meet up with them on the other side of the world—in small well-heated hotels in Paris and London, in a pension overlooking the Mediterranean. They were living in England when the war broke out and I never saw them again. The last time I remember them together they were stooping to pick bluebells in an English wood. A few yards down the lane a car and chauffeur were waiting to drive them back to town. They had begun to tire easily and my Mother was growing increasingly vague and frail. The civilised English loveliness of the little glade had greatly moved them and as they strolled back arm-in-arm to the car I noticed the tears of pure pleasure in my Mother's eyes.

On a flying war job that included three crowded weeks in England Daryl wired the Professor that he would make a superhuman effort to go down to Devonshire—by train—to visit him and my Mother, if only for a few hurried hours. T. G.'s answer was characteristic. In the firm classical hand that never wavered even in advanced old age he wrote: 'Come and see us my dear Daryl, by all means, we shall be delighted to put you up. But why be in such a hurry? Even a fortnight is hardly enough for inspecting the really beautiful scenery of this district.' I quote from memory but such was the substance. The strains and stresses of wartime transport the bombing and other nightly terrors before they reluctantly moved from Tunbridge Wells to Devonshire had not greatly incommoded them. Seated side by side for long cosy

123

hours in their sitting-room with T. G. reading aloud from Longinus or perhaps my Mother delightedly assisting in the annotation of his monumental, as yet unfinished Dictionary of Classical Philology, they inhabited a world of the spirit over which Hitler had no control. The Professor's Hellenic acceptance of physical danger and my Mother's childlike faith in his judgment as to just where the bombs were going to fall made possible an unexpected serenity in their old age. They died within a few years of each other in the land of their birth.

6

OUR SCHOOL

The busy hum of children's voices from the little ginger schoolhouse floating out over our paddocks had soon become as much a part of life at Mulberry Hill as the clucking and cackling from the fowlyard and the continuous bellowing of Fulton's bull. Although the main ingredient in the school's symphony was the basic hum—like the murmur of our own bees under the roof—there were recurrent overtones pauses and changes of tempo with the jangle of the school bell that evoked a clatter of boots on the hard clay of the yard, the staccato shrilling of the teacher's disciplinary whistle, the bursts of throaty warbling of magpies in the school pines. The scholars recited *The Inchcape Rock*, shouted and sang, saluted the flag at the gate with suitable patriotic sentiments every morning at nine o'clock, droned out the multiplication table—even now the triumphant singsong 'ten tens a *hun*dred' calls up a drowsy summer afternoon at Mulberry Hill and the shuffle of children's feet on bare boards.

Our first introduction to the Baxter school children was through the Bengal tiger who, for reasons best known to himself and the carrier, had arrived from Bruce Street alone at our front gate, a few days after the move, and been left realistically draped over a tea-tree bush with his ferocious stuffed head peering out through the leaves. The children on their way to school, confronted with gleaming tusks and yellow tiger eyes, screamed fell over backwards or simply stood agape in the middle of the road, according to age and temperament. In the mid-morning break I walked across the school paddock climbed the three-rail fence and explained to the teacher that his new neighbours didn't go in for pet tigers in the garden, whatever he might hear to the contrary and some of the younger children were brought up to the house to see for themselves the monster lying peacefully stretched out on our drawing-room floor. The tiger incident established us all on a friendly footing and we soon got to know most of the scholars by sight and many by name, exchanging waves and shouts over the hedge as they walked past on their way home from school. Some stopped for a chat, others never got beyond a shy grin.

Certain key figures persisted and I have no doubt their kind can be seen coming home from any country school today. Ever present are the lingerers and procrastinators by the roadside, who stoop to tie an imaginary shoelace, or shift the school satchel from one shoulder to another as if bowed down by the weight of a pencil case and two or three books. Here come the men of action—the Flash Harrys, riders of deliberately wobbling bicycles to scare the girls, who react with suitable squeaks of terror—the pushing punching full-blooded boys who yell through cupped hands to a buddy half a mile down the road: 'Hi! Charlie! See yer ter-morrer!' just for the hell of it. These boys can whistle as loudly as the Stony Point Express approaching our crossing and make full use of their remarkable talent. And there is always a quota of silent bullet-headed boys in clumping boots who have to milk when they get home from school, walking a little apart from the female trail, with whom they will have no truck for many years to come. Amongst the girls there is always a beauty stepping daintily over dust and puddles, retying her hair ribbons after school and conspicuously ignoring the bullet-headed fraternity as she will later ignore at the Saturday dances all but the best dancers in light shoes.

For us two adults in the new white house on the hill, busy with a thousand small exciting tasks, summer came all too soon. Down at the schoolhouse the long chalky dustladen inky days dragged slowly to a close, with the children penned up in their little yellow desks counting the days weeks and months before the holidays began. All round were summer scents and sounds: but not for them. Sometimes as I leaned on my spade in the vegetable garden on a fine morning when school was In, and I, fortunate adult, was Out and free to dream and loiter, I would see a child emerging from the schoolhouse door, to be joined a few seconds later by another from the door at the other end thence to stroll arm-in-arm in friendly converse towards the little wooden shed with its peaked tin roof known in the Victorian country as the 'dunnekin'. The school dunny was placed discreetly at the further end of the yard so that a leisurely trip, unless at the urgent dictates of Nature, could be made to spin out nearly ten minutes. What Australian country child doesn't remember the sudden overpowering urge for freedom and the sunlit paddocks outside the schoolhouse windows, the upflung arm and hypocritical 'Please, Teacher, may I leave the room?' and Teacher's faintly suspicious 'Very well Johnnie—if you're not away too long...' the joy of leaving the droning voices behind, of dallying in the bright morning air, the illicit orange or candy bar, the brief companionable session chatting side by side in the two-seated 'dunny'—one compartment for girls, one for boys—the slow-footed return to the prison house where if the visit has been properly timed Teacher is even now ringing the releasing bell for recess.

Soon after our arrival at Mulberry Hill the peace of the quiet country night had been shattered by the scrunch of wheels and flash of kerosene lanterns down at the school. From the open windows came an ominous buzz as from an illuminated wasps' nest suddenly disturbed, rising to a crescendo of shouts thumpings and presently the unmistakable crash of falling chairs. 'I hear the fur was flying down at the Protest Meeting last night,' said Jim the Butcher expertly trimming our cutlets on the drying green next morning. Jim who drove a four-wheeled cart from one isolated housewife to another supplied us with first class meat and most of the local news. I asked him what they were protesting about?

'Same old story,' said Jim. 'Sure you wouldn't fancy a nice bit of rump steak for your breakfast?' (Big healthy rosy-cheeked Jim fancied six to eight chops for his own.) 'Some of the parents want the school shifted and some don't.'

Jim told us how the school acre, originally bought from the old McCubbin property, had been selected as the most accessible site for the several families with school-age children. Since then the infant population had gradually drifted towards Langwarrin and Pearcedale so that today most of the scholars were walking three or four miles to school. Some were barely six years old and some had to give a hand with the milking when they got home. The chair throwing was caused by a belligerent minority of parents still living close by, who were opposing a majority petition to the Education Department for removing the school to a more convenient site. Last night things had come to a head with the announcement that the Inspector was actually coming down in person to sum up the position for himself. We asked when? 'Anytime now,' said Jim with a wink. 'Some of them reckon next week' and closing down the lid of the fly-proof cage in which tripe sausages and kidneys were laid on a bed of fresh parsley for our temptation, he jogged away down our drive. Twenty years later the school was still on the old site.

'Anytime now' was a phrase often heard in Baxter. It gave hope and confidence to the listener without committing the speaker to anything so rash as a date. Sewerage, electric light, the new tarmac road, the bus service: all or any of these amenities were said to be coming 'anytime now'. For some of them we waited for twenty years. Progress in our part of the world had a habit of going backwards instead of forwards so that the local Progress Association had to be always on the alert to pin it down before it slipped through their fingers, like the new Recreation Hall, dumped down in the natural bush setting of the old Langwarrin Camp, going surely and steadily downhill until the only socials within its flimsy wooden walls were held by possums rabbits wallabies and snakes and it was sold and carted away leaving the heath and bachelor's buttons and wild fuchsias to take over the trodden ground.

The children had lost no time in presenting themselves with the freedom of Lindsay's paddocks and all living things thereon: magpies lizards grasshoppers ants rabbits cats dogs cows horses eels frogs and tadpoles in the dam. There were no 'Learn to Swim' campaigns for country children and hardly any of the Baxter young could keep afloat. Against all rules and regulations, they paddled and skylarked in our new deep and dangerous dam. Ringed with wattle and eucalypts, the icy brown water bristling with leeches tadpoles mosquitoes and an occasional snake, was an open invitation to a non-swimming child to drown itself in the utmost comfort far from prying adult eyes. Except for the inevitable cricket in the matchbox and the frog in the hot hand, we never saw the children ill-treat an animal or bird. Anything on four legs was coaxed petted and stuffed with cake and sandwiches from the school lunch boxes. My pony N—r developed a passion for fruit cake and old Mary who hated carrots would nibble condescendingly at a scone. One morning a hand had shot up during a spelling lesson: 'Please, Teacher! Nell Lindsay's taken my lunch!' A few minutes later a little boy near to tears was at our kitchen door where our Dalmatian Nell had just laid at my feet a limp packet of half-chewed sandwiches neatly extracted from a jacket in the cloakroom. This was going too far even for the adored Nell. But so mutually tolerant are children and animals that even the owner of the sandwiches bore the thief no grudge.

The Baxter Mothers' Club, a hard working little group of local ladies, did their best to raise money for amenities for school and playground. Money was tight round Baxter and it was uphill work. One afternoon two of the school children called at the house selling raffle tickets for 'a pair of ducks, delivered to your home'. We had only a few ducks of our own and I hopefully took several tickets. Christmas was coming and a nice young duck always comes in handy. A few weeks later, when the raffle was drawn, I was rung up by the winner—a Somerville housewife—angrily demanding why I hadn't delivered her Christmas dinner? Unfortunately the Mothers' Club had forgotten to ask us if we were willing to donate the prize! Daryl was away painting with George Bell—it was fiendishly hot and nothing for it but to select two prime birds from our tiny flock to be killed dressed and driven over to Somerville by Syd in the jinker. We heard afterwards that the lady who had taken possession of our own Christmas dinner for sixpence was very much annoyed that the ducks were not delivered cooked!

Nothing is more rigid than the seasonal activities of children. Mysteriously, the hopscotch season opens, as mysteriously closes. There is a time for silkworms football rounders skipping cricket and marbles. When the first leaves showed on the mulberry tree children began appearing at the courtyard gate carrying cardboard boxes pierced with holes for ventilation in which there lay dying amongst their own droppings pallid silkworms deprived of their natural diet of mulberry leaves. It was many years before nylon put an end to the keeping of silkworms as a surefire source of pocket money to the thrifty young. In spring and early summer gardening was carried on at the school with mounting enthusiasm. The children always came up to our door in pairs, like members of a religious order, trotting backwards and forwards across the paddocks to ask for the loan of a spade or a wheelbarrow. 'Teacher says please have you any jonquil bulbs left over?' 'Teacher says have you any marigold seedlings because you can have some of ours.' 'Teacher says please have you any old flower pots?' Year after year we watched the current teacher hopefully trying to make a few flowers grow in the starved little beds. As soon as the really hot weather set in the sunbaked clay of the schoolyard was more suited to a parade ground than a garden, the school tank dried out and nothing was left when school reopened after the long waterless holidays but a few straggling geraniums.

So the children of Baxter amused themselves in their own simple way. They were no less happy or sad than the country school children of today although there was no TV to hurry home to after school and the nearest picture theatre was five miles away at Frankston, where the dialogue from the cheaper seats was likely to come through as the chattering of distant monkeys and the adults brought rugs and hot water bottles on winter nights.

For Baxter youth, apart from strolling along the quiet country roads there was practically no week-end entertainment except the mild excitement of an occasional flower show, the fortnightly dances at the Baxter Hall, and now and then a local horse show (or gymkhana) a cheerful family affair with boys and girls arriving on anything they could find to ride, and Mums and Dads Aunties and Grandmas following in traps jalopies delivery vans and a sprinkling of big shining cars from fashionable Mount Eliza. Not everyone at our gymkhanas was horse-minded—there was something for everybody: sometimes it was combined with a fruit flower or poultry show, and for many of the onlookers the events in the ring, of world-shattering import to the local riders, were simply an excuse for an all-day picnic under the gum trees. Prize money was small, there was hardly any betting and not much beer. There are gymkhanas still on the Mornington Peninsula but they are much more elaborate and not nearly so gay. There were always a few well-turned-out diehards who rode with their toes hardly touching the stirrup irons, in hard hats and polished boots, but for the most part the dressing was a mixture of hunting caps fancy blouses top boots head scarves jodhpurs and navy serge suits. The judges paid much more attention to the actual management of the horses and the horses themselves.

At most of our local horse shows, certain characters, like Charlie Hill and Bob Fishwick, were a standing dish. Charlie, a wiry crooked-faced little horse dealer with bandy legs ending in large military boots, always wore a heavy fireman's coat that flapped about his ankles as he mingled with the crowd at the rails. Charlie usually arrived at the showgrounds in a low-slung cart on two old motor car wheels. He seldom drove the same horse for more than a few days or weeks. Rumour said that he had once sold for a pound to a Baxter resident a U-necked animal so ancient that it had dropped dead walking to its new home. Charlie who fancied himself as a ladies' man despite his far from prepossessing appearance lived alone in a rather sinister two-roomed house shaded by one scraggy tree from which more often than not hung the carcase of a newly slaughtered horse, the boiling down of horse flesh being one of his many sidelines when money was running out. We had no great love for Mr Hill but it was impossible not to sympathise with his loss of what he always referred to as 'Me Fortune'—a considerable amount of hard cash slowly accumulated over the years, tied up in a canvas bag and carried for safety in the pocket of the fireman's coat, whence it had unaccountably vanished one day at Dandenong market, never to return.

Of the same profession, but a very different character, was Bob Fishwick, a long-legged sallow-faced Irishman with sad black eyes and a melancholy cast of mind. Unlike Charlie, he sincerely loved a good thoroughbred horse as well as knowing its market value to the last halfpenny. Few people had ever been known to get the better of Mr Fishwick in a business deal. Once, after hours of wordy battle on the subject of a coveted mare which Daryl had finally refused to sell, Bob had actually thrown in his hand to say with a weary sigh, 'By jeeze! You're a hard man, *you* are. A real hard man...' Coming from Bob, himself as hard as the proverbial stone, this was a compliment indeed! Mr Fishwick not only regarded himself, and rightly, as an expert on horses but as a skilled handler of bees. The last time Daryl called on him at his spotless home on Mount Eliza poor Bob came tottering out swathed like an Egyptian mummy in bandages from head to foot with nothing visible but two swollen black eyes. 'Good Heavens Bob,' said Daryl. 'What's wrong?' Through cracked and swollen lips came the lugubrious croak: 'Bit be bloody bees!' It was no laughing matter and a cruel blow to his self-esteem. There were never any hard feelings between Daryl and Bob who had a mutual respect for each other's abilities. I think it was one of the happiest days of Bob's life when Daryl agreed to paint on the dashboard of the Fishwick jinker a lifelike portrait of a bay horse. Whether the painting was in part payment of a horsy transaction or whether it was a straightout pledge of friendship I never inquired.

Bob Fishwick and Charlie Hill, Eileen Coffey (a former Australian champion who sometimes came from town to judge) Jack Mann from Mount Eliza, still driving his buggy and pair, old Bill Langdon—half blind now but still dressy in hard grey hat and the pointed patent leather boots of his youth—with Ray the chauffeur and a champagne luncheon in the old Daimler car, at which we were often guests... How their names bring back those crisp autumn Saturdays, with cold blue-faced children from Baxter and Langwarrin, Tyabb and Somerville, waiting their turn beside their mounts on the still wet grass; or the hot summer days when the thundering hoofs in the arena threw up clouds of dust on the spectators watching from the rails or sitting on the dry grass under the flickering shade of the gums on the other side...the younger children who came in droves,

135

darting in and out like mice almost under the horses' feet, the balloons and penny whistles, the refreshment tent with free hot water and delicious cold corned beef and home-made scones, the pie stall, the toffee apples and penny ice-creams...the musical chairs on horseback, the flag and barrel race, the brush hurdles, the riders mounted on anything from Shetland ponies to 15-hand farm horses...in the middle of the ring the judge and his assistants, bellowing against the din through a megaphone until the last event is lost and won, the last electroplate trophy and satin ribbon presented. Then out come the horse floats, the carriers' van taking away the hurdles and wooden forms, the big refresh-ment tent comes down, and the hot happy riders go jogging home along the dusty roads with the late afternoon sun in their eyes...

For years we must have gone to every gymkhana for miles around, often on horseback. In the studio two faded streamers testified to Daryl's Champion Hack at Lang-warrin. Later on, as an old resident respected for a sound horsy knowledge and commonsense, he was sometimes invited to judge.

Although Daryl always enjoyed a day out at a local gymkhana, he had no stomach for the evening entertain-ments in the Baxter Hall, when a sudden unaccountable attack of intense pain—backache toothache or a sick head-ache—was likely to confine him to his own comfortable fireside an hour before we were ready to start. Isolated on an unfenced strip on the Baxter-Pearcedale Road—in winter a slithering sea of mud and trampled grass fatal to female finery—the hall was about the only public meeting place in the district and most local activities took place within its thin wooden walls. In winter an ice box, in summer a frying pan, the hall was the focal point of community life. In architecture, it was in the same lamentable government rococo as the state school. Inside, little more than an empty shell furnished with a few wooden forms and across one end the little stage. Behind the stage, a tiny unlined kitchen where the ladies boiled up gallons of tea and coffee in kerosene tins over a wood fire. There was never enough money in those days to get the interior repainted but a long long time ago somebody with an urge towards better and brighter entertainment had strung up strips of coloured paper from the ceiling where fly-specked and bedraggled they dangled year after year above the farewells jumble sales concerts piano recitals and meetings of the Baxter Fire Brigade. On the stage, Miss Somebody's pupils perspiring in velvet tam-o'-shanters through the intricacies of the Highland Fling, a conjuror from the city in a boiled shirt, our own little amateur ballet group, were all obliged to do their stuff in front of the one stage property—a tattered backcloth of an English garden, flanked in the wings by brooms suitcases hats coats and the compulsory fire buckets, all in full view of the audience.

The Saturday night dances were very popular and always well attended. There was no public transport but Baxter youth was hardy and thought nothing of walking several miles to a ball, swinging a hurricane lamp or riding over the rough country roads on a push bike. On dance nights the long straight Baxter road twinkled with the lights of a few local cars jinkers and traps. Kate and Terrence, a devoted admirer on the Railways who later became her husband, went on foot and if no transport was available even the Cockney born and bred Hilda would bravely conquer her fear of the dark bush paddocks in tight fitting peach satin, hurricane lamp in one hand, a paper bag with her best gold shoes in the other. A much sought-after dancer, light as a fairy on tiny feet, there were plenty of admirers to escort her back to Mulberry Hill.

Music for the dances was supplied by willing amateurs like Bill Marshall with wrists strong enough to wrest from the vitals of the worn-out piano a continuous volume of non-stop popular airs to which the dancers could at least keep time, even if much of the melody was lost through the several faulty keys which could have been struck with a sledge hammer and remained dumb. Treble and bass were in a different pitch so that a wily pianist who knew his instrument would try to keep on safe ground in the middle register. Bill was enough of an artist to draw from this frustrating instrument a tinny sweetness that could be heard two miles away on still nights at Mulberry Hill. The programmes were mostly 'Old Time'—lancers, Alberts, barn dances and valettas with waltzes and foxtrots thrown in as a concession to contemporary tastes. As soon as the evening got really under way with the dancers relaxed and perspiring, the music, particularly during the 'One two three: Hop!' of the barn dance, was all but obliterated by the tramp of heavy boots worn by most of the males although a few dandies slabbed down their hair with pomade and danced in light shoes. Another musician in demand on Saturday nights was Alec Vince. Of Austrian descent he had a natural talent for the accordion—an instrument perfectly attuned to the brittle silence of the Australian bush. Sometimes when the solitary candle at Alec's window was burning late we could hear across his orchard the harsh wheezing cry of the accordion with certain phrases repeated over and over again, like the cry of some lonely bird of the night. Down at the hall his own music acted on Alec like a drug that kept him playing away in his allotted corner of the dance floor hour after hour, only pausing for an occasional gulp of very sweet tea or a bite of cream cake. Unconscious of the jumping stamping boys and girls swinging partners under his nose, the strong greying hair curling about the gently swaying head, the periwinkle eyes seemed fixed on the stream of music flowing in and out, out and in, between his two hands, as a boy leans over a bridge on the Danube watching the water sucking in and out against the stones.

From the ceiling the kerosene lamp with the tin reflector swung up and down on its iron chain in time to the dancing feet, its black shadow rising and falling on walls and ceiling. On two or three wooden forms people not actually dancing sat wiping their foreheads and sweating palms. Under the business-like direction of the M.C. on the stage—a personage something like the 'caller' at square dances—the complex figures of valettas and quadrilles were performed with great skill, especially by the older generation who were critical of the rowdy lancers which tended towards midnight to get out of hand with the girls, squeaking like guinea pigs, being swung off their feet round and round on the slippery sawdusted floor. Amongst the boys and girls there was a curious atmosphere of prudery and skylarking. After each dance the female partner was dropped like a hot potato and deposited on a form to sit there chatting with her girl friends until the next item on the programme. The girls were not as smartly dressed as they would be today. A dash of lipstick, a light dusting of chalk-white powder the only artificial aids to beauty of sparkling eyes and flushed rosy cheeks.

Tickets cost five shillings double, an excellent supper included, ('ladies, a plate please!') No liquor except a surreptitious beer gulped down in the darkness outside. The homemade cakes and sandwiches were always finished to the last crumb and by the stroke of twelve—it cost a pound extra to hire the hall after midnight—the ladies would have collected the supper baskets washed up the cups and plates emptied the giant enamel teapot turned down the lamps locked the piano and both doors and be standing on the sandy strip at the roadside waiting for their men to take them home, some on foot, some behind a slow jogging farm horse, boys and girls on ponies and bicycles, a party in an open car with side curtains flapping in the night breeze that smells like Heaven after the dust and kerosene fumes and heated bodies inside the hall. Crunch of wheels on sand, ring of horseshoes on the road goodnights and catcalls echoing over the silent paddocks that line the road from Baxter to Pearcedale where the farms and orchards lie invisible in black velvet darkness, all too soon to lighten into the bleak Sunday dawn with the sun coming up over the barn and cows waiting in the yards to be milked Sunday or no Sunday, pigs and poultry to be fed—the same old

Sunday routine and the memory of last night is put away until Saturday fortnight comes round again.

Sunday is always a long dun-coloured uneventful day with a strange flat light of its own. A depressing day for the Baxter young that should by rights have set the angels singing in Heaven. Most adults worn out after a full working week spent a good part of it just lying around the house while Grandma dozed on the horsehair couch in the front room—not yet christened 'the lounge'. The very cows seemed to be resting; the dogs, let off the chain because the family is at home, lie down quietly in the dusty backyard. A few families take the children to church in the mornings if they can find a church service of their own denomination—the local halls being worked on a kind of roster system. In the afternoons, boys and girls take aimless walks along the well-known paths they travel all week to school. A lucky few with ponies or bicycles set out on desultory rides to nowhere in particular, tea being at half past five. After tea Mum gets ahead of herself by putting the Monday washing into soak and everyone goes early to bed. So ends another Baxter Sunday of thirty years ago...

I have a large shiny photograph taken for some special occasion by a professional photographer who came all the way from Melbourne. About thirty children obviously in their best clothes—no T-shirts bare legs and sandals—every leg and arm is sleeved or booted. They sit there shyly smirking or staring straight ahead out of the stiff dark grey mount. No widascope, and every child at the end of a row has come out a monstrosity almost twice the width of its neighbour. (All group photographs if the rows were long enough used to come out that way in my own school days when the prefects in their serge tunics looked like pregnant toads.) I can still remember most of their names. Here is Gordon Bryant, always a safe bet as a prize winner, good at the writing of neat fact-filled essays, a studious ambitious boy who later became exactly what might have been expected—a Member of Parliament. Jack Fletcher, his bold blue eyes here reduced to the communal stare of the photograph—always brave and reckless and strong, who enlisted early in the Second World War and was lost forever in the Malayan jungle. And here is his young brother Russell, a shy solemn little boy who used to bring me bunches of violets from his mother's garden on the hill opposite the school. A little further down the row is our cook Hilda's son George, even then something of a dandy with a face wiped clean of expression by acute shyness and a too tight coat. I can remember his mother buying that coat and George insisting on wearing it on a scorching summer day. Dorrie Dicker, a handsome dark child whom Daryl had once painted in a scarlet blouse, the two Dawson girls whose home had been burnt out one spring afternoon as they sat in school three miles away, Jean Marshall long ago married and living in Sydney with a child of her own, lovely fair haired Violet Lee, Beryl and Charlie Scott... I hope that when the photographer let them become human again they were going to enjoy themselves for the rest of the day! Has some important visitor from Melbourne given them a half-holiday or are they just about to start on a school picnic? Or will they get rid of their finery and go soberly back to school?

When the first Christmas came round at Mulberry Hill and there was still no sign of the Inspector nobody seemed surprised but ourselves. With Christmas less than a week away the parents' thoughts were all on the festive season. The annual school picnic, a bazaar organised by the Mothers' Club and, shining night of delirious excitement, the Christmas breakup in the Baxter Hall. In stifling midsummer heat, a local pine tree gay with tinsel and coloured lights was set up in a tub swathed in crinkled paper and the Union Jack, the branches nearly touching the ceiling. On the top was that almost extinct and lovely thing, a fairy doll. The good-natured stationmaster as Father Christmas, heroically suffocating in scarlet robe and cottonwool beard, almost frightened the little ones into hysterics with his lolly pink cardboard face and painted smile as he bent over them with a few kind words and a toy from the tree. Long remembered in Baxter was the Christmas when Daryl, who had designed the first commercially-produced moulded doll's head in Australia and had an interest in a small toy factory, came to light with an assortment of koalas kangaroos and blue-eyed dolls in pink and blue velvet dresses and lovely gold or ink black curling hair.

On the day following the Christmas party, the school was closed down for the long summer holidays and silence reigned in the deserted playground. No more newspapers lunch wraps paper bags and ruled pages of exercise books sailing over our fences on the north wind, no three o'clock bell breaking the stillness of a languid afternoon under the mulberry tree, no horses waiting in the school paddock to be patted and fed with apples and jam sandwiches and the

143

dogs, who from the first had enthusiastically adopted the school lunch hour as their own, tightened their belts and lay dozing all day in the courtyard waiting for tea. I found myself listening for the eleven o'clock whistle and the daily procession past our sundial at the little white gate.

7

RETREAT TO BACCHUS MARSH

Cousin Edie's lilacs had begun to flower, the new tea-tree hedges were racing ahead, we had acquired a cow of our own and two blue-tongued lizards a foot long, who lay sunning themselves all day in the courtyard dreaming of the good old days when the world was practically red hot. Life at Baxter followed its uneventful way, uneventful except that local farmers were complaining about the low prices brought by fruit and vegetables. A neighbour who got up at four one morning and drove a truck of first grade cauliflowers to the wholesale market in Melbourne drove back the same day with the same load. A record crop of peas became for some mysterious reason unsaleable and had to be dug into the ground. There was nothing wrong with them peas and the weather was just right, too. Old-time farmers like Andy Fulton and Charlie Scott looked inquiringly at the sky which for country people usually supplies the answers to droughts floods and other seasonal disasters known to insurance companies as 'acts of God'. In this year and season it told them nothing.

An expensively travelling widow in quest of a flower piece for her Riviera drawing-room called on us at Mulberry Hill and with a certain reluctance the artist allowed her to carry back to her suite on an Orient liner one of his special favourites. I remember that picture very well—honeysuckle like clotted cream on a deep indigo ground—because it turned out to be the last picture sold from the studio for a very long time. The man-made calamity called in Australia simply 'the Depression' had hit our little community almost overnight.

The poultrymen and farmers were as unprepared as the bankers and politicians for the tidal wave that engulfed millions of unsuspecting people all over the world and even ruffled the quiet waters of our own little Bay. In the country round Baxter and Langwarrin people seldom died of active starvation—the hated 'Sussy' or government sustenance saw to that. Many families we knew were sucked down into the black depths of unemployment and near despair. One family lived courageously in an old railway carriage right through the Depression. Whether the economists ever found out the underlying reasons for this calamitous muddle I don't know. But what is the use of facts and figures—after it is all over—to people like our neighbour Alec Vince, peering in innocent bewilderment into the little purse on the mantelpiece which for twenty-five years had always held enough shillings for a bag of chaff for his horse and now, astonishingly, didn't...That year was a wonderful season for cherry plums—I have never liked them since. They grew in wild profusion in Alec's neglected orchard and in old deserted gardens where the children picked them by the gallon for the making of glutinous pale pink jellies, as they did the small blackberries transformed by thrifty housewives into black boot-button jam. People came from town to gather windfall apples and pears and we ate the oldest and toughest hens and sold off the rest because fowl feed was too dear.

Art, compared to bread and petrol, tea, meat and beer, is a luxury product in a financial crisis. We didn't need an economist to tell us that nobody was going to buy pictures until it was all over. We talked over the situation at the kitchen table one evening under the swinging oil lamp with the last bottle of Scotch between us. Before we went to bed Daryl had written out a starkly truthful advertisement for the papers in which he refrained from describing Mulberry Hill as a Gentleman's Desirable Home in the Country. We just called it a Furnished House to Let. The only person who answered this masterpiece of brevity was a Miss MacIntosh, one of three Scottish sisters, who appeared to have made up her mind to take the house even as she walked up the front path and knocked at the front door. Miss MacIntosh was the tenant agents dream of and seldom find. She was all for signing a six months' lease at a rental that seemed to us fabulous almost before she had crossed the threshold.

'I'm sure it will do very nicely...oh no thank you, I don't think my sisters will want to see it...oh what a charming view you have over those fields!...'

147

Over afternoon tea from the best Minton cups we conscientiously stressed the shortage of the summer water supply and any other disadvantages we could remember, including bees in the chimneys and possums in the walls. Nothing disturbed Miss Annie who even professed to a liking for oil lamps and cooking on a one-fire stove. Syd agreed to stay on in the garden and drive the sisters to the station when they so desired. They were fond of dogs and only too happy to keep an eye on mine. Never were three elderly ladies more accommodating. I don't know if they went so far as to enjoy our blowflies and mosquitoes—there were no complaints about anything the whole time they stayed at Mulberry Hill.

The Misses MacIntosh were ready to move in at once and we promised to be out in a week. The obvious choice for an enforced busman's holiday was Bacchus Marsh, a cosy little village ringed by sombre folded hills that Daryl had always wanted to paint. The artist Remus Fullwood had once denounced Sydney's palms as 'damned amateur trees'. The almost treeless hills surrounding the Marsh are strictly professional, repudiating the timid pencil and fuzzy brush of the amateur—age-old outcrops of volcanic rock, gashed by deep ravines, cracked and fissured by natural erosion with here and there a solitary windmill turning beside a dam with banks of raw yellow clay or a stark little farmhouse and sheep scattered like grains of rice on the slopes. We had passed them often on our way to the Lindsays at Creswick on the other side of Ballarat and they were always beautiful and always different. The traveller has his first sight of the Marsh from a breezy plateau on the Melbourne-Ballarat

Highway where the road that has been gradually climbing for several miles suddenly unwinds itself steeply into a lush green valley, where the red and white roofs and chimneys fringed by clumps of willow and elm are suspended in a bowl of aqueous light. The cheerful bustling little market town goes about its business ringed by stillness and silence and soft windless airs. Before the coal mines brought commuters and a harsh new prosperity you could hear the cherries dropping into the grass in the orchards or a fish jumping in a willowed pool a mile out of the town. It was seldom windy in the Marsh itself—only away up on the open hills at Ballan and Blackwood and Pyke's Dam.

Bacchus Marsh is an old settlement by Australian standards with comfortable brick and whitewashed houses and the patina that only comes to a dwelling that has been lived, loved and died in, tempered by summer suns and winter winds. On the outskirts stands the snug little two-storied brick house once the home of Captain Bacchus for whom to my disappointment the Marsh was named, and not as I had always supposed for Bacchanalian revels under the Lederderg willows. The final approach to the township from the Melbourne end is a mile-long avenue of tall branching elms, in summer a cool leafy tunnel where the pedestrians' faces look sea-green in the shade. On either side of the avenue between the dark boles of the trees orchards of peach and apricot, cherry and apple fan out and slices of river flats, with cattle standing motionless in the lucerne, stereoscopic in the valley light.

Now we were standing in the avenue with our suitcases beside us, peering over the broken wooden gate of

149

The Laurels—a four-roomed wooden cottage fronting the Highway. At the rather odd rental of sixteen shillings a week, The Laurels had been the only vacant cottage on the agent's books. He had written: 'I think I should tell you if you wish to rent without inspection, the house is reasonably clean but in bad repair.' We didn't mind it being unfurnished so long as the roof didn't fall in before our lease was up, and we told Mr Macpherson we would take The Laurels on chance. It was a house devoid of character except for the fact that all its main lines were slightly out of plumb including a sagging six-foot verandah in front and a picket fence onto the street. It stared at us blankly from two uncurtained windows, one on each side of the front door, and told us nothing. In the chilly twilight an army of snails was chewing away at the rank weeds and marigolds of the narrow garden strip. I decided then and there that whatever else I left undone at The Laurels I would get rid of those snails. Two scrubby bushes like down-at-heel Christmas trees were aflutter with paper bags and scraps of old newspapers blown in from the Highway. Although tightly wedged between two nondescript if slightly less shabby neighbours, the house had a curious air of isolation. We stood for a moment on the rotting verandah before going inside. For better or worse The Laurels was to be Home until we were safely Out of the Red.

The key turned on the clean stuffy emptiness of a long disused cave. The four box-like rooms bore no trace of human occupancy—not so much as a dead match or a nail in the wall. Even when we had set out our few household possessions—two deck chairs, two camp beds, a seagrass mat, three wooden boxes and one all-purpose broom, it still felt like a cave and stayed that way till the end. In the lean-to kitchen at the end of the narrow hall the vital parts of a rusty iron stove lay fossilised on the bare boards. The kitchen opened onto a little yard, enclosed by a high paling fence, with an elm tree and ivy-covered dunnekin marooned in a sea of long grass and self-sown cabbages with tall yellow flowers. There was no back to the stove but Daryl soon had a fire roaring dangerously through a sort of blowhole on which I later learned to cook at lightning speed without singeing my eyelashes. We put my typewriter and Daryl's painting things into the two back rooms which we christened Studios One and Two and went, rather forlornly, to bed.

Next morning in brilliant sunshine The Laurels looked almost gay, with bacon and eggs sizzling on the blowhole and the crooked kitchen window festooned with rainbow cobwebs sparkling with dew. In the dark narrow bathroom where long trails of anaemic ivy had forced their way through the unlined wooden walls and the water in the old tin bath was icy cold, the musty floorboards had given way, leaving me standing knee deep in rubble and scurrying black spiders. We never got round to mending the floor, but if we once began mending anything at The Laurels we could have been employed on necessary repairs from dawn till dark. Because of the tall trees in the avenue the house was so dark that Daryl had to take the Woolworth mirror onto the verandah and shave within a yard of passersby on the Highway.

We had just finished our first breakfast when Jack Macpherson the agent appeared at the back door—a big gentle man accompanied by Whisky, a big gentle dog—and carrying rather shyly a bunch of roses from his wife. 'Ollie thought you might like a few flowers…Anything you want just let me know. Best butcher far end of the street on the right.' There were no curtains at the windows and no rugs on the floor nor ever would be. Always the soul of tact Mr Macpherson refused to step inside. We assured him we wanted nothing but milk bread and chops and set out to inspect the town.

Looking towards the village where the trees began to thin out and the shops started we could see from our gate the blacksmith's old white horse which Daryl later painted, standing all day under the same tree like a live advertisement for White Horse Whisky. The blacksmith's hammer rang out above the chatter of children on their way to school, the circular saw whined in the woodyard of the house next door which the agent told us was the parsonage, the hens were clucking so close to the dividing fence we could almost have reached over for a fresh egg. In the lime green tunnel of the avenue the sun danced amongst the leaves and a roadside stall opposite was set out with apples and lettuces to tempt the passing motorist to stop and buy. The Highway cuts clean through the town—at the beginning of the avenue: MOTORISTS SLOW DOWN PLEASE; out and away over the hills at the other end. For half a mile it is called Main Street with shops brimming over with local produce—yellow-box honey newlaid eggs apples walnuts juicy cuts of beef pork and lamb. Even in the Depression nobody in the Marsh went hungry. Out on the Lederderg people were fossicking for gold in the worked-out claims and the grocer sold frying pans axes and tin billies as a sideline. Over a little slit of a shop at our end of the town was written the one cryptic word BOOMAKER, where a stocky Germanic dwarf presumably mended the local BOOS. Outside the Border Inn a truck of calves was waiting while the driver had a quick one with Cyril Jones. Busy Main Street was dominated on one side by the red brick post office topped by a large white-faced clock and on the other by the two storied Inn, whose old wooden balcony hung dangerously above the pavement below.

Our two back rooms reeking with paint and turpentine were looking and smelling like working studios when George Bell turned up at The Laurels for a few days' painting. George who normally lived amongst well-polished antiques and shining silver—to say nothing of Edith's delicious food—was perfectly at home in his spartan quarters in Studio Number Two, furnished with one wooden box and a broken blind. He had brought his own camp bed and painting gear and the inevitable garlic sausage for the communal kitchen. Like most artists George had a chameleon capacity for settling down almost anywhere if the working conditions were right. With no furniture to be dusted and swept under nothing ever got mislaid as it did at Mulberry Hill. A piece of manuscript, a half-finished sketch, could be found in exactly the same place where the owner had left it a week ago. And how quiet it was in the two back rooms! Although the traffic rushed past all day long on the Highway its raucous scrapings and scratchings were treacle soft as background music because we knew that no car-load of jolly visitors from town was likely to be disgorged at our gate. No telephone disturbed the cave-like calm of The Laurels when the painters were at work and nobody knocked on our awful front door with *The Laurels* printed above the fanlight, except now and then the postman bearing glad tidings of the Misses MacIntosh and Mulberry Hill, or Jack Macpherson whose office was next door to the post office in Main Street. The agent had a rare perception and was always a welcome guest who never stayed too long when there was work on hand. He confided to me after we got to know him better that he had more or less invented the rental of sixteen shillings a week as likely to attract an artist to the Marsh. He was one of those sensitive laymen who has an almost holy respect for art. The sketches and drawings stuck up all over our walls were a continual source of wonder. How was it that a chap like Daryl who could talk shop with farmers about crossbred ewes and fat cattle could dash off a lifelike drawing of the dog Whisky on the back of an envelope—or the recognisable painting of Smith's Farm, later hung at the Royal Academy in London? Jack's invariable comment after prolonged gazing was in essence the same as my own: 'Beats me how the old so-and-so does it!'

A visitor too small to reach the doorknocker was Snowy, the blonde toddler from the woodyard. We would find him playing like a kitten amongst the paints and paper on the studio floor, and once diligently scrubbing our rotting verandah with my hairbrush. Like a kitten he knew by instinct when one of our doors or windows was left open and if Daryl put him out on the mat with instructions to run along home now, he was back within a few seconds. Snowy's father drove the municipal night cart as a sideline to the woodyard and in his gayer moments went fishing in Pyke's Dam, occasionally bringing us a welcome gift of blackfish or trout. At Pyke's, the artificial reservoir folded into the hills above the town, a man-made waterfall dashed winter and summer into a deep rocky gorge under a stone bridge. Daryl was painting by the roadside on the way to Pyke's one morning when the driver of a laundry van with a long country day ahead and to hell with starched shirts pulled up and strolled across the grass to stare in hard-breathing silence at the unusual sight of a real live artist at work.

'Do people pay you for a photo like that?' he presently inquired.

'Sometimes—if they want it badly enough!'

Next morning the painter was back at the same place and again the van pulled up.

'How about you coming along to my place some Saturday and doing a bit of painting for me?'

'What sort of painting?'

'Something right down your alley! You come along Saturday and bring your traps.'

Next Saturday it was raining cats and dogs and Daryl made his way as requested to the Swan Laundry in Lederderg Street where Bill Miles and his wife were awaiting him on the doorstep of a small corner shop sheltered from the deluge by an iron verandah. There were two windows—one facing onto each street. The job was to paint on each of them a large lifelike swan. The first black ('Before the wash. Get the idea?'). The second white ('After the wash'). All objections were airily waved aside as the artist got out his paints and brushes and a crowd of Saturday afternoon stragglers closed in under the verandah. By the time Swan Number One was finished and loudly applauded it had grown too dark to go on with the job and Mr Miles agreed after a little expert tuition to tackle Swan Number Two himself with Daryl outlining the lettering and feathers and topping off the beaks of both birds with a neat professional yellow. The finished product visible from the Highway nearly half a mile off put the seal on the artist's reputation in the Marsh. As he had refused to accept payment for this rather unusual commission Mr Miles and his wife generously insisted on doing our laundry free of charge for as long as we stayed in the town. A clear case of medieval barter. Another was the sketch of a racehorse from Sol Green's nearby Under-bank stables, paid for by mutual consent in a truckload of meadow hay.

So the days became weeks, the weeks months, and we were content in our crazy wooden shell. Now we belonged to the daily life of the Marsh where the locals had become accustomed to the lean springy figure of the artist striding down Main Street with haversack and sketching stool. 'Hubby out painting today?' asks the man where we buy our eggs. 'Saw you up at Pyke's yesterday,' says Snowy's father, and Putt Malcolm and Ollie Macpherson stop for a chat under the post office clock. The clock was our only reliable timepiece but it might just as well have stood permanently at ten to three like the famous clock in Grantchester. Meals at The Laurels were at any hour of the day or night, according to the painting programme. Sometimes Daryl went off alone on foot in search of a watercolour subject, sometimes in the car heading for the hills with oils and canvas and a packet of sandwiches. Sometimes I went with him to lie stretched out amongst the dandelions and dry sheep droppings on the windswept paddocks above the gorges, reading, dozing under a pine tree in the heat of the day, boiling the billy for tea. As the days grew longer and warmer we often ate out of doors at the cottage, sitting on our two boxes under the elm in the backyard where the long grass had been laboriously cut down with a hatchet borrowed from Snowy's father, and my nail scissors. Now and then when we had had a specially economical week we would indulge in the small extravagance of Mrs Jones' excellent three-course dinner at the Inn—soup meat and two vegs apple pie and cream, the beautifully cooked country meal spoiled as so many good meals are spoiled in Australia by being served on the stroke of 6. An hour later not even the Angel Gabriel would have got anything out of Mrs Jones but cold meat and tomato sauce. The Border Inn which had belonged to the Jones family for three generations was a favourite halfway house for discerning travellers on the Ballarat-Melbourne Road. There was an atmosphere that invited lingering in the little secluded garden of lawn and fruit trees and old-fashioned flowers. A feeling of homely comfort in the way the big kitchen opened onto the scrubbed bricks at the back, the tree ferns in tubs, the cockatoo, the white-washed Ladies and Gents reached so discreetly by a little bricked path bordered with geraniums and hanging begonias. The spacious rooms upstairs had access to a wide balcony overlooking the street in the best tradition of Australian pubs, where a summer afternoon could be agreeably spent watching the life of the little town unfolding

157

itself below—people driving into market in cars and jinkers and family trucks, travellers from Melbourne and Ballarat pulling up in a citified bustle demanding a quick drink; others lingering for Mrs Jones' famous homemade scones and tea. Sometimes a sad-faced country horse, the reins slung over a post outside the Inn, over its neck a sugar bag with bread meat newspapers and presently a bottle or two when the rider has finished a beer with Cyril Jones; and in the bar below a never-ending conversation between two or three regular patrons is droning on in the clean shady room where the afternoon sun comes filtering through vine leaves, and in the front hall with its shining lino and brass jardinieres Mrs Jones and young Nance are dashing up and down with trays, answering the telephone, telling travellers how far it is to Ballarat or Blackwood, whether the fish are biting out at Pyke's Dam.

Cyril showed us the cellar under the bar and we spent an hour inspecting the stock of imported wines whiskies and liquers not often found in a modest country hotel. He took a connoisseur's pride in his collection and when we got to know him better would sometimes show us a new buy or forgotten cobwebby find. The bar trade was exceptionally heavy but always orderly and under control, Cyril being an expert handler of tough or abusive customers. Although he often appeared to be fast asleep he was never surprised at anything. From behind thick round glasses the myopic little owl eyes missed nothing even as he sat apparently semi-tranced listening to the trots or the scores at Albert Park rifle butts in the little room behind the bar. Only rarely did he let fall a laconic comment on human frailties. The Jones family all did their share in various capacities in the smooth running of the hotel—Cyril in the liquor department, his active little parrot-blonde wife in the kitchen, the mother a tall dignified old lady in a neat black dress supervising the bedrooms and the boarders' comforts, while young Nance the schoolgirl daughter who enjoyed a friendly chat with the clients flew up and down stairs on a thousand odd jobs. To young Nance and her mother, both quick movers, on the run from morning till night, Cyril's almost constant air while on duty as of one reluctantly roused from slumber must have been exasperating, particularly on a warm afternoon when the women were washing up or baking or sorting the laundry and he sat draped over a high-backed chair in shirt sleeves and braces, rising now and then with a sigh of martyrdom to shuffle out in his easy slippers for a breath of fresh air. Hotelkeeping was in his blood and nobody knew better than Cyril Jones how to attend to the special needs of an old client. Unless he was in the mood for conversation his sentences had a disconcerting way of petering out before they were completed—they were simply professional patter, part of the job—like the obligatory nips of gin and water with a customer. These things belonged to his public and business character. In private life there existed another Cyril Jones, a man of action and firm decisions, a pigeon shot of international class who had carried off prizes at Brussels and thought nothing of paying vast sums for a particular type of gun that took his fancy. He was a generous free-spending man.

The Jones family took an immediate liking to the young Tasmanian Professor Leicester McAulay. Cyril asked: 'Why

do they call you Doctor McAulay if you're a professor?...
Oh I see—then I shall call you Doc. Sounds more friendly.'
This was one of the longest and most articulate speeches
I ever heard him make.

At always unexpected moments in my life Leicester
had been appearing on stage like the Demon King in the
pantomime who shoots up through a trapdoor, makes a few
profound remarks to the audience and as suddenly disap-
pears. Although he could calculate to the millionth part of
a split second such cosmic problems as the speed of light or
how long it would take a bunch of atomic dust to reach the
moon, he was less conscious of man-made time than anyone
I ever knew. He habitually wore as a bangle on his lean wrist
a rather too large watch that somehow gave the impression
of a child's toy and which I never saw consulted. I imagine it
was worn more as a gesture to the social order to which his
family belonged than as an instrument for keeping track of
the details for which lesser minds have need of a watch. Few
human beings are so free of the twenty-four-hours-in-a-day
complex that they can eat and sleep, work and play, equally
well or badly in any one of them.

Leicester arrived in the Marsh late one afternoon from
his home town of Hobart, Tasmania. 'I'm going to Tahiti...
Actually it seemed an idea to go via Bacchus Marsh.' We
hadn't seen him for several years in which many things had
happened to all three of us and there was a great deal of talk
to be got through, though with Leicester one never had to
waste time explaining. The chasm of the years since our last
meeting would simply close up and we would go on from
there. Daryl asked how he knew our address?

160

'Perfectly simple, my dear Watson! When I got off the plane in Melbourne I rang Mulberry Hill and a woman with an awfully charming voice told me you were at Bacchus Marsh so I simply went along to that nice-looking pub down the road and asked where the artist was living.' At times maddeningly vague he could be unexpectedly practical in small things. Now his bright heavy-lidded eye swept the empty cottage in one penetrating glance accepting everything that it was or wasn't. He had no idea why we happened to be living like this but made no unnecessary comment.

'I'm awfully sorry but I left my bed in the luggage room at Spencer Street Station...I'm quite happy sleeping on the floor you know.' Usually he travelled the world like a self-contained fast-moving snail with his house on his back—a small conical folding tent and sleeping bag. As we had no spare bed and no extra bedding it was arranged that he should live and eat with us at The Laurels and sleep at the Border Inn. We hoped he was staying at least a week?

'Well...you see...*as a matter of fact*...if I remember rightly my ship sails tomorrow. No, Hell, it can't be! I've got it written down somewhere...probably the day after. From Sydney.'

Evidently this was to be another trapdoor appearance. Pushing back a crest of curly black hair that was forever falling over one bright dark eye he began tracing the ocean route from Sydney to Tahiti with the toe of a large black boot in the sand of the backyard. Leicester was the only person I ever knew who used his feet to express himself as other people use their hands. '*As a matter of fact* Tahiti is quite a long way from Bacchus Marsh…You go up here somewhere…East of that tuft of grass…'

Dumped down on the marigolds inside our gate was a string bag containing a few unwrapped toilet articles a bottle of Scotch and a newspaper parcel with which he set off to arrange for a bed at the Inn, returning presently minus a boot and limping on one foot. '*As a matter of fact…*I took one of my "boos" to your excellent "boomaker" on the way. I have only one pair so he says it will be ready in time for Tahiti.'

'Did you tell the boomaker *when* you are leaving for Tahiti?' I asked.

He gave me a withering glance. 'And here's a garlic sausage for *you!* Now we can relax and talk all night! So this is The Laurels!…*As a matter of fact…*I don't think I like it *quite* as much as Mulberry Hill. I suppose *you* do or you wouldn't be here…It looks like a good place to work.' Extraordinary how everyone had the same idea about that house as a workshop!

The evening was what Daryl's father used to call balmy. While I prepared a meal in the kitchen the two gentlemen dragged the boxes out under the elm and began to talk in earnest with a bottle of whisky between them on the grass. Daryl, relaxed in paint-stained flannels, refused to pull his conversational punches. 'To Hell with the neighbours! If they had the sense to listen in to Leicester it would do them a power of good!' He may have been right. I don't know why but there was a midsummer madness in the air of The Laurels backyard. In the house itself people tended to be over-serious: in the backyard they let themselves go, discussing the most

162

abstruse and unconventional subjects with such wit and brilliance that I would abandon my two iron pots if I was cooking and come out to sip my drink under the elm.

I had to keep poking my head out of the kitchen window: 'For heaven's sake you two! Not so loud! Do please remember the parsonage drawing-room is on the other side of that fence!' I hated missing any of their conversation when Daryl and Leicester were really extended and now and again I went out into the yard to listen…Einstein. God. Aunt May Butler. Sir Ernest Rutherford (as a brilliant youth Leicester had helped that great scientist to split the atom at Cambridge). God again. Bach. Something really *low*. Roars of Rabelaisian laughter mingling with the dust coming up golden from the ground on the last beam of evening light to float amongst the elm branches as the black boot got busy tracing again in the sand. After dinner we showed our guest our two studios and some of the paintings. *'As a matter of fact…*I really *prefer* Studio Number One. More atmosphere! When I get back from Tahiti I might come to Bacchus Marsh and start painting myself. Or I might write a novel in Studio Number Two. It has a certain macabre charm of its own…' He never minded being teased and would say with mock humility: 'I know what I like…*As a matter of fact* I happen to like a rather large painting—I think by Marcus Stone—called Somebody or Other with her Pale Eyes. Do you know it?'

I reminded him how the first time we had ever talked about art he was going through his Highland cattle stage and I was a highbrow schoolgirl and dedicated disciple of Sir Baldwin Spencer as my aesthetic guide.

163

'No. No. You mock me! I don't like Highland cattle *much* now. Daryl, is it all right if I admire Gauguin? I shall have to, anyway, when I get to Tahiti.'

As a matter of fact as he would have said himself, his penetrating mind could nearly always pick out the essential qualities in anything which he really set himself to understand and analyse although at the time he had no technical knowledge of painting. He once succeeded in explaining to us in very simple language the basic idea of Einstein's Theory of Relativity, approaching it not purely as a mathematician and a scientist but from the human angle and its ultimate relation to all life.

We sat up very late talking that night and when Leicester was at last persuaded to go limping back in his one 'boo' to the Inn it was locked up for the night and in total darkness. Ever considerate he decided that rather than rouse the sleeping Joneses to let him in he would climb up one of the verandah posts to the first floor balcony over the street and steal silently into his room through the French windows. All went according to plan except that he stole into the wrong room. Lightly passing his hand over the pillow in search of the light he touched the face of the sleeping Mrs Jones who uttered a shrill feminine scream as he hurried away still in the dark. When he apologised for his mistake next morning Mrs Jones gave him a kind motherly look. She told us afterwards, 'Poor fellow—you must have got him ever so drunk that night! Such a nice quiet young man too!' The Professor's midnight climb up the verandah post was told and retold with appropriate embellishments for years, always ending with, 'And such a nice quiet young man too!'

There were certain days when I sat at my typewriter in the empty green-aired room feeling like a deep-sea fish suspended in its natural element. Not only in my fish tank but outside in the sheltered valley all natural objects seemed in a state of suspension as they do immediately before an earthquake. It was a characteristic of the Marsh and perhaps had something to do with the old volcanoes seething and boiling so far below the earth's crust that even the geologists hadn't discovered them. Whatever the reason those still windless days were ideal for painting out of doors when not a twig stirred in the orchards and little round pink clouds would hang hour after hour above the same fold in the hills as if they were already painted on the backcloth of pale luminous sky, and in the flat brown pools of the Lederderg the sudden leap of a fish scattered the languid air like a pistol shot. These were the days that brought back memories of Greystones where I had so often stayed as a child.

Greystones was a sheep station five or six miles out of Bacchus Marsh belonging, when I knew it, to the Molesworth Greenes. Most of us have a nostalgic vision of one particular house of our childhood: Greystones was mine. To begin with the two-storied bluestone house was exciting because of its snug fitting coat of close-cropped ivy that exactly fitted round every Gothic window and door excepting only the neat white architraves. The columns of the verandah which ran round three sides of the house and even the chimneys, crowned by tall yellow chimney pots, wore dark green ivy coats. The house stood on a little rise bang in the middle of the rich volcanic plains, backed by a gentle slope masked by feathery wattles

165

and gums looking down on garden and orchard. The colon-naded verandah had special enchantment because of the way it was seen in individual segments through the ivied arches so that there seemed innumerable little scenes of garden and orchard, hill and plain and glowing flowerbeds intensified as in a Florentine painting, The long terraced garden, reached by shallow flights of steps, ended in shrubberies and a row of pines that cut off the homestead garden from the paddocks and far away the thin blue line of hills—for my Mother and me simply the Greystones Hills—probably the You Yangs. Towards the back of the house the bluestone outbuildings were free of ivy and neatly tuckpointed in white. Here was a powerful windmill that drew the yellow water from the dam for house and garden and close by was a big wire cage where full-grown peach and cherry trees were growing, with red and green parrots and white cockatoos darting and chittering above the forbidden fruits. Under the study window at the side of the house, beds of wallflowers seemed perpetually in flower, their spicy fragrance seeping into the house like the scent of Christmas pudding. In the vegetable garden I saw for the first time cabbages growing in the rich red soil and ripe strawberries carefully banked up with fresh straw.

Inside the house was always a smell of beeswax from the polished floors and dark old furniture. On the round cedar table in the hall stood a bronze statuette of the Dancing Faun, though I didn't know who he was till I came to draw him many years later at the Art School. There were always flowers beside him arranged by Miss Cora. She adored flowers and carried a pair of scissors and open basket about the house in the mornings and wore a wig of

166

tight chocolate-coloured curls which I greatly admired. On another table lay neat piles of the English and European newspapers and magazines that my Mother loved—the *Revue des Deux Mondes*, the *Spectator*, *Observer* and *Sunday Times*. Unlike most of the station owners, the Greene family were interested in a great many things besides their own sheep. They were the sort of people who bought expensive books about Art and Poetry and had them lying about for a visitor to browse through and there were many paintings in heavy gold frames. I mentioned in another chapter how Sir Baldwin Spencer had made me for the first time conscious of pictures as things to be looked at. I had forgotten how my dear old friend Mr Molesworth Greene would take his five-year-old house guest to stand before an early Streeton of Venetian gondolas or the Italian lady with long black hair stabbing herself in a milk white bosom adorned with realistic trickle of scarlet blood—I think a genuine Guido Reni. I used to lie awake in the room where this picture hung over the mantelpiece wondering why the poor lady was so unhappy. There was also a suit of Japanese armour on the landing which I had to pass, sweating with terror, on my way upstairs to bed when the grown-ups went in to dinner. I was convinced that a real man was shut up inside waiting to pursue me up the dark staircase. Running down to breakfast in broad daylight I paid it no attention, my thoughts fixed on a miraculous contraption called a dumb waiter laden at breakfast time with hot scones clotted cream butter honey and strawberry jam.

We must have sometimes arrived at Greystones in bad weather although I think of us invariably getting out of the train at Bacchus Marsh on a perfect summer evening. Bob the coachman would be waiting for us on the platform to escort us to the shiny black Greystones wagonette standing a little way down the road outside the station yard so that the always high-spirited horses who hated the train could stand with their backs to the engine. The evening train by which we always travelled gave my Mother time to dress for eight o'clock dinner and me to be put to bed in a fever of exhausted anticipation by old Elsie the Irish housemaid. Mr Molesworth Greene was fussy about his horses and Bob, cracking his whip and looking smart in leggings and a fawn driving coat drove the well-matched pair of bays at a good bat out under the tall railway viaduct to the open plains faintly gilded with summer light, the near paddocks barred with long blue shadows of post and rail fences where clumps of half-seen startled sheep scattered at the clop of our horses' hoofs on the hard red road. Oh! that moment of almost painful joy and excitement when Bob pointed with his whip to the glint of a Greystones dam reflecting the sky and the Greystones windmills flashing high up in the pale golden air as we turned into the gravelled drive, past the iris bed near the gate and the lemon scented gum where the magpies were going to bed, and the wheels of the wagonette scrunching on loose gravel—the sound I can still so clearly hear—as Bob pulls up exactly opposite the front door flanked by two bronze cranes and everything is just as it has always been only better and lovelier than ever, and curled up in my dark corner of the wagonette that smells of sticky waterproof and fresh hay I want to cry.

The front door is opened to the summer night and old Mr Molesworth Greene is coming out to greet his guests in a white linen jacket, dark trousers and scarlet cummerbund. He lifts me down from the wagonette and sets me right side up on the gravel like a little doll and takes my hand. He is my first love. 'Just time for you and me to pick strawberries before Elsie takes you up to the Lighthouse' and in the fading light we pick them very carefully for my supper, laying each one onto a fresh cabbage leaf. The Lighthouse was the octagonal bedroom always allotted to my Mother. She liked to look out at the plains and in the early morning before Elsie brought us China tea and wafer-thin bread and butter and pulled up the Venetian blinds, we would get up in our nightdresses and lean far out of the window with the ivy brushing our cheeks and hair.

At this exciting hour, the garden looked half asleep with no gardeners about and dew lay on the terrace and on the glistening flower beds gay with solid masses of creeping geranium, scarlet mauve and pink, spilling over the clipped ivy borders. If we poked our heads out far enough we could see the tennis court where later on Miss Cora and my Mother would be playing tennis in flowing skirts frilly calico drawers and whaleboned corsets, or they might take their books and sewing into the little pagoda tennis house covered with passion vine, starred with flowers like pink and purple Japanese parasols.

There came a period of glorious emancipation when I was thought old enough to stay at Greystones alone, heavily guarded by an elderly moustached governess known as 'Kitten' belonging to the visiting children of 'Cocoa'

Greene, then Lady Allardyce. Sir William Allardyce as a visiting Governor of the Falkland Islands was treated to a certain amount of local limelight when we were all taken by train to Ballarat to go down a gold mine. Blown out with a mayoral mid-day feast of chicken, trifle and long speeches, the children trailed along behind the official party dressed in miners' trousers and caps and carrying stumps of candles. Our trousers were so dangerously long we could only just waddle like ducks in the narrow dark tunnels where there was no room even for children to stand upright. The rotting wooden supports looked as if we could have pulled them over with one hand. Water dripped from the rock walls and once we almost fell over a man lying on his stomach tap-tapping with a little hammer beside a feeble lamp.

When the holidays came to an end I was allowed to go home alone by train in a purple beaver hat and coat feeling very grown up. Sir William bought my ticket, kissed me through the open window and—oh, abandoned moment of ecstatic guilt!—pressed into my hand a shining half crown. I had committed the unforgivable sin of Taking Money from Strangers. It never occurred to me that an old family friend could hardly be called a stranger any more than dear old Uncle Ted àBeckett who tipped us handsomely every Christmas, and for the rest of the journey I sat clutching my little purple kid purse in which the half crown burned like a live coal. I was to go to school in Melbourne very soon and though I didn't know it this bright morning was the end of a chapter. Within a few months my dear old friend Mr Molesworth Greene was dead and Miss Cora gone to live in town. I never saw Greystones again.

Our stay at the Marsh was nearing an end. The weather had turned sour for out-of-doors painting, our bank account was at least convalescent and the MacIntoshes' lease was up. With many promises to return next summer—who but the swallows ever return next summer, or the next?—we said goodbye to the Macphersons, the Joneses at the inn, Snowy, the surly little 'Boomaker' who had never yet recognised us as regular customers, Mr and Mrs Miles at the Swan Laundry where we called to collect our washing for the last time.

Looking back on it now I can see that The Laurels where we were so absurdly happy, and even comfortable in our own way, had a very special quality that was in itself an experience. It was not only a house without time—it would have been the same if it had been crammed with striking clocks. It was a house so adequately and uniquely filled with its own emptiness that nobody, not even Mr Macpherson, seemed to notice that it was never furnished. At The Laurels emptiness was not a negative statement but a positive affirmation of truth and beauty like the holes in a Henry Moore sculpture. So that when we finally came home to Mulberry Hill and sat down to dinner at the shining cedar table on whose dark depths the Georgian glasses floated like lilies in the candlelight, I knew that although I would go on loving and desiring these things it was possible to live fully and happily without them. Twenty years later in a Florentine monastery the memory of the empty cottage in the Marsh

171

came suddenly back and I understood, almost as if I had painted those exquisite frescoes with my own hand, how a masterpiece can be conceived in the cool emptiness of a whitewashed cell.

8

ANTWERP TO AINTREE

Daryl had just settled down to paint one morning when a cable arrived from John: dear improvident John for whom money was just something you had to have if you wanted to keep a string of polo ponies for Hurlingham and stay at Claridge's when Mollie and the kids came up to London. John suggested, as if we had only to step on a bus, that we should come over to England and see the Grand National as his guests from the family suite at Liverpool's Adelphi Hotel. Neither of us had ever seen the classic race and as Daryl hastened to point out, Aintree was practically on the way to the other National in Trafalgar Square.

The only available ship that would get us to England in time and incidentally the only one we could afford was the *Anna Spitzen*, a German cargo boat sailing almost non-stop from Melbourne to Antwerp and carrying only one other passenger besides ourselves. The three Lutheran nuns who joined the ship in Adelaide never appeared on the passenger lists. An illustrated book showed a magnificently panelled smoking room and library, the food was described as simple and wholesome in the German style. There was plenty of room for the luggage which in the thirties presented no practical problems. Europe was full of semi-starving porters with handcars ready to trundle anything anywhere for a few cents. In London sixpence for a railway porter was still a handsome tip. Although we had very few actual garments we seem to have set off with a fantastic amount of luggage by present-day standards. Two immense iron wardrobe trunks studded with brass nails, cushions coats rugs, half a dozen hastily bought suitcases, my typewriter, Daryl's painting gear in a bulging knapsack, an easel, a hat box, parcels for friends and the friends of friends all over the world. Hardly anyone bothered to ask just where we were going. It made them feel happy to give us a letter of introduction to a dear old cousin in North Africa who never sees a white man—actually he won't see us either but we don't say so. I feel morally bound however to deliver in person the Spode teapot for somebody's aunt who lives only 45 miles from London by Green Bus.

It was several years since we had had to catch anything so rigidly scheduled and urgently un-missable as the *Anna*, now loaded with Australian wool and headed for Antwerp (via Adelaide and Port Said) at 11 a.m. on a Saturday morning. The Lindsay boat-catching technique (which nearly had us stranded in Naples on our honeymoon) consists of strolling up the gangway just as the sailors are

174

tearing it to pieces and hanging it over the side ready for the next port. Eric, an Irish cousin, used to drive his car onto the Newry station and leap on board the already moving Belfast train. Lionel, en route for Spain, racing in a hired car to catch the Orient liner at Port Melbourne—funnels belching smoke, sirens hooting, passengers waving goodbye to friends below and wife Jean long since on board—had carried on a spirited one-man analysis of the current situation in India. ('You know, Joe, the whole thing began with Warren Hastings...') Or the missionaries—or Mr Nehru. For once I wasn't even listening.

We had made a good start for the *Anna* and were just passing the Melbourne Town Hall with ten emergency minutes in hand when the driver slowed down and Daryl jumped out dashed up the steps of the portico and disappeared. A quarter of an hour later he dashed out of another door and told the driver to step on it. 'Pity you didn't come in Puss! I'd promised Gengoult last night I'd have a farewell glass of champagne with him in the Mayor's room on the way to the ship!'

At the top of the gangway with exactly two minutes to go we were confronted by a notice in German: Sailing 4 p.m. A few faithful friends had turned up to see us off. According to Basil Burdett, the *Anna* was reputed to carry a genuine German Pilsner and we all assembled in the panelled smoking room of the booklet to try it out. The small dark windowless cabin already reeked of beer and stale German cigars. It had begun to rain, the Pilsner had soon given out and the bar closed down. Basil had the far-away look in his sad Spanish brown eyes that always came over him on a wharf or a railway station where the very sight of a departing traveller was enough to set his feet itching. Nobody could look more French, more English, more Spanish than Basil. This morning the long Hapsburg face was definitely Spanish crowned with a small black beret in which only a few weeks before we had seen him at Mulberry Hill looking exactly like an Italian count in a flowing cape. If somebody had pressed a ticket to Antwerp into his hand he would have set sail then and there (for Madrid and the Prado—after all Daryl, you can go anywhere in Europe for a few pounds...). An informed knowledge of the galleries of Europe and a rare ability to take on the art and culture of any country where he found himself would later make Burdett of the Melbourne *Herald* an outstanding critic of the arts.

The usually pleasant city of Adelaide was sizzling under a heat wave when the *Anna* decided to stay there for several days instead of the six hours of the schedule. We caught a bus with seats hot enough to fry an egg—a luxury we were never to see on the *Anna's* menu—and went for a swim at a suburban beach where the cold green water washed the *Anna's* coal dust out of my hair. We were sitting under a tree in North Terrace trying to stretch our meagre shore-going budget to include three unscheduled nights away from the stifling heat of the *Anna* with every porthole closed when a tall figure in a tussore silk suit alighted from a car on the kerb. It was Frank Downer whom I had met for the first time at the races in Melbourne, elegant in grey topper and tails. There are fashions in faces as there are in hats. Frank Downer belonged to the Edwardian period when it was fashionable for a man of the world to be handsome and well turned out. When we knew him he was a widower, living in a large cool house in a large cool garden at the foot of Mt Lofty, waited on by a staff of adoring elderly maids. In this delightful oasis we spent the rest of our enforced stay in Adelaide. Frank was a marvellous host and connoisseur of most of the good things of this world where he had already contrived to enjoy himself for nearly seventy years. He was mad about horses and a former polo player of world class and conversation at his table was apt to stick at racing and horses no matter where it had started off. Over the carefully selected South Australian brandy he produced the kind of stories that King Edward VII would have called risqué—the bold laughing violet-blue eyes across the candlelit table still the eyes of an Edwardian lady killer. Generous, easy-going, a pillar of Church State and the Morphetville Racecourse, our kindly host was a perfect specimen of his class and age. It was well that he died before his particular world had been engulfed in a flood of plastics and nylon shirts. He was no reactionary—would have bought the maids a washing machine and probably accepted the atom bomb as a necessary evil. But how he would have hated his brandy in a plastic container—even at a country race meeting!

The *Anna Spitzen* finally sailed at midnight and after a farewell supper of lobster mornay and French champagne Frank drove us down to the wharf. Already the siren had begun the belligerent howl we later grew to know so well and Frank who was thoroughly enjoying himself had twice been officially requested to go ashore when Daryl, on the top step of the companion, lost his footing and fell with a sickening thud onto the deck below. There was no doctor on board but somebody tightly bandaged the leg and later applied rightly or wrongly a plaster of Paris cage in which he spent the greater part of the voyage. Frank was unceremoniously bustled ashore and the last we saw of Australia was his disconsolate figure waving under a lamp as the ship drew slowly away from the pier.

Our third passenger showed up next morning at breakfast—a trim little blonde in shorts, armed with a skipping rope and a German dictionary, two articles in constant use throughout the trip. Leonore was the perfect fellow traveller *à trois*. She appeared to have no difficult moods of her own, which allowed the Lindsays to indulge in sulks or silence for three. When we became impossible—the atmosphere of the *Anna* was flat but never relaxing—the wonderful girl simply picked up her skipping rope and the dictionary and left us to recover.

As Daryl was glued to his chair and as the only form of amusement for the ladies was a walk round the always vibrating and none too clean decks Leonore and I went down to explore the library. The Chief Steward, in charge of the passengers' literary fare as well as our stomachs (the *Wholesome Food in the German Style* was mainly fat, water, pickled gherkins and excessively salt herrings) was a lugubrious individual with an egg-shaped head and pale bulging eyes who solemnly unlocked the cupboard in the smoking room to disclose two technical handbooks and the Bible—all three in German. We had all been counting on the *Well Stocked Library* of the booklet and in sheer desperation Daryl unpacked his pencils and began half-heartedly to make some drawings, waylaying passing sailors and prevailing on them in dumb show to sit for their portraits. However the caste system on board was so rigid that only two or three of the ship's company were allowed to exchange more than a curt 'Morgen' with the passengers and, on the whole, seagulls perched on the rail and the ship's cat who didn't know the rules were just about as inspiring and less trouble. The Captain—small vain and plain—and the Chief Engineer—tall vain and handsome—were both childishly pleased to pose for their portraits. The two men were poles apart in character and social background. The Captain was a perfectly transparent type of the kind known on the stage as a straight part—a bad-tempered humourless stocky little bully singularly devoid of charm. The Chief was something of a mystery man who had been through World War I and Heaven knows what else: well educated, unpredictable as to moods. Although it was easy to imagine him in a tight corner doing dark things with a knife— he had strong well-shaped hands—with us three passengers he was always polite and even a little shy, revelling in the infantile game of Halma which Leonore had taught him. All four of us soon became passionate Halma addicts for sheer want of anything better to do. I can still hear the Chief's triumphant cry of 'In calaboos! In calaboos!' (in prison!) when a throw of the dice sent one of his enemies back to the starting point.

Needless to say, the nuns who must have stolen silently aboard when we were skylarking at Adelaide, were out of bounds, either as sitters for the artist or anything in the conversation line. An almost visible silence enveloped the three gentle creatures who never appeared in the dining saloon, and I hate to think of the wretched meals served to the uncomplaining women in the privacy of their own cabin. (The food was deplorable. A frequent item on the breakfast menu was a large pallid pancake drowning in thin mauve jam. An unforgettable mid-day meal in the tropics was pea soup followed by pale fatty stew.) The nuns were a drab little party returning to their German convent after a stretch on some tropical mission station. In all weathers they sat still as woodcarvings from a medieval cathedral, in an enclosed corner of the deck where perhaps deliberately—they must have belonged to a very strict order—they could see nothing of such scenery as from time to time we passed. Their faded black serge habits looked shabby and in hot weather woefully unsuited to life on the ocean wave. One warm morning when they were taking a silent constitutional round the deck the Captain who had his knife into these most unassuming and law-abiding of passengers remarked in an audible whisper as they passed by, 'Dem nuns! Dey stink!' In stormy weather when they were obliged to go below the wind blew their voluminous skirts about their black cotton stockinged legs as they descended the steep companion that had been Daryl's undoing. How they must have suffered through the long weeks at sea! Or were they so far advanced in spiritual grace that they were less aware of physical discomforts than Leonore and I?

One of the exasperating regulations on the *Anna* was the compulsory weighing of everyone on board, passengers and all, though mercifully excluding the nuns. The ceremony took place on Sunday mornings on deck with an officer standing by with a notebook and pencil beside the scales. The Captain thoroughly enjoyed the weighing routine as an exercise of authority, particularly over his two female passengers! His wife who was making the trip at the company's expense in honour of a wedding anniversary made a point of turning up to see the fun. As far as I know, the stout rosy-checked *Haus-frau* was never publicly weighed. Speaking no word of English she sat all day knitting in her husband's stateroom over the bridge, never mixing with the common herd even at meal times, and evidently preferring the company of her white cockatoo. It was soon noted—officially and unofficially—that Leonore and I were getting thinner every week. At the table all eyes fastened upon our half-touched plates, not in pity but in scorn. 'Why do not you eat, you ladies? You have the appetites of mice!' We were getting tired of being publicly lectured and one Sunday morning the Chief was persuaded by Leonore to lend us some lead weights which we sewed into our corset belts. Again and again we were ordered to step onto the scales. Though we still looked as skinny as rats the scales recorded an increase of nearly a pound each. Although we felt certain the Captain (to say nothing of his wife) suspected something, short of having us publicly stripped and searched he could do nothing about it. Next Sunday the weights were a fraction heavier after which we were left in peace to turn into a couple of live scarecrows at our leisure.

Soon after crossing the Equator we awoke to a sickening stench wafted all over the ship. The refrigeration had broken down. A vital part was missing and could only be replaced when we reached Port Said. The Captain was furious, stomping up and down the decks and shaking his fist at the flotilla of rotten cabbages riding the calm blue sea. As we jogged through the Red Sea quantities of putrescent meat and vegetables were daily dumped overboard. First to go were the brussels sprouts (oh dem sprouts! How dey stink!) soon to be followed by the entire meat supply, later replenished at Port Said by a few choice cuts of camel and donkey to see us through for the rest of the voyage. The stench of rotting food and fresh paint under a tropic sun was appalling and meals a thrice daily torture of nauseating boredom. There was no nonsense of shading the portholes from the noonday glare off the shining sea, the dingy white tablecloth laden with cheap Britannia metal dishes rose and fell, the water in the carafes was lukewarm and as flat as the Captain's incessant guttural wisecracking at the head of the table. At three o'clock, as a sop to the three fussy Britishers, afternoon tea was grudgingly served by the egg-headed steward, in an elaborate Britannia metal coffee pot, looking like weak sauterne and tasting of nothing at all. (The Chief told us it was brewed from dried cherry leaves.) We spent practically the whole six hours in Port Said in Simon Artz's store drinking cup after cup of good strong tea with real milk.

The large cool store on the waterfront, something like a Middle West barn with its high ceilings and bare board floors, was the Mecca of every traveller through the Suez Canal. At Artz's we bought limejuice and chocolate and sweet biscuits to eat in our cabins and were never quite so hungry after meals again.

The tourists' Port Said is a town of cardboard ready to be folded up and put away as soon as the daily tide of travellers has been sucked back into the ships lying alongside in the Suez Canal. In the dusty streets behind the waterfront, where the conscientious tourists take a hasty drive in a hired car, the lacy shutters of the paper-thin houses are closed against the mid-day heat and a few dejected palm trees slant towards the sea. Who lives and dies and makes love in those pink white and yellow houses? What goes on in the streets when they are bare of tourists, no shipping tied up on the waterfront and no gullible strangers to feed swindle or guide? What does the future hold for little boys like the dark pretty child in the tarboosh who insists on Daryl making a sketch of him outside Simon Artz's? Or the panther-slim youth who spends the whole day following a likely-looking subject in the hope of selling him a packet of *feelthy postcards* before the ship sails?

It was tantalising to find ourselves in the Mediterranean bumping along on that fabulous sea almost within cat-swinging distance of the invisible shores of Egypt and still nothing to be seen from our porthole but the same little scampering waves. A few days later we changed our course, with the *Anna* running parallel and within a few miles of the North African coast. The weather had grown pleasantly warm and even the glum and usually silent crew seemed mellowed under the magic of the Mediterranean sun and fragrant breezes wafting in from the shore. Leonore and I spent hours hanging over the rail in sunglasses, watching the coastline slip slowly by, sometimes so close we longed to jump ashore and run barefooted beside the ship on the ribbon of clean yellow sand. After a few hours the endless honey-coloured foothills, the belts of grey green brush, the swamps, the forlorn tidal lagoons produced exactly the same sort of coma as a ride in the Chapel Street cable tram on a summer afternoon with the unchanging line of dun coloured shops and pavements slipping past the windows and little Miss Hebden fast asleep in her corner seat...The *Anna's* engines thump like tom-toms, the tropic sun beats down on the vibrating decks. Ping ping: Ping ping: go the ship's bells over the flat glaring fields of the sea, setting the creatures of the deep stirring and darting, the sea snakes uncoiling in the darkness as our shadow blots out for a space the pale sea light, while on some remote desert shore a wandering tribe sees far off a phantom ship dancing above the desert palms of a mirage.

Leonore, who had the fancy to skip at sunrise before the heat of the day, came running down to our cabin one morning to report a new and unmissable view. The motionless turquoise expanse of the sea was streaked with pink and from it rose an all pink scene of such exotic beauty it might have been a slice of the Old Testament in technicolour. Against a pink sky towered like Babylonian skyscrapers mile after dazzling pink mile of terraced rock formations, huge square-cut vertical blocks and slabs outlined at varying levels with deep violet shadow where arches and gateways gaped in the pink façade. When the Chief came off duty an hour later we were still hanging over the rail with the terraces still pink under the mounting sun. He told us the rocks were fretworked with vast caves inaccessible to man, where generations of lions had been living as long as God

184

made lions in Africa. He had heard them sometimes in calm weather, roaring across the still water.

A flock of tiny humming birds from the African forest attached themselves to the ship, fluttering and hovering like a cloud of butterflies some thirty feet above the open deck. All through a windless morning the exquisite little creatures—some so small they could only be seen clearly through Daryl's race glasses—kept up an incredible pace through the blue air with only an occasional weakling pausing to rest a while amongst the ropes and spars. Where were they bound and why? As the day grew hotter and the sun beat down on the frail indomitable wings we began to fear they might never reach their destination. What if by trustfully following the course of the *Anna* they were to find themselves a week later madly off beam in Birmingham or Tunbridge Wells instead of the jungle reaches of the Upper Zambezi or wherever they were heading? One by one the brave little travellers began to flag and soon the tiny jewelled bodies were dropping exhausted into the green foam of our wake. A few fluttered feebly onto the deck, stunned or already dead, to be swept up later by a sailor just as we used to sweep up a panful of dead bees on the verandah at Mulberry Hill.

It was dusk when we passed into the shadow of the Rock of Gibraltar and out into the chill grey Atlantic. For the first time since we left Melbourne it seemed worth while to consult a calendar and start ticking off the days before Antwerp London Liverpool and the Grand National. There were no more ports on the schedule and Daryl calculated we should reach Antwerp with a couple of days up our sleeve if the *Anna* kept up an average pace. There was no available radio for the passengers and we could only guess at the weather the favourites and the state of the tracks at Aintree. We had read every scrap of print on board including the two handbooks in the library, deciphered all the notices in German and eaten the last of our sweet biscuits. My impressions of the Bay of Biscay are mainly crouching over a Halma board, tilted at a dangerous angle above small angry bottle green waves.

We had got so used to sleeping through flappings and bangings creakings groanings bumpings and thumpings that an unexpected burst of silence woke us at dawn as effectively as an alarm clock under the pillow. Last night we had gone to bed in the Bay with the waves slapping against the sides of the ship, the water carafe rising and sinking in its wooden cage, our two suitcases sliding up and down under the bunks. Now suddenly, all was stillness and unnatural peace. The *Anna* was positively gliding, smooth and silent as a black swan between the level banks of a pleasant river, with little grey chateaux and vineyards running down to the water's edge. The light was that clear luminous unmistakeably French light of Monet and Boudin. In short, the *Anna* had embarked on a leisurely trip up the River Garonne. A French pilot had come on board during the night—a little dark-faced man with a ragged moustache, now taking an early breakfast in a battered straw hat. It seemed a golden opportunity to try out my indifferent French on a real live Frenchman. Alas, the two beady black eyes stared back at me without a glimmer of comprehension. I tried again, slower—still no response.

With a defeatist 'Au revoir, monsieur', I left him to finish his coffee in friendly international silence. After breakfast, the pilot, who had been up all night and looked in the clear morning light like a seedy small-town doctor, still in his music-hall straw hat and carrying a little black bag, was rowed ashore, presumably to await the *Anna's* return in his native village where the Chief told us the inhabitants spoke and understood a patois known only to themselves.

The rest of the day was spent gliding slowly up the river, playing three-handed Halma on deck and wishing the Chief or Captain would appear to tell us where we were going and why. In their usual corner sat the nuns, their heads bent over their prayerbooks as the sunny vineyards and chateaux drifted by. It was dark when we creaked into a little wharf and a makeshift gangway was let down, swinging above a little dark jetty lit by a single lamp. A sailor came up with orders from the Chief not to stray from the wharf as the *Anna* would be sailing within an hour. There was an open shed at the end of the jetty whence a solitary figure emerged to sell us, in dumb show by the light of a kerosene lantern, a bottle of brandy. We sat down on a wooden bench facing the dark water, the three of us taking little nips from the bottle by turn. It was bitterly cold and the cheap fiery liquor helped to keep us warm. As usual we were hungry. Leonore and I would have traded the best vintage brandy in all France for a plate of hot fish and chips. A hundred yards away the dark shape of the *Anna* rose and fell under the light from the big swinging lamp over the open hatch where the crane dipped and swung above the gaping hold. It was long after midnight when the last crates and barrels were unloaded and we heard the pad of rope-soled feet on the deck over our heads, goodnights in French and German, the shattering cry of the siren that must have roused the sleepers in the vineyards for miles inland. In the morning another stop to take the pilot aboard, another to put him off again onto a dangerously rocking tub with its one funnel belching black smoke in all directions and so out into the tossing waters of the Bay. One way and another the excursion up the Garonne had cost us two valuable days.

We were within ten miles of Antwerp on the morning when the *Anna's* engines suddenly ceased to thump, the ship made a half right turn and stopped dead. Sailors appeared from nowhere, running and shouting. From the bridge the Captain's voice could have been heard halfway to Australia. No sign of the Chief. Then an ominous silence that lasted until lunch time when we ate alone in the saloon. No information was given either then or ever afterwards to the passengers—what really happened down in the engine room was never divulged. Hour after hour the *Anna* continued to ride at anchor on the chilly waves of the North Sea. We only knew that we were going to arrive late at Antwerp. Very late. Very very late...With suitcases packed ready for a flying start down the gangway, passport to hand, the dreary uncommunicative steward tipped, poor Daryl limped up and down the deck in a frenzy of frustration. At Aintree every blade of grass would be in place for the great race. Horse boxes and floats would be pouring into Liverpool from all over the British Isles. At the Adelphi our beds were being made up. So another day passed. We were still riding at anchor when we went down to lunch for the last time. It was no longer funny, as it had been for the first few weeks, when the egg-headed steward bent over our meagre plates hissing through broken teeth: 'Pliss! A little chiss and sussich?' The original 'sussich' which had somehow survived the lack of refrigeration in the Red Sea was now wafer thin like the dry soapy 'chiss'. Even Leonore who was worrying about the date of a women's conference in Sweden, looked glum.

When we finally tied up amongst a tangle of smoking funnels and swaying masts we had missed our chance of seeing the Grand National not by hours but days. We never had another.

The medieval towers and roof tops of Antwerp traced on the soft morning air raised our drooping spirits. There was also the exquisite pleasure of going down the gangway of the *Anna* for the last time. We followed the porter trundling our luggage over the cobblestones without a backward glance, piled into a rattletrap taxi and went off to collect our first mail since we had left Melbourne. There was a letter from the Westys, who had moved in as caretakers at Mulberry Hill while Hilda Reynolds had a holiday in England, where she immediately fell off a merry-go-round on Hampstead Heath. Mrs Westy's letter was full of small exciting happenings. The fowls were laying like tigers, Donnie my lovesick spaniel had refused to eat for the first week, the garden was real good, twenty points of rain last night...We read it sitting on a stone seat in a chilly little square while the lovely smell of gum leaves after rain came drifting in from Australia ten thousand miles away. Another from Sydney: 'I have written about you to my old friend Monsieur Fernau. If you have any time to spare in Antwerp I think it might amuse you to call on him...' And one from Monsieur Fernau himself, exquisitely illegible on hand-made paper—inviting us to stay with him for a week before going on to England. Characteristically, it seemed that everything had already been organised with meticulous attention to detail: Monsieur Fernau was not accustomed to having his invitations turned down. It was arranged that we should call at his city apartment in the Grand Place where the low mellow buildings, unchanged for centuries, gave it the unreal look of an expensive film set. Almost too perfect to be true. From here our host was to drive us out to his country house which in one of his rare moments of facetiousness he had christened The Lark's Nest. The Antwerp flat was known as The Crow's Nest. Monsieur Fernau of the exquisite Crow's Nest was one of those anachronisms to be found in every period of civilisation—a survivor clinging to the raft of an already vanished past. Banker, connoisseur of medieval art and twentieth century wool, he had long been the ruling force in the famous Belgian firm of Kreglinger that had its roots in the Middle Ages and tentacles all over the contemporary world.

The atmosphere of the reception rooms in the Grand Place—the original linen-fold wood panelling and sixteenth century gilded leather on the walls, the deep piled carpet—was one of such chilling perfection that we were prepared in some degree for the fantastic tempo of the next few days. It was impossible however to be prepared for the actuality of Monsieur Fernau himself, limping majestically into the room and holding out a manicured hand in welcome:

a plump pale hand that had probably never done anything more physically strenuous than signing documents, turning the pages of medieval manuscripts or helping its owner to a soufflé. On first sight and ever after (he was precisely the same in shops or restaurants as he was in his own private kingdom in the Place) Monsieur Fernau proclaimed himself by very lack of proclamation as a person accustomed to authority. I was glad even as we shook hands that we were awaiting his pleasure not as suppliants pleading for an overdraft, but guests, and guests only.

In pre-war Europe it was still possible to live as Monsieur Fernau lived in two distinct and separate worlds. Physically the rather ungainly body dwelt in the twentieth century world of banking and wool broking, organising, directing, arrogantly and brilliantly interfering and virtually ruling over the great firm from an arm-chair padded with Utrecht velvet. This was only one half of his life. The other was lived out mentally in quite another climate to the world of men and affairs, in which he breathed the rarefied atmosphere of his personal tastes and pleasures: the collecting—and reading—of strange and rare books, of jewels, ivories, old silver, carvings and prints—the kind of things that are bid for at Christie's or Colnaghi's by international collectors. This was the world in which he discussed French verse with beautiful sophisticated or specially intelligent women, for whom he had the same unerring eye as in every other department. A cultivated taste backed by great wealth made it unnecessary to suffer fools of either sex gladly or otherwise and it was still comparatively easy to shut out most of the unpleasant things that were happening all over Europe—preposterous little revolutions amongst the lower classes—even strikes on the waterfront where men were unloading the firm's wool...Imagination boggled at the thought of Monsieur Fernau in his dark London suit and soft-brimmed black hat riding in a bus or being ticked off by a taxi driver. If there was any ticking off to be done it was by Monsieur Fernau of The Crow's Nest.

He was unaware of himself as an anachronism and when I grew to know him better I realised that it was just no use expecting the normal reactions, mental moral political or anything else, from this extraordinary link between two worlds. His values were simply not those in fashion in the nineteen-thirties. Ruthless by contemporary standards, he probably thought of himself as humane—perhaps even kind: had he not entertained the two young Australians with all possible courtesy! One could picture him carefully planning the ruination of a business rival, drawing up and signing the fatal words and delicately sniffing at a tuberose on his writing table. As we sat drinking China tea and wafer thin Belgian pastries preparatory to taking off for The Lark's Nest I noted the powerful head dominated by eyes like splinters of blue glass—hard appraising eyes continually on the watch, missing nothing, and in this rarefied setting I felt suddenly uncomfortably aware of my unpressed travel suit and far-from-Paris hat. A few minutes' conversation in which he inquired briefly after our mutual friend in Australia—we gathered a barbaric country scarcely on the map of the civilised world—revealed the egoist who finds it unnecessary to boast or even to speak of himself. His prints his library his *objets d'art*, were not only his own world but perforce the world of everyone with whom he came in contact. Everything from The Lark's Nest to Gothic cathedrals where from time to time he immersed himself in the past were all alike a background for Monsieur Fernau of the Grand Place. Tucked under a heavy bearskin rug we drove out to The Lark's Nest for dinner, covering the flat Belgian roads at an incredible speed. He began talking to Daryl of Flemish art. His astonishment that the young Australian painter could converse on Memling and Van Eyck with knowledge and conviction was thinly disguised. He asked: 'How do you, as an Australian, come to know anything about Old Masters?' When Daryl began telling him about the Felton Bequest his attention wandered. Australia was altogether too far away. Next day after Daryl insisted on visiting the Antwerp museums alone our host was not specially pleased on going over our marked catalogues to find that we had picked out most of his own particular favourites as our own.

The Lark's Nest turned out to be less frivolous than its name implied: a smallish perfectly appointed well heated country house filled with rather too many objects of rarity and value. Everything proclaimed the personal taste of the connoisseur. We were waited on twenty-four hours of the day by a Belgian couple, the dark silent wife an inspired chef, the dark silent husband, no matter what time we returned to the Nest at night or sat up talking at home, respectfully awaiting our pleasure in white cotton gloves. The two sallow faces were expressionless as the faces of two West African zombies. When I remarked in all innocence, 'How lucky you are to have such a wonderful couple!' he raised his pale tufted eyebrows: 'I consider they are fortunate in their employer!'

An hour before dinner one evening Monsieur Fernau came up to our room in high good humour carrying over his arm an exquisite Spanish shawl with instructions that I should wear it to the meal. He was infuriated when I found it impossible under his watchful eye to drape it effectively over my simple dinner frock, saying sourly: 'My dear girl! You simply have no idea of wearing your clothes!' He was right of course—he had an infallible sense of costume. (It only occurred to me long afterwards that most of the women he knew had ladies' maids.) After a dinner beginning with wild duck and ending with fresh pears stored all winter in the ice house in a cave at the bottom of the garden, a backgammon board was produced by the zombie with appropriate brandies and liqueurs and I was forcibly instructed in the rules and regulations of this diabolical game—if such it can be called. For me it was an embarrassing evening, sitting upright in my exotic shawl secured at key points with safety pins, trying not only to keep awake after the Burgundy and rich food—no wonder our host suffered from gout—but to master the complicated technique of the board. From time to time Monsieur Fernau thumped at it in fury: I have no head for even the simplest game beyond throwing a dice, in which luckily I had had long practice on the *Anna*. Daryl meanwhile, uninhibited by our host's indifference to all but the game in hand, settled down to browse happily amongst the rare and beautiful books under the shaded standard lamp. It was no collection for the squeamish or uninformed.

Whatever their social shortcomings, our host was indefatigable in the entertainment of his Australian guests. Perhaps there was even a certain titillation in being occasionally—very occasionally—contradicted, since he was constantly asking us to extend our stay at the Nest. Why hurry? Surely there remained many fine things in Antwerp worthy of our attention? And we could always cancel a hotel reservation out of season. Personally, he never had any trouble of that sort at Claridge's...

We were taken one morning presumably to admire a singularly unattractive large two-story house being put up in a near-suburban wood for a wealthy Parisian friend. The architecture—contemporary French-Belgian with plenty of black marble and no expense spared—was a hotchpotch of Sweden Versailles and Shepheard's Hotel in Cairo, of a style that mercifully disappeared with the outbreak of the Second World War. To our astonishment Monsieur Fernau insisted on extolling its charms which must surely have been anathema to his sensitive taste! Our lack of enthusiasm was no doubt infuriating from young people who had probably never had a chance to see a fashionable modern house in the wilds of their native land.

More successful was the eighty-mile drive to Brussels in the long black Daimler under a fur rug, in brilliant sunshine, with Monsieur Fernau, assured of an excellent lunch ahead, at his conversational best. Our host and hostess were charmingly civilised people with an unpronounceable name; the women guests, dressed by Lanvin and Schiaparelli and dripping with pearls, so prettily mannered that I felt perfectly at ease in my one and only Australian suit.

195

The whole atmosphere of the house was typically Parisian from the moment the butler opened the door of the faintly scented drawing-room, over-heated and over-furnished in pale honey coloured wood and gilded mirrors. No flowers. At the table everyone spoke French except ourselves and it was easy to understand why Brussels has been called the Little Paris.

After lunch we left Monsieur Fernau gossiping with the ladies by the drawing-room fire while we went off for an hour's wandering through the town, dominated by the huge classical building—I think the Law Courts—of which the story is told that a visiting Indian rajah, impressed by its size and grandeur said to his equerry: 'Order two of those palaces to be built for me at home.' For us, one was enough, as there were several pictures we specially wanted to see. The nightmare collection of Hieronymus Bosch might easily have been painted in the twentieth instead of the fifteenth century. The blood red devils with pitch forks, lifelike monsters and strange beasts are pure surrealism—neither dream nor reality. Driving back to the Nest we passed many small allotments each with its own vegetable patch. Thinking of our Australian vegetable garden I asked innocently how the Belgians managed to make such tiny plots produce so much? To which Monsieur Fernau replied: 'I have no doubt the peasants do whatever is necessary.' I should have known. It was a subject in which he could have no possible interest.

On our last night, there came to dinner a sort of fairy tale princess of dark-haired pale-skinned beauty, a member of the family firm (a melancholy young man who looked like a painting by Ingres), and several other guests. Their world, far apart from ours, was connected by a bridge almost too slender to cross at a single meeting, but the Princess's calm oval face lit up with real humanity when we talked together over coffee. The melancholy young man, the elderly Belgian frustrated painter whom we visited in his studio, even the young Princess—all of them, including our host himself, were characters left over from a novel by Marcel Proust. Monsieur Fernau and his circle were my first and only contact with a small slice of European society that was virtually wiped out—as well as much that they represented—by the Second World War.

The galleries and museums of Antwerp are an inexhaustible treasure house but time was running out. I would have liked another morning at the Plantain Museum—whose saints and madonnas reminded me of the still beauty of the Princess—and many more amongst the Flemish carvings. I still have the engraved copy of the charming French verse that hangs in the museum, given to me by Monsieur Fernau and the little old French silver vinaigrette which brings back so clearly this unforgettable week on what now seems like another planet.

In the street on our last morning in Antwerp we passed a huge shaggy bear being led on a chain over the cobblestones on its hind legs. I knew better by this time than to ask Monsieur Fernau if this was a common sight in Antwerp since nobody but ourselves batted an eye as the poor creature shambled past. Bears on chains, overworked servants, the cabbage patches of peasants...These things were definitely not Monsieur Fernau's affair...

The shadow of Monsieur Fernau and his kind lay heavily upon the city of Antwerp which seems lit in memory not by the living warmth of the sun but the cool grey light of a medieval painting, its snug gabled houses, prim gardens, sober churches and monuments never wholly real under a cloud canopy of the down-pressing past.

9

PEOPLE, PICTURES AND PLACES

In London it was early spring with Hyde Park floating in a mist of palest green and Piccadilly gay with tulips in newly painted window boxes. Nothing seemed changed since we had last driven down Bond Street on our wedding day. The shops entrenched in long tradition of exclusive trading still felt no need to advertise themselves. Why bother with window dressing when everyone knows that at Lock's and Asprey's, Walpole's and Cartier's, can be bought the best diamonds handbags jewels umbrellas and top hats in the world? Nor is there any need to tell the passer-by that behind the discreet façade of Tooth's or Colnaghi's vast sums are changing hands for a Dürer, a Rembrandt, even a Cézanne. In Piccadilly the glass doors of the Ritz still swung open to reveal an Edwardian flashback of Turkish carpet and potted palms. The windows of Fortnum and Mason's were piled high with hothouse fruits, hearts of palm, truffles, special Continental cheese arrived that morning, like ourselves, on the boat train.

In Trafalgar Square the same overfed pigeons or their great-great-grandchildren were still fluttering round the fountain. The top of Nelson's column and the portico of the National Gallery were frosted white with their droppings. The same sense of excitement carried us on winged feet up its narrow stairs, through the turnstiles and past the postcards and umbrellas into the little room on the left where sits enthroned in pure blue glory Leonardo's *Madonna of the Rocks*. And this moment of rare piercing joy on a spring morning long ago in London is everlasting. In a parched Australian summer twelve thousand miles away I can take it out and gloat over it as I could take out of a jewel box—if I had one—a single gem. Whereas the once-dragging hours (which I will spare the reader) of a three-handed session in Fowlis Terrace with my Mother's old friend Miss Dinely are now mercifully reduced to a mere flea-bite on the surface of time. 'Oh that!' says Miss Dinely dismissing by the very tone of her voice the photograph of Whistler's exquisite Little Miss Alexander in a silver frame on the piano. 'Cream, Daryl? Sugar?...That picture used to belong to my family but none of us liked it and we gave it away.' Daryl says: 'Puss and I were admiring it only this morning at the Tate.' Which is all I can remember now of an abortive two-hour conversation. So are we compensated for the inequalities of our pleasures and pains.

Art galleries—if you go there to look at the pictures— are exhausting places as we had found out on our honeymoon when half an hour at the Louvre had reduced us both to the state of gaping exhaustion known to gallery directors as 'museum fatigue'. We were going to spend a lot of our time in London looking at pictures and needed a modest home base where we could relax in cheap uncluttered peace. After a morning with a limp bowler-hatted little agent in Kensington it appeared that uncluttered peace was about the most expensive commodity on the market. For the visitor on a modest budget, plain cost twice as much as fancy and the smaller the rent the more every inch of space was crammed with dreary gimcrack furniture fringed pelmets painted lampshades and kidney-shaped cushions. It was the same at Woolworths where even the teapot we had to buy had a kitten painted on both sides. Armed with the agent's key we peered, hopefully at first, into furnished flats with drawn blinds smelling of soot and mice where ancient gas heaters howled like dingoes at the touch of a match. Constant hot water so loudly called for by British travellers on the Continent was evidently still a luxury at home. A flat we inspected in Holland Park—the last—stands out as a masterpiece of its kind although I hope its pink poplin curtains and worn black carpet trellised with roses have long since crumbled to dust. Someone with a taste for the Glamorous East had furnished it largely with cheap Indian brasses and rickety brass coffee tables, brass Buddhas squatting on lace mats and on the mantelpiece a procession of brass elephants going nowhere. It was a period of dismal bad taste without the comfort of the Edwardians. Not only in London but in practically every city civilised people were living in places like this. With or without brass elephants it made no odds. In Australia they would have been Kewpie dolls.

In 'rooms' as distinct from flats the landlady was usually willing to toil up several flights of stairs with a chop on a tin tray. The lease of an unfurnished flat was anything from two to ninety-nine years. In so called 'private hotels' (no privacy and no liquor) there were lace curtains and maids in black stockings and enormous mob caps, where the boarders evidently lived in perpetual fear of scurvy, judging by the array of lime juice bottles on the dining-room tables which would have delighted Captain Cook, each with its owner's label round its neck like a pet dog. Meals were usually served in dungeons lit by artificial light, and watery coffee taken after dinner amongst the potted palms in the LOUNGE. (Gentlemen are requested not to smoke in the LOUNGE.) Many of these Kensington private hotels had started out as well-appointed Victorian dwellings with plenty of servants, nannies and governesses, with a carriage and pair stabled in the mews at the back. The rooms were often elaborately handsome with gilded cornices marble mantelpieces and massive cedar doors. It was sad to see these once cheerful houses fallen in the social scale.

Meanwhile in fashionable Sloane Street for reasons equally mysterious most of the houses seemed to have survived as private dwellings, handsome and a trifle smug, knowing themselves to be situated at what used to be called a Good Address. Some of them faced onto garden squares with iron railings laurels lilacs summer-houses and private keys and here the children of the well-heeled amused themselves under the supervision of nannies in coachmen's capes and stiff straw hats. Still homeless, I found myself waiting to cross Sloane Street one sunny morning penned in amongst a scatter of nannies and perambulators opposite one of these coveted garden islands. Beside me stood an elderly nannie wheeling a shiny black perambulator as big as a hansom cab in which reclined at full length a plump rosy-cheeked boy of perhaps ten years old who regarded the world about him with the languid disapproval of one already 'down' for Eton or Harrow. In a few moments the haughty little passenger would be alighting from his chariot to enjoy a game of cricket behind the screening laurels at an age when many a Baxter ten-year-old would be walking home from school to milk half a dozen cows before tea.

Chauffeurs were waiting beside the doors of expensive cars, a footman with a feather duster, like an extra in a Mozart opera, was flicking at a vase in a drawing-room window, housemaids were on their knees scrubbing spotless white steps, a florist's shop sent out whiffs of early hyacinths and hothouse lilac from the south of France. I was examining a shining brass knocker on the white panelled door of Number 77A when to my embarrassment it began to knock of itself and a tall rangy woman in tortoiseshell glasses was opening the door, tossing a dustpan onto a gilded console table on which stood a vase of white tulips and asking me to 'Come inside, do, the buses in this street are appallingly noisy—I suppose you've come to see the flat? It only came vacant last night.'

I said: 'It's a miracle! We do most desperately want a flat.'

'Most furnished flats in London are plain hell,' Mrs Harrison said with a grin—not the professional land-lady smile I was beginning to recognise that melts away like

203

rancid butter in the sun. 'You're from Australia? I thought so! My husband and I knew some terribly nice Australians once from Sydney. I daresay you know them?' (Like a great many other people in pre-war England the Harrisons always expected everyone in Australia to know everyone else.) We began climbing up several flights of stairs chatting all the way. On every landing stood a piece of good old furniture— a Georgian sofa table, an oak dresser.

The flat, once the servants' quarters, was on the very top of the house with a bedsitting-room overlooking Sloane Street, a bathroom looking into the top of an elm tree and a tiny square hall. Hardly any furniture except divan beds and two more antiques—a vintage tin bath and Regency mirror. Uncluttered peace!

'You say your husband's an artist? What fun! Is he good at fitting into small spaces? I thought artists had easels and things.'

I assured her mine was on holiday and wouldn't be painting in the flat. When he was produced for mutual inspection a few hours later Mrs Harrison said: 'It's so tiny, I can't charge very much' and quoted a rent unbelievably low. We moved in next day.

The Harrison family consisted of a pretty petulant blonde who came and went from boarding school and disapproved on principle of the tenants, a thin dark student son at London University and a gentle tweed-jacketed pipe-smoking husband with a greying moustache. I remember them because all three might have been stock characters in a drawing-room comedy on the West End stage. It was Mrs Harrison with her tireless broom and her sense of humour and her long active legs who supplied the driving power for the whole establishment, assisted by a pasty-faced youth with the stamina of a Swiss chamois and a little old German ex-governess with a merry walnut face and tight curly hair dyed jet black, who pushed the old-fashioned carpet sweeper from floor to floor and slept for free in a sort of broom cupboard under the stairs. The brave little creature had suffered damnably during the war, was as poor as a rat and thankful for Mrs Harrison's roof over her head.

One of our first callers at Number 77A was our old friend Professor Henry Tonks. He stood for a moment on the threshold taking in the whole establishment with shrewd hooded eyes. An impeccable skeleton of a man with long-boned hands and feet, in an old very well cut tweed jacket that hung in folds over his long frame. 'What a climb! How on earth did you find it, my boy? I suppose you two know you have one of the best addresses in London?' Tonks an elderly bachelor who knew his London inside out and himself lived in an exquisite small house in Chelsea's much sought-after 'Vale' had an unexpectedly worldly streak. Whether Tattersall's historic sale-yards, close by, were also a 'good address' I don't know. Only a Londoner can understand how the same street can be U at one end and definitely non-U at the other. Daryl was delighted to find himself only a stone's throw from the pagoda-like building under whose glass roof there was perpetual free entertainment, equine and human. It wouldn't have greatly surprised me if, like the man in the *New Yorker*, he had come back to Number 77A one day leading a newly-acquired horse upstairs. 'Just look at his quarters! Picked him up for a song!…I've already asked Mrs Harrison if I can put a bag of chaff in our bathroom.'

We went one Sunday morning to watch the riders in Hyde Park's Rotten Row. Tiny children in their West End breeches were bobbing up and down on ponies led by grooms and riding masters, elderly gentlemen shaking up their livers before the Sunday roast beef, nervous customers on hired hacks patently in need of something to cling to as well as the reins. A heavily made-up grandmother in a hard hat and smart black habit cantered past ablaze with diamond brooches and pins. At a distant turn a female figure was flung onto the tan by a large galloping horse obviously out of control. Except for a sprinkling of well turned out foreigners from the nearby Embassies and one or two diehards from private mansions backing onto the Park, the traditional glory of the Row had departed.

At home in Australia, when Daryl wasn't painting or riding through the bush on Pompey or working in the vegetable garden or cutting wood or digging potatoes, there was always time to note the shape and quality of the clouds, to watch the ants crawling up the side of the woodshed and wonder if it was going to rain. In London he became a man of affairs—always in a hurry, always going somewhere, leaping with tireless energy from tube to taxi, taxi to bus in a hard hat; in his hand a rolled umbrella, in his pocket not grass seeds and drawing pins but little notebooks full of addresses that sent him flying from one end of London to the other and often beyond. What with the Thames winding through everything and turning up in unexpected places without a bridge and the trains plunging underground and coming up miles away in the opposite direction, not one of the great London galleries and museums can truthfully be described as 'on the way' to another—even for a Lindsay. A never-ending source of interest pleasure and at times exasperation, that kept him in almost perpetual motion, was the Felton Bequest. Looking back on it now I realise that he was fascinated even then—as he would always be fascinated—by the Felton with its vast resources and clumsy complicated mechanism that often made decisive action impossible at the London end. The Felton would always be a flame at which Daryl would find himself— unofficially—buzzing and now and then singeing his wings. Long before he had more than a purely personal but none the less devouring interest in the Melbourne collection, a bundle of his early letters from Australia to Henry Tonks, preserved until the latter's death, testifies to his doubts and fears. The latest acquisition for Melbourne could keep him awake all night at Mulberry Hill if he felt that Randall Davies or later Sir Sydney Cockerell were making a bad or injudicious buy. He was fast becoming acquainted with the inner workings of the London art market. He knew that London salerooms in the thirties were full of impor- tant works of art that could still be bought at a reasonable figure if one knew how to go about it—great paintings rare prints and drawings that had hung on the walls of private mansions hitherto unseen by anyone but the Duke and his butler and perhaps a handful of house guests when the Long Gallery or the Blue Drawing-room was opened once a year. The American market was tempting and an increasing number of gaps were showing out on the faded brocades and wallpapers of the stately Homes of England as Gainsboroughs and Reynolds, Constables and Van Dycks changed hands under the guidance of international experts like Bernhard Berenson and Joseph Duveen. A few years ago we had watched a daily procession of Britishers mournfully filing past Gainsborough's Blue Boy on view at the National Gallery, soon to leave for California. So did they file past the draped coffins of the Duke of Wellington and Queen Victoria.

Davies had succeeded Rinder as the Felton's London adviser and his rather petulant demands on Daryl's time and judgment were strangely revealing. Would Daryl meet him at ten o'clock tomorrow morning and take a look at a chalk drawing at Tooth's? A doubtful Old Master at Wildenstein's?...Won't take us long, old chap...Oh thanks...Thanks most awfully...He had no 'eye' for painting and perhaps rightly lacked confidence in his own aesthetic judgments. If Daryl had a strong enough hunch that a certain picture was aesthetically 'right' nothing would change his opinion. For him the picture itself was the thing that mattered: he never claimed expert knowledge of provenance, authenticity and all the rest of the solemn sale room pronouncements which could be safely left to scholars and experts in their particular fields. Randall who dwelt in a perpetual twilight of doubts and fears must have suffered hell during his brief term of office with the Bequest. His diffident English charm caused us both embarrassment, making it all the harder to sidetrack his often ill-timed requests. A few years later the whole process was to be repeated, in a slightly different key, with Sir Sydney Cockerell, then a somewhat pompous elderly scholar living near Kew Gardens who often summoned Daryl to advise—unofficially of course—on possible purchases for Melbourne. Sir Sydney however was a very different cup of tea from the hesitant Randall. A former Director of the Fitzwilliam at Cambridge his real forte lay in the acquisition of rare books and manuscripts of which he had a vast knowledge and experience. He was perfectly aware of his limited knowledge of painting and liked to enlist the help of Daryl as a practising painter and an Australian who had been a close friend of Frank Rinder in his brilliant buying days and evinced a surprising understanding of the needs of the Melbourne Gallery. It was surprising to other people besides Sir Sydney. To quote Sir Charles Holmes, the Director of the National Gallery in Trafalgar Square: 'Where he [Daryl] gets his judgment about art from, Heaven knows! considering he spent most of his life amongst sheep and cattle in the back-blocks of Australia.' Although Holmes, himself a fine painter, like many untravelled Britishers probably thought of Australia as a land of droughts bushfires and kangaroos, he was to some extent right. Australian artists as such were virtually unknown out of their own country. In the war 'the Aussies' had been magnificent if unconventional soldiers and now in peace time wore strange clothes and spoke with a harsh faintly American accent.

Holmes knew nothing of the family background in the small up-country mining town of Creswick, Victoria, where Daryl and his nine brothers and sisters were born. The streets of Creswick were wide and grassy, leading out and away to the goldfields and the Chinese camps on the outskirts of the town. There were several rambling wooden hotels, an assortment of well-attended churches, the hideous Masonic Hall, sporadic outcrops of low wooden shops with iron roofs lit by gaslight or oil lamps. From a wooded hill overlooking the town the two-storied Forestry School flanked by plantations of pine looked down on the bustling little town of neat weatherboard cottages, with a sprinkling of solid mid-Victorian houses each with its own hedged and shrubberied garden and stables. There were two or three doctors in Creswick with flourishing practices that took them miles out into the bushy foothills on horseback, or like Doctor Robert Charles Lindsay behind a good strong horse in the buggy with a groom or perhaps young Daryl beside him to open the gates on the lonely farms of Smeaton or Cabbage Tree Flat. The nearby Chinese encampment with its traders and kindly opium-smoking old men who gave the young Lindsays ginger and strange sweets and sent them home when it grew dark; the miners, the fireworks, the annual procession with the dragon winding its way down the main street between gaping children and straggling livestock gave the little town a background of perpetual excitement, a faintly exotic and distinctive flavour, enhancing the normal country joys of ponies and dogs, picnics and rabbiting and those long dusty golden afternoons fossicking amongst the worn-out mining claims where the once raw yellow clay, now covered with rank weeds, lay humped beside the overgrown shafts and feathery stunted trees that Percy Lindsay was later to record with a wistfully authentic charm. Close by, fringed with reeds like rusty swords, the deep and treacherous Creswick Lake lay flat as a tin tray under the open sky. The nearest town was Ballarat ten miles away, where came celebrities like Mark Twain to lecture, Adeline Genée to dance and Nellie Melba to sing. Local transport depended on the horse or one's own sturdy country legs (Ruby Lindsay, beautiful and shy, insisted on walking across the paddocks to her own wedding because she feared an admiring crowd at the church's front gate on the street). And so the young Tremearnes, the Lewers and the Lindsays grew up free as summer morning magpies, making their own entertainment at each other's houses. It was dated of course—in the sense that every breath we draw belongs irrevocably to a particular day and hour—but it was first-class entertainment just the same. For Percy, warbling the 'Wandering Minstrel' in the old tin bath, G. and S. was as much a part of contemporary living as the chip heater in the bathroom or the mahogany sideboard. Acting and music were in the air and what boundless energy and invention went to the home-grown production of *The Mikado*, beautifully sung and smartly dressed! what side-splitting amateur scripts charades impromptu turns and always classical music! There is a photograph of Daryl's brother Reg with a mandolin, another of Lionel, even then incredibly Spanish, with a sprouting dark moustache and guitar. Percy most expertly played the flute, sister Mary was witty and inventive backstage, and apparently the whole family except Daryl the youngest boy could sing. A pale little creature long of face and leg in half-mast trousers and lace-up boots, he enjoyed in silent admiration of his betters the gargantuan party suppers with claret cup lobster and his mother's

211

famous trifles; and once, at the age of nine, secretly downed with spectacular results a large tumbler of the Doctor's best port. There seems to have been an amazing supply of local talent—even Doctor Lindsay in genial mood would sometimes oblige, by special request, with the sole item in his repertoire, the rollicking Irish ballad 'Barney O'Hay'.

The Lindsay children were brought up on a robust diet of Rembrandt and Turner, Constable and Dürer, Cervantes Rabelais and William Blake, as other children are brought up on Red Riding Hood and the Three Bears. They were familiar from earliest youth with the large exciting engravings of Gustave Doré in the family Bible, knowing God and Satan and Adam and Eve as other children know Peter Rabbit and Winnie the Pooh. All in varying degrees had an instinctive respect for what could be produced with a stump of pencil or a penny bottle of ink. One hot afternoon in the summer holidays when an unnatural stillness had fallen upon the house Janey had opened the door of the dining-room, there to stand for a moment in silent wonder, close it and steal away. The children were all there, even the little ones in petticoats and singlets and underpants, all drawing away for the lick of their lives. All had pencils, bits of charcoal or crayon and pieces of paper. Some lay full length on the worn carpet, others face down—with stomachs pressed for coolness against its dark shiny surface—on the mahogany dining table. Scrape of pencils, crumple of paper, a child without a handkerchief—probably young Daryl—snuffling happily in a corner. Finger of yellow sunlight falling between the long heavy curtains onto the hard-breathing children tranced in their own timeless Heaven…Long long afterwards—her beloved Reg and beautiful wayward Ruby were dead—the Mother of the Lindsays was to call up for me the unforgettable quality of that summer afternoon…

Apart from Robert (soon to leave for exile in a country bank) who loved all objects rare and beautiful, none of the boys except Daryl appear to have become visibly excited by photographs of antiques in old numbers of the *Studio*. As a child of ten he was intrigued by the craftsmanship of a finely plaited headstall for his pony, the Tremearnes' mahogany sideboard, his mother's few pieces of Victorian jewellery. When he left home at eighteen to work (for ten shillings a week) as a jackeroo on a cattle station in faraway Queensland, the family was already scattered. Money was scarce now in the old white wooden house under the pine trees. The mines were no longer working and many of the shops in the once busy streets were closing down as the population dwindled. The old carefree days of fun and laughter and charades and family jokes and feuds and going reluctantly to church in stiff white collars were already in the childish past and only Janey serene as a Buddha in voluminous black silk skirts was unchanged…

In Queensland it was a red letter day for the young jackeroo from Creswick when the station mailbag brought him an odd number of the *Connoisseur*. At night, stretched on an old iron bedstead on the homestead verandah, he read it from cover to cover by the light of a candle. The black velvet heat, the aching weariness of a long day in the saddle, the buzz and flutter of singed insects dropping into the tin candlestick were forgotten as he pored over the illustrated advertisements of Albert Amor of Bond Street and Mallet of Bath. Reading about the sales at Christie's and Sotheby's, exhibitions at Tooth's and Colnaghi's and the Royal Academy, he noted and ever afterwards remembered that Lord Redesdale's collection was to be sold at Exeter on the fifteenth, 'including a very fine pair of Famille Rose vases, thirteen and a half inches in height'. His memory for this kind of information, apparently useless to a Queensland cattleman twelve thousand miles away, enabled him thirty years later to identify a piece of porcelain in a New York collection or the provenance of a portrait in an English manor house. Such was the private world into which he escaped as the other stationhands might escape into the world of racing and the study of form in the Brisbane papers.

A few years later war broke out and he had his first taste of the great London galleries as a private on leave from France.

It was good to be in England together, enjoying pictures in our own time and way. Both of us hated using a catalogue in an art gallery. Daryl would spot a painting twenty feet away and go and stand in front of it, agape with single-minded concentration, exactly as I had seen him pick his fancy in the Birdcage at Flemington Racecourse, judging a horse on its conformation without consulting the odds.

This is not the place for describing the pictures we loved best. Enjoyment and understanding of a picture come by looking at it, not reading about it in a book unless the author is a Ruskin or a Kenneth Clark. When I was about ten years old my Mother, who had a natural bent for music but very little for painting, was all for the Arts as part of our education. To stimulate our interest in the Old Masters, my sisters and I were given a course of forcible feeding from a book called *Great Masterpieces of European Art*. It was a terrible book with small blurred photographs accompanied by a text that went something like this: 'To the right, the figure of St Buzz Fuzz—or Cardinal This or Lady That—stands with the left arm raised parallel to the vertical column of the temple in the middle distance, while in the foreground can be observed...' It was years before I could bring myself to look an Old Master in the face. Now in joyful uninformed ignorance I looked at them in the National Gallery (then upholstered in crimson brocade) where the deathly chill was soon forgotten in the glow and glory of the walls. Until the onslaught of museum fatigue would send us wobbling out on frozen feet into Trafalgar Square in search of hot strong tea and that brightest jewel in Queen Victoria's crown, the toasted muffin. South Kensington, crammed to bursting point with treasures, was less like a museum than a maze where every dim-lit corridor led back to the Great Bed of Ware no matter where the visitor started out. At the Wallace Collection the gilded rooms seemed perfumed by the warm scented breath of Bouguereau's pink-fleshed nudes afloat on sky blue clouds. In the draughty Tate there was as yet no window dressing and nothing to waylay and beguile the earnest seeker after the Turners—only the pictures themselves to be studied with backbreaking concentration in the reflected light from the river on whose banks Turner used to sit and paint. At the Tate I saw for the first time a room or maybe two filled with portraits by John Singer

Sargent. They looked almost indecently alive, embalmed for ever in their own juicy paint, the celebrated sitters as easily recognisable without a catalogue as the waxwork figures at Madame Tussaud's.

Sometimes, in the Holy of Holies at Colnaghi's or at the historic house of Agnew's in Bond Street, we would be shown behind the closed door of a pleasant panelled room a single masterpiece set out like a diamond on a length of velvet—to be savoured at Agnew's with a glass of Mr Agnew's brown Spanish sherry. Now and then a contemporary painting—mostly French. An English artist, unless he married a duchess or otherwise came into the limelight, could expect very little support from the British public. Men like Tonks and Steer and Augustus John and the Nashes had their own private buyers and their work was rarely on show. Occasionally, in one of those dark muddled shops that sell old frames and artists' materials and lay figures, an original oil or watercolour could be picked up, usually with its face to the wall, traded in for a few pounds by some unfortunate professional artist on the breadline. Sometimes a well-tempered palette or a set of the classics with faded yellow fly leaves ideal for watercolour drawings turned up. (Lionel, prince of bookstall prowlers and pouncers, had once in London bought for seven pounds an old volume containing prints valued at seven hundred pounds.)

Daryl was avid for the kind of specialised knowledge with which I had no concern—knowledge that can only be got in a great city like London. In London he could learn to know—as Harold Wright of Colnaghi's would know by a sort of sixth sense of acute perception, fruit of long experience—the exact state of a Rembrandt plate and the price it was likely to bring at auction. In London he could handle a carved Italian frame with the original gilding intact, early silver and glass, Boule and Wedgwood, Minton and Ming—everything you touch and handle and stroke has its own distinctive feel and texture.

The West End antique shops were filled with real antiques at fabulously low prices where knowledgeable young men in striped trousers discussed in B.B.C. accents and with enormous gravity the finer points of Jacobean needlework and Empire wall brackets. Every shop had its own special character and special excellence. Best of all was Churchill's poky little room stuck like a barnacle to the wall of an immense warehouse in the Edgeware Road where, incidentally, a Queensland dugong had once been inadvertently stored for several years with dire results. At Churchill's was simply set out in row after row of its own natural grace some of the finest and rarest pieces of old glass in the world. The whole of Mr Haines' set-up was typically English in that hardly anyone outside its own exclusive clientele knew of its existence. There was no showmanship, the glass was left to tell its own story against a background of the profound precisely expert knowledge of the proprietor. At Haines' a client was invariably treated as a gentleman and an honest one at that. It made no difference if he had money to spend or not. Nothing was locked up. Things were seldom dusted or broken. I watched Mr Haines handling a rare piece with the same sure touch as Mr Chant long ago in Chapel Street, Prahran. Priceless fragile pieces were sent off to international collectors as far away as Australia with no more fuss than posting off a pair of boots. Haines, having attained his own particular pinnacle of international prestige, was content to sit back and enjoy his collection, occasionally favouring an old client with half a dozen clarets or an engraved goblet. Actually he was already, when we met him, rather allergic to new clients and we were honoured when he allowed us to take home a modest purchase of some Georgian table glass to Mulberry Hill. How well I remember the bleak winter afternoon when we lunched together in his cosy little private room above the shop. The coal fire, the pork chops and apple pie, the white wine in superb seventeenth century glasses.

At the opposite end of the aesthetic pole was the beautiful house in Grosvenor Square where Madame Fernau dwelt in luxurious elegance. Although the Fernaus preferred to live with the English Channel between them most of the year, they had a mutual respect for each other's taste and business acumen. As Monsieur Fernau had specially instructed—I won't say asked—us, we went to call on his wife. The whole house was furnished from attic to cellar with valuable pieces from which Madame would now and then part, a little reluctantly, albeit at a good stiff price, with a cabinet or a set of spoons. Her clients were mostly wealthy Americans. Like her husband, she had impeccable taste though rather less austere. Selected clients—by appointment only—were served with afternoon tea and cocktails by the butler and the silver tea service was genuine Queen Anne. Over China tea and cinnamon toast, Madame unbent a little, noting a large blue Australian eye resting on her favourite pieces. When her guest questioned the authenticity of the handles on a Chinese Chippendale cabinet her own eyebrows under the elegantly coiffured hair flew up. This young man from Australia actually seemed to know something about antiques...

We were both happiest in the less pretentious second-hand shops scattered all over London where Daryl soon had innumerable friends in 'the trade'. I wonder how many of those shuttered shop fronts on which we used to knock after business hours are still functioning today? Somewhere in Paddington or Notting Hill a bell jingles, a light springs up in a back room and a man in shirt sleeves and carpet slippers carrying a cup of tea or a candle in a bottle opens the door. 'Oh it's you, sir—come in—just let me put a bit of newspaper down for the lady to sit on. That chest's a bit dusty.' It was the old Chapel Street treasure hunt all over again. The same sitting in friendly half darkness behind the closed shop, swapping experiences of worm holes and false chair bottoms and faked legs, two paintings stuck together in one frame, a set of fruit knives 'absolutely in mint condition! Be-eautiful'. A silver tankard amongst the jellied eels and reach-me-down suits at the Caledonian Market, then the most rewarding hunting ground in London. From these friendly people, who accepted Daryl as a fellow enthusiast with no axe to grind, we learned something of the inner dealings of London's antique market. Most of them, I'm sure, were honest, except when a client or another dealer treated them badly, when no holds were barred. It was a self-contained strangely exciting little world as exclusive and its members as carefully graded as the members of White's or the Reform Club.

In vast storehouses sacred to the trade, unknown to the general public, were often deposited for long unloved years the contents of some family mansion. Here were crystal chandeliers mounted in ormolu, Adams mantelpieces, tapestries, carved and gilded cherubs clinging to tall mirrors and four-poster beds, Aubusson carpets reeking of naphthaline, their garlands of lilies and roses still fresh and glowing under the sudden naked light of an electric bulb. All these treasures once hotly disputed by the heirs—tied up in Chancery suits, now unwanted, forgotten, who knows?—but left to rot and fade amongst the spiders and mothballs in Pimlico or Paddington until the war comes and they are burned, hosed down, blown up or otherwise destroyed—only a little more quickly and thoroughly than by the gentle hand of time!

In London, history is very close to the surface. One is constantly confronted with historical personages mounted on bronze horses or standing erect on handsome pedestals in streets and squares. So *that* was what Mr Gladstone looked like! And there, over and over again, is Queen Victoria with her little pursed-up mouth, hanging onto the heavy Royal Sceptre as if it were as much a part of her everyday attire as her umbrella. Daryl introduced me to his favourite equestrian statue in London. King Charles on an elegant pedestal at Whitehall, very much a king, and very much alive, which can't be said of Earl Haig stiff on his clumsy charger at Victoria, or for that matter of most of the twentieth century statues in city streets.

English history kept coming up at me at unexpected moments. Waiting for a bus in Piccadilly, I suddenly remembered that the tall house opposite the bus stop had once been the home of the Duke of Wellington, the gift of an adoring nation. After his death, it was opened to the public who came, I think, on Thursday afternoons to gape at his ornate gilded furniture, gold and silver plate. Perhaps in that very house the same Weigall who had made our bust of Mr Carlyle had done his drawing from life—not a very good one—of the Duke. That house, stiff and unlived in as it was when I saw it, did bring Wellington to life as a real person.

At the Reform Club where I went to tea one Sunday with Uncle Bob, history oozed from the walls. The old old waiter who brought our tea and thin bread and butter and fruit cake, and even the club cat, belonged to the last century. It was a new and startling innovation to allow the ladies over the threshold once a week although my host appeared to be the only member availing himself of that privilege. Uncle Bob, who had been a Member of Parliament for as long as I could remember, and a passionate advocate of Free Trade for over fifty years, was nothing if not contemporary-minded: which is one of the more endearing traits of the English character.

In the Temple, where Charles Lamb and his friends lingered beside the fountain and Sam Pepys ogled the women coming out of the exquisite little Temple Church on Sunday mornings, our friend Allison Russell had a flat in King's Bench Walk. A species of legal Beefeater stood just inside the high always locked gates, ready to receive the tenants' parcels and carry them up the steep dark flights of stairs. Like many other Temple dwellers, Sir Allison sent his laundry and dry cleaning to a famous firm in Scotland by train in large wicker baskets, returned a fortnight later for special 'quick service' but normally taking three weeks. We made this fascinating discovery the year he lent us his flat and we wanted something cleaned in a hurry. These are some of the tremendous trifles that made the pre-war English the delight and despair of their opposite numbers in Australia.

10

MORE PEOPLE AND PLACES

My cousin Martin Boyd was occupying the first floor of a Queen Anne cottage in a quiet street at the back of Kensington High. He had a genius for finding pleasant little houses where he contrived to live in a certain modest elegance on whichever side of the world he happened to be. As a bachelor free to take off for 'foreign parts' whenever the spirit moved him, he seldom remained long at the same address. It wouldn't have surprised us to hear he was living in a hollow log in the Australian bush or in an Anglican monastery in France. It would have been a comfortable log and the beds in the monastery not unduly hard. Although *Lucinda Brayford* and *The Cardboard Crown* had not yet been acclaimed as bestsellers in England and America, Martin—who was always becomingly modest about his writing—was already well enough known to English readers to be photographed by the shiny papers coming out of the Dorchester on the arm of a duchess or gloved and top hatted on a fine Sunday morning strolling in the park—perhaps on his way to lunch with a mutual relative Dame Maud McArthy. Dame Maud was an elderly lady with whom he had for years indulged in a warm gossipy undemanding friendship. Having made a unique success as head of the British Army Nursing Service during the First World War—she died before there was another—she was living in a cosy little house in Kensington overflowing with signed photographs of generals and crowned Heads, all of whom she had accurately summed up as human beings. Authority had never gone to her head and when the war ended she was still as funny and direct as when I had met her long ago in Australia.

Not long after we had settled in at Sloane Street Martin, who was planning a retreat to West Wittering to sail his boat and finish his current novel—probably *The Lemon Farm*, offered us his Holland Street flat while he was out of town. We were sorry to leave Mrs Harrison of whom we had grown very fond. Martin's flat, of course, was charming, with small paned windows overlooking the street.

As a young man in Melbourne studying for the Church and afterwards architecture before settling down as a professional writer, he had always had a nose for odd and unusual pieces of furniture and queer old paintings picked up for a few pounds. During the war he had embellished his dugout in France with a large statue of his favourite Dancing Faun, dragging it from one filthy hole to another until forced to abandon it forever in the oozing mud. A splendid Norman fireback survived however to adorn the family country house in Victoria which he later bought, restored and lived in for a few years. On the walls of this house his nephew Arthur then a schoolboy in Victoria later painted with wit and distinction lively scenes from the Old Testament with members of the Boyd and àBeckett families in some of the star roles.

Holland Street was very pleasant with its almost countrified air small shady gardens and a friendly little shop or two where the customers and their dogs all knew each other by name. The lower story of Martin's house— it really *was* Queen Anne and had once been occupied by an admiral—had long since been wantonly deflowered by a small dark shop beside the front door whose original fanlight was still intact. Here lived and worked with antlike diligence a Mr and Mrs Gittens, in a perpetual mouldy twilight, the fitful gleams of the English sun seldom reaching beyond a dusty rectangle of light in the window of their newsagent's shop. A water closet downstairs dripped unceasingly behind the scenes, enhancing the cavelike atmosphere of the Gittens' two back rooms, into which we once had a horrifying glimpse of grey discomfort. Their tiny backyard was a-bulge with unsold newspapers and discarded furniture, lengths of wood, rusty iron, sacks of coal. The Gittens belonged to no guessable age group. Both had pale pleasant rather greasy faces, probably through living almost entirely without fresh air and eating hastily snatched irregular meals. The shop was never shut except for an hour or two on Sunday mornings. Both husband and wife looked cold even in warm weather, perhaps because of the seeping damp from the original Queen Anne foundations which luckily didn't affect us upstairs. The newsagency had a small regular clientele of customers of which we soon became a part. As well as newspapers the Gittens sold magazines, light—very light—literature and a fantastic assortment of unrelated odds and ends evidently in request by the Holland Street public, such as darning needles, ruled writing pads, envelopes with crinkly edges, fireworks—quite a wide choice—sealing wax, safety pins, hair nets, striped peppermint lollies, tinned soups and the Union Jack in ever so many sizes, presumably for those elaborate processions when the English will stand happily all day in the rain. Except for trifling differences in the stock it might have been the little shop round the corner in an upcountry township at home. Through their association with Martin of whom they were touchingly fond and proud, they had a lively interest in Australia and even, I think, had visions of emigrating to that far-off land that Mr Boyd was always talking about. Long after in Australia, when the London Blitz was at its height, I had a sudden vision of the Gittens imprisoned in their dark narrow shop—the drip of the cistern at last defeated by an awful roaring in the sky...

A few doors round the corner lived the balletomane Arnold Haskell who had stayed with us at Mulberry Hill and whose latest book was illustrated by some of Daryl's drawings. Arnold used to drop in on us for a cup of tea and news of his many Australian friends, a small exotic figure squatting on a cushion on the floor in his dark London clothes. It was said he had Armenian blood. For a short time he had been a dancer himself. Haskell was literally obsessed with ballet and every least detail of that mysterious organism from the length of a *tutu* to the latest ballet 'mamma' to cause trouble backstage. His great liquid brown eyes dilated as he regaled us with spicy morsels of ballet 'shop' with a seriousness typical of the dedicated balletomane. He had a real knowledge of choreography and at this time was spending practically every waking hour backstage at Covent Garden or Sadler's Wells. He was recognised as a world authority and much sought after by aspiring young dancers in need of the right word in the right place. He was a kind little man who liked to help the young and talented when he could. His gossip was lively and feminine but seldom malicious. He had lived so long in the unreal half-world of the theatre where he himself had no creative outlet that he seemed hardly flesh and blood: a Petroushka stuffed with sawdust with no substantial life of his own. We dined one night with Arnold and his Russian-born wife in a dining-room that might have been a stage set by Bakst—all black and purple and gold with tall thronelike chairs of painted wood, in which the host as he sat at table was almost engulfed.

London was ballet mad that season, as it was right up to the outbreak of war. Covent Garden Sadler's Wells Drury Lane, the tiny Marie Rambert Theatre, once a church in Notting Hill Gate—we went to all of them. At Covent Garden Daryl made working drawings of the dancers in action, in *tutus* and practice tights, sometimes sitting with a pencil in the darkened auditorium—he had to wait till the lights went on again to see what he had got down—or

227

standing up in the feeble light of the wings so close to a line of sylphides floating off the stage he could smell their breath and feel the light brush of their muslin cloud. For Daryl, who had the privilege of drawing backstage whenever he liked, just as he did in Australia, all this was valuable experience. For me, the bubble of illusion was pricked by familiarity and I preferred to watch ballet from a stall, as pure theatre. I never wanted to know, as the stately Queen of the Willis glided onto the moonlit stage, that in real life she was suing her husband for divorce or that the Swan Princess was suffering from a carbuncle. When any of our special friends were dancing I wanted to think of them as the Magician or the Sugar Plum Fairy—not Algie and Edna with whom we were scrambling eggs after the show. Pavlova who remained sealed in her hotel suite when she was dancing in Australia, except to drive in a closed taxi to the theatre, knew the importance of the magic gulf that separates the professional from the public.

No other theatre had the glamour of Covent Garden, where the crystal chandeliers the crimson hangings even the little gold chairs in the shadowy tiers of boxes had the audience in exactly the right mood of excited anticipation before the curtain went up. I remember a first night when the lights went up at the interval and the whole theatre seemed to be sparkling, so brilliant were the women's jewels, so white their long kid gloves. Near the entrance to the supper room a woman wearing a long greenish cloak and crowned with a sort of Tudor head-dress caught my eye. Round her neck was an antique necklace of enormous size, garnets or turquoise— no diamonds. The expression in the strong featured face from which large clear eyes looked out and over and away, the concentration with which she was talking to two men in a clear rather husky voice, gave her a sort of splendid isolation in the crush of satins and black coats—a monumental figure of solid green rock washed over by the waves of talk and laughter and ballet chat that rose and fell unnoticed. I asked Arnold Haskell, who knew everyone, who she was? The poet, Edith Sitwell. We were always running into Arnold at the theatre, often with his friend Captain Bobby Jenkinson, who will be remembered by balletomanes of his generation as a rich and generous bachelor who attended practically every performance of a ballet he liked, in very long tails, looking exactly like a drawing of a handsome 'masher' by du Maurier. Bobby had a house at Virginia Water where he gave Sunday parties to his friends in the ballet. I think he married one of them—a beautiful talented girl whom he loaded with jewels. How Edwardian it all sounds and how much time Londoners spent in enjoying themselves! Leslie Goode, another bachelor, then a director of Covent Garden, and one of the chain-store Sainsburys, were two other well-known balletomanes, party-givers and bouquet-providers of the thirties who thought nothing of running over to Paris or Monte Carlo for a special performance.

There was a matinee of *Coppelia* not long before the war that held a huge audience clapping and stamping in a frenzy of applause as Karsavina, one of the last great Russian prima ballerinas, dropped her final curtsey to a changing world. After the war something warm and vital went out of classical ballet as we knew it, leaving a cold emptiness at the core.

Whereas the pre-war ballet soared to dazzling heights of perfection, the legitimate stage was at a low ebb—the theatres filled with saccharine so-called drawing-room comedies. These plays were nearly all tarred with the same insipid brush. (Scene I, Act I. The drawing-room of Lady Watterstone's house in Kent. To right, French windows open onto a rose garden etc. A parlour maid or a butler, invaluable for getting the stars on and off, were invariably 'discovered' when the curtain rose, dusting the chintz covers or fiddling with the paper flowers.) Usually there was a popular star heading the cast, trailed by a Milky Way of nobodies. So long as established favourites like the Boucicaults or Dame Edith Evans were in the lead—great artists already belonging to a dying theatrical tradition—the London audiences seemed perfectly satisfied to see them afloat on a waste of waters, unsupported by anything but their own wits and personal magnetism. The few plays containing ideas which appeared at this time were short-lived, except the incomprehensible Bernard Shaw who had come to be accepted as a yearly offering along with Shakespeare and Barrie's *Peter Pan*. A feature of West End matinees was the afternoon tea tray passed hand over hand like a fire bucket by patrons seated in the darkened auditorium, the tinkle of glass and china and rattle of teaspoons mingling with the light English voices on stage. Coming out into the thin pale sunlight at five o'clock there was an indefinable sadness in the air. Perhaps even then, they sensed—these matinee-going housewives retired civil servants and elderly ladies from the country—something of what lay ahead of them in slaughter and suffering. Many of the gloved and

230

toqued women and umbrellaed and bowler-hatted men who now sat sipping tea and exchanging gossip in the stalls were a few years later to perform incredible feats of bravery and physical endurance.

Not only the theatre but English shops newspapers and all forms of advertising stressed the importance of class and money. Social magazines like the *Tatler* were read in the Underground by white-collar workers who would have called a hunting coat 'red' and a table napkin a serviette. The *Tatler's* hunt balls and Piccadilly night life at third hand spelled desperate escape from the drabness of life in the suburbs. The outward and visible chasm between rich and poor, upper and lower, was ever present in the streets, where little groups of out-of-work coal miners sang for coins thrown into a shabby hat held out to passersby. Some of the Welsh coal miners had been out of work for years on end. In Kensington, beggars held out tins and cardboard box lids as we had seen them do in Italy until it was made a punishable offence to beg publicly on an Italian city street. I was haunted by the bitter-sweet tinkling tune ground out from a terrible little piano on wheels by a hollow-eyed ex-serviceman from the First World War.

Most of the better class shops didn't bother about window dressing, although coal was appetisingly set out on plates in a window in Kensington. Each plate bore a neat label with the price and variety—Best Durham... Direct from Cardiff...and so on. Everything but the garnish of parsley. In the fishmongers', crayfish on strings walked about on marble slabs, while hares pheasants and turkeys hung side by side brushed by the damp coats of passersby.

It was hardly ever warm enough to worry about flies. Dogs walked in and out of the most exclusive shops just as they did in the old Baxter store—although in Baxter a fox terrier snuffling amongst the flour and sugar bags was liable to be sent flying through the door by an infuriated customer's boot. In Kensington it was a dog's right not only to go shopping but to occupy a seat in a bus. Even so, I felt it was going a little too far when we saw a live panda looking out of a taxi window in Hyde Park. Worthy of Charles Keene was the ritual evening stroll of West End maids and butlers leading the family pet on a leash and standing by, while the animal lifted a leg at its chosen lamppost, with expressions of mingled boredom embarrassment and scorn. But the apotheosis of animal worship was surely reached on the day we watched a shabby little cat of no social standing hold up the river traffic below by entangling itself on the iron jaws of Tower Bridge. The bridge was just about to open up for the ships to pass through when somebody on the Embankment spotted the cat. In a few seconds the poor creature would have been mincemeat for all to see. To the watching crowd, the humane costly and triumphantly British solution of holding everything until a specially summoned policeman climbed up and literally tore it from the jaws of death, seemed perfectly normal. No wonder the London policeman has a world wide reputation for good old-fashioned human kindness! Like the bus conductors and taxi drivers, close contact with the public sandpapers down the traditional British reserve to an easy friendliness, as it does in the markets in the back streets where we found an almost Rabelaisian climate of real wit, as jellied eels haddocks mussels and second-hand clothing changed hands under a crossfire of Cockney wisecracking. The stallholders were sharp as needles, summing up the customer's bargaining potential in a flash. Much of the good fresh country stuff was doomed to be boiled to a watery paste whose rank miasma lingered nightly in a thousand front halls. Ordinary English middle-class cooking was probably at an alltime low, and the Express Dairies were filled with white-collar workers lunching off pastries and 'phosphates'—pale green and yellow syrups fizzed up with tepid soda water.

Lunch hour in London was apt to last from two to three hours for business and professional people in top level jobs. At any hour of the day from the top of a Piccadilly bus, fascinating glimpses were to be caught of the heads of clubmen bent over *The Times* at the long windows or seated at white clothed tables in vast half empty rooms. The pace of the thirties was still more or less Edwardian although that pleasure-loving monarch had been in his grave for over twenty years. Although every Londoner above the breadline wore a watch and Big Ben down by the river boomed out the hours and quarter hours the public clocks in the streets often differed from each other by as much as half an hour. Now and then somebody who had missed a train wrote to *The Times* about it. In the better class shops the customer was expected to take a long time making up his mind and an Anglo-Indian with time on his hands could spend an entire morning in Bond Street choosing a tie or an umbrella without remark. Daryl treated himself to the time-devouring extravagance and enduring satisfaction

233

of having a pair of riding boots made to measure by a small exclusive bootmaker in the West End—one of those typically English pre-war specialists who summed up the human race in terms of their own profession. ('If I may say so, sir, your friend Major Body is a very fine gentleman. He hangs a good boot.') Luckily Daryl himself hung a reasonably good boot at the time: in other words, like Dick Body, who had performed the necessary introduction of a new client, he was the possessor of a pair of fine-boned legs thin enough to be literally poured into a shining leather mould. The smaller London shops produced some Dickensian characters seldom met with behind the counters of the department stores, where polite poker-faced robots would serve a cannibal chief with a meat axe or a bishop's wife with a hairnet with the same lack of human curiosity.

Outside Harrods, the huge Knightsbridge store which in the thirties reigned supreme amongst the County, Rolls Royces and Daimlers of uncertain vintage lined the kerb of Hans Crescent for half a mile while a uniformed commissionaire stood at the entrance to the jewellery department with an open umbrella to protect the ladies' toques—sometimes the most famous and beloved toque of all on the tightly curled head of Queen Mary herself. At Harrods an almost holy hush prevailed. No woman would dream of trying on a blouse or even an overcoat except in the privacy of a curtained cubicle. A stranger's cheque was cashed immediately without question and anything from an ermine coat to a pith helmet would be instantly despatched to the remotest corner of the globe. An article a customer had bought paid for and gone sour on overnight could be brought back a week later and the money civilly returned. Almost equally imposing though of a different calibre were the Civil Service and Army and Navy Stores where retired colonels could buy calves-foot jelly and consommé in glass jars, on some complicated per cent basis which allowed their wives and daughters to buy raincoats and other worthy garments.

A pre-war visit to an English country house entailed much complicated arranging before the right train could be caught on the right day at the right railway station. A week-end with the Stradbrokes at Henham Hall involved the choice of two or three railway lines—unless of course a guest was arriving in his own *motor* as Lady Stradbroke always called it. We had no *motor* in England and never have I written or received so many polite notes before we finally arrived at Wangford Station en route for Henham.

Set in the wide free-rolling Suffolk landscape beloved of generations of English watercolourists the house stood in a semi-wild park with enormous trees where foxes rabbits and pheasants enjoyed themselves according to their fashion until the season of annual slaughter came round and the gentle Earl as Master of Hounds gathered his forces for a day's hunting. The original Hall had been burned down over a century ago but the three-storied mansion that replaced it was handsome enough in its way with rows of long heavily pedimented windows and well-proportioned portico facing the gravel sweep where the hunt assembled under a spreading cedar...The great landowners were not yet much concerned with making every acre carry its share of crops and pasture, cattle and sheep. Certainly there was a vegetable garden at Henham where apples apricots peaches and pears were espaliered on warm brick walls, although Mr Bully would have been shocked at the undisciplined foxgloves and hollyhocks running riot amongst cabbages and lettuces. It was in this garden one summer evening that I heard my first English nightingale prodded into ecstatic song by Lord Stradbroke with a shooting stick. His old tweed cap that always reminded me of my Father's crammed down over his eyes—the late evening sunshine still lay upon the flowering tangle at our feet—on his face a charming expression of simple pride at having conjured up this marvel of liquid song for his Australian guests. Like so many Englishmen of his class and age Lord Stradbroke truly loved his birds, went into raptures over the larks and nightingales and even cheerfully endured the screeching of his wife's peacocks on the lawn. Pheasant and grouse, quail and woodcock had so long been the legitimate prey of the masters of Henham that their wanton destruction was simply never questioned. The English have a special genius for keeping their emotions in watertight compartments.

The annual Hunt Ball at Henham which threw everybody except the Countess into a ferment of happy excitement was probably exactly like a hundred other hunt balls all over England. The whole affair was a perfect period piece with young girls floating through candlelit rooms on the arms of broad-shouldered sailors and soldiers and young men in pink coats with complexions almost as rose-leaf as their partners. Seated on gilt chairs against the panelled walls or vigorously waltzing, grandfathers and grandmothers and elderly aunts—most of them still hard riders to hounds—were having the time of their lives. The

Scotch whisky, the claret cup for the younger guests, the red roses all over the house in tall silver vases, the silver pheasants set out amongst the trifles and fruit salads and cold meats on the supper tables, even the family butler, were exactly what I had hoped and expected.

There was little formal entertaining and we were free to wander about as we liked. We slept in a high-ceilinged gilded room downstairs with windows opening out onto a little private balustraded court facing a great cedar whose boughs swept the turf. The vast double bed appeared to be supported by solid gold cherubim with the torsos of heavyweight boxers. The head was draped with crimson velvet and topped off with a golden coronet. The rest of the furnishings were a comfortable mixture of odd chairs with rather faded chintz covers, velvet stools with more crowns and gilded legs, Victorian mahogany marble and mirrors and always on the dressing table a little jug of country flowers. I think it was during our last visit to Henham that we went for a picnic to Norwich where Daryl wanted to show me the cathedral. Lady Stradbroke who loved picnics insisted in spite of the chilly weather that we ate our Melton Mowbray pie sitting on the damp grass by the roadside: 'Just like Australia!' while the chauffeur boiled up a tea kettle on a spirit lamp.

I like to remember the Stradbrokes as we saw them out riding together one autumn afternoon in the park at Henham. The Countess rode side-saddle in a dark flowing habit, sitting her big black horse with a careless elegance, her husband on a bay a few lengths behind. Against a background of sombre evergreens and streaming clouds the two cantering figures made an equestrian composition worthy of Velasquez at the Prado. When I think of Henham now, it has the quality and texture of one of those old French tapestries whose colours still retain a sort of faded brilliance in which the Countess is forever riding side-saddle on her great black horse in the park...In the end, Henham Hall was pulled down stone by stone. It was too large, too hopelessly impractical for contemporary living.

Certain parts of England have the kind of immediate beauty easily assimilated by a busload of tourists bowling down a Kentish lane in spring...drifts of primroses, an apple orchard in bloom. The country Constable and Turner, Cotman and Gainsborough liked to paint was of sterner stuff. The great landscape painters of the English School were not specially concerned with the recognised beauty spots starred nowadays in the guide books along with the best hotels. Cotman gave immortality to a solitary rock in mid-stream, Gainsborough to a single tree laced with shadows and windy airs. As artists, they were fascinated not so much by the object itself as its relationship to other objects and the elemental forces of Nature—the rock shaped inexorably by secret watery rhythms, the tree rooted by the pull of gravity in the dark earth.

Of this distinguished company were two contemporary English painters, Henry Tonks and Philip Wilson Steer. Both were accepted as part of the tradition of English painting as few English artists have been accepted during their lifetime. Although Tonks was not really a landscape painter except for a handful of lovely spontaneous watercolours, he was as sensitively aware of every nuance of English light and English weather as Steer himself. When he placed his solidly built English nymphs in a woodland setting it was an English stream, an English wood enveloped in English sunlight. Outwardly austere, Tonks was a romantic at heart. Strangely enough, he had trained first as a surgeon before throwing away at twenty-seven the prospect of a brilliant surgical career and switching over to the serious study and practice of art. Within a few years, he was holding the coveted post of Professor of Drawing at the Slade where he was loved and hated respected and feared on account of his witty inspiring and often vitriolic tongue. Female students had been known to faint and falter under his withering scrutiny and in one tragic instance to leap from an upstairs window. Himself a superb draughtsman, his insistence on drawing and yet more drawing can be seen and felt in the work of his distinguished pupils Orpen and Augustus John. Dürer and Leonardo, Rembrandt and Ingres were his gods. No smudgy charcoal was permitted at the Slade and only the bravest and strongest of purpose could stay the course. The sharper the point of the searching pencil or hard-nibbed pen, the more admirable to the Master was the artistic adventure in which every fumbling stroke left the student stripped bare of disguise.

Daryl had been singled out by the gods for a meeting with Tonks at the precise period of his intellectual and emotional life when he was most in need of exactly the sort of wise counsel and instruction that Tonks was so well able to give. The young Australian was making wartime drawings of plastic surgery at Sidcup Hospital under the critical eye of Sir Henry Newland, then performing life-giving miracles in this still little-known field. Sir Henry had introduced his draughtsman to Tonks who happened to be visiting the hospital. His first words were characteristic: 'What are you doing?' Daryl said: 'Trying to draw, sir.' It was the perfect answer for Tonks, who told him: 'I'm glad you said *trying*... However, I may be able to help you.' In this brief exchange both men far removed in background age temperament and experience understood one another perfectly. Tonks must have found something to interest him in the long Australian face, then pale from sessions of continuous work in the theatre and long hours at the drawing board in a tiny room at the hospital where he had once been taken by surprise by a visit from Queen Mary. As the artist was wearing nothing but his underpants at the time, he had leaped as nimbly as possible through the window into the snow. Her Majesty's reactions were, alas, never disclosed! Whatever Tonks' reasons he had requested Newland to grant one day a week special leave for his draughtsman for personal tuition at the Slade. To Daryl's everlasting gratitude, this unconventional request was granted. It was a decision that was to change the subsequent pattern of his whole life.

The eagerly anticipated weekly lessons at the Slade were hardly less valuable than the informal talks with the Professor beyond the classroom, where now and then Tonks would relax and let himself go to a chosen few. One day in class, he was explaining to the students the quality and meaning of a line and had suddenly fixed on Daryl a fierce hooded eye (Daryl has elsewhere likened him to a wedge-tailed eagle). 'Lindsay! I don't believe you're understanding a word I say!' Daryl said truthfully: 'I'm afraid I'm not, sir.' Later in the privacy of Tonks' studio he had the temerity to add, 'You know, sir, I wasn't the only student who couldn't get your meaning this afternoon. Only the others weren't game to say so to your face.' Tonks took it in good part and was even fair-minded enough to admit that for once his own explanation might have been at fault.

When the war ended and Daryl was at last free to leave the Army, Tonks advised him to scrap the past, take up art as a professional career and start on the bottom rung. As related in an earlier chapter he *did* start at the bottom—with Mr Thompson's teapots.

When Daryl had introduced me as the girl he was going to marry, Tonks had asked, 'Where did you get her, Lindsay?' He seemed pleased and rather surprised that the Australian fiancée showed a passionate interest in the drawings that lined the walls of studio and staircase at the Vale. Ignorance—so long as it wasn't joined to the arrogance of the Art Boys—he didn't mind. He often talked to us about the Australian country, particularly the quality of the atmosphere which he was convinced was 'too hard'. He used to say to Daryl: 'Your Australian sunlight would never do for me, my boy. I could never get the *feel* of it.' He was probably right. I don't think Australia could ever have been his spiritual home. Another day when Daryl was showing him a watercolour which hadn't come off, Tonks said, 'Never forget, the sky fits over the land like a bowl or a dome. It isn't a backcloth. *Do you understand* what I say?'

To dine with Tonks at the Vale was always a highlight of our visits to England. Behind the closed door of the studio at the top of the steep narrow stairs, the host awaited his guests, rising from the high-backed leather chair in which he usually sat in his red leather slippers, the sherry set out on a little table before the fire. The simple meal was perfectly cooked and served by a devoted elderly housekeeper in the small elegant dining-room to the accompaniment of carefully chosen wines. There were seldom more than three dinner guests, as carefully selected as the liquor. The host's conversation swooped and darted and soared, falling like the wedge-tailed eagle with precise and savage joy on the prey of the mood and hour—perhaps the contemporary London Art Boys for whom he reserved a special brand of Tonksian scorn. And sometimes in the candlelit room, there would emerge a glimpse of the lesser-known Tonks for whom the gilded palazzos of Florence spelled romance. In Tonks' day, conversation—not the casual small talk of today—was still one of the pleasures a civilised Londoner could enjoy at leisure at his own table. When TV has finally put a stop to such happy occasions, Henry Tonks will surely be remembered as a great conversationalist in the same way that Dr Wilmarth Lewis of America, Sir Kenneth Clark and my brother-in-law Lionel Lindsay will be remembered. All were at their best talking together over a few choice bottles in the company of friends.

A frequent dinner guest at the Vale was Tonks' life-long friend and crony Philip Wilson Steer, for many years a valued colleague as Master of Painting at the Slade. Although the two men were at one as to aesthetic aims and ideals they were poles apart in their personal approach to the student at work. It was common knowledge at the school that rather than embarrass an incompetent student Steer would prefer to mutter something quite irrelevant and pass on to the next easel—partly through a natural dislike of a 'scene' partly through sheer kindness of heart. A classic example of this evasive technique in the classroom was his comment—if such it can be called—to a fumbling female student awaiting his verdict on a drawing. After a long painful silence: 'How's your sister?' said Steer and shuffled away. How different to Tonks' often quoted: 'Have you ever done any needlework, Miss S...? Then don't you think you're wasting your time here?' Although Steer had a singularly tolerant approach to painting he just couldn't take some of the more advanced work of the *avant garde*. Looking at an exhibition of Cubist and abstract works, he said, after a long silence: 'I suppose all these painters have private means?'

Steer lived not far away from Tonks in a snug little house overlooking the Thames at Cheyne Walk. Like Tonks, he was ministered to by one of those superb and selfless housekeepers whose destiny seems wholly fulfilled in creating and maintaining the perfect background for the rare spirits under their care. Steer's house was naturally very different in character and general atmosphere to Tonks'; comfortable, homely—even a little stuffy—the owner having a mild phobia on the subject of draughts and fresh air. This, for an English landscape painter who liked to take copious colour notes and when possible paint out of doors, must have been a distinct drawback. On the few occasions when I went to his house, he gave me the impression of being bundled up in several lavers of garments, the ill-fitting jacket on top somehow giving a shawl-like effect, as of a large docile bottle-shouldered baby. Like all great men his quality was universal, unrelated to any particular age.

Afternoon tea at Steer's was brought into a pleasant little drawing-room upstairs, infiltrated with reflected light from the shining surface of the river, by Mrs Raines, the housekeeper of the masterly portrait now at the Tate. There was nothing of Tonks' rather austere eclecticism in the Queen Anne teapot and old English flowery tea service. For Steer, a certain cosy comfort was all important. The walls of the drawing-room were dotted with trivial little Japanese fans, probably collected on some long ago journey to the East, or perhaps a former tribute to the fan-loving painter James McNeill Whistler whom Steer greatly admired. Numerous pairs of boots and odd or beautiful shells completed the décor. Everywhere exquisite casually framed watercolours hung in indifferent lights or, not framed at all, proclaimed the painter's complete lack of personal vanity. His was one of the most self-effacing personalities I have ever met and one of the most compelling. Steer's long comfortable silences, his apt word flung into the talk at exactly the right moment, were just as effective in their way as Tonks' brilliant conversation. When Steer opened his mouth to say something, everyone else at the table stopped talking.

If Tonks were a conversational eagle, Steer was a gently cooing pouter pigeon. Finding himself in a company in which he had no particular wish to talk he would very sensibly close his eyes—not I think because he was bored but from a sort of chronic distaste for unnecessary physical exertion. Nobody who produced such a number of important paintings to say nothing of hundreds of sketches and drawings could be called physically lazy. Steer's manner with 'the ladies' as he would probably have called any women friends, was invariably courteous but I don't think he was particularly easy in their company and was probably much more talkative alone with Daryl or Tonks or their mutual friend the writer George Moore. Tonks himself had a wide circle of friends and for social relaxation moved in a rather worldly milieu of amusing intellectuals that included the painter Vanessa Bell, Bess Norriss (Mrs Nevin Tate, a former pupil) and the celebrated criminal lawyer, St John Hutchinson and his wife, at whose lovely house in Regent's Park we once dined with him. Steer, in contrast to the mobile Tonks, was deliberately static, preferring when not at work in the studio or the Slade, to stay at home and keep warm. Lunching with Tonks one day at Sir Geoffrey Blackwell's country house at Berkhampstead, we were admiring our host's collection of some of Steer's finest oils. It appeared that the artist, well wrapped up, had actually consented to stay at the Blackwells' one summer for a season of serious outdoor painting—a triumph indeed! Steer, who had private means, belonged to that class of Englishmen who have a proper respect for money and can yet be amazingly generous. During the war he lent the British Government a large sum of money free of interest and left an unexpectedly large fortune when he died. He lived simply and well and enjoyed the pleasures of the table. One of his keenest pleasures was shopping and he could often be seen in Church Street on Saturday mornings, with a string bag, looking carefully at the cheese and fruit, or prowling amongst the antique shops where I daresay he relished bargaining for a Greek coin, a Japanese print or a rare piece of Chelsea porcelain. He could afford to live as he pleased and had no use for the well-meant patronage sometimes extended to a painter. Years ago he had allowed us to select for a trifling sum the splendid watercolour that hung in our drawing-room at Mulberry Hill. I can see them now, dozens of unmounted sketches and drawings, scattered all over the drawing-room carpet at Cheyne Walk. 'Just pick your fancy,' said Steer. He was the least possessive of men. Painting was his life and if he wasn't actually working or teaching he was thinking about painting. I once asked him, when he must have been really old, whether he had ever considered writing a book about his life and work? It was a foolish question, to which his answer was perfectly logical: 'You don't know what you're talking about! Why the deuce *should* I write a book? I should hate to! No, no, I'm a painter. I think in *paint*—not *words*.' It was the first time I had ever seen him ruffled out of his customary calm and quite the longest speech I ever heard him make.

The last time I saw Steer was just before the outbreak of war and I was about to go back to Australia. He was nearly blind and I had brought him a pot of white cyclamen whose fragile blooms he touched, very gently, with his square-fingered sensitive painter's hand.

Looking long and often at Steer's richly textured canvasses, in which even the scents and sounds of the English countryside seem imprisoned, the hidden secret beauty of England unfolded for me: slowly, truthfully, just as Steer himself was slow-moving and truthful. Long after, when both our old friends were dead and we were once again in England, a shadow falling across an English meadow, the light on an English cloud could bring them back...Tonks pointing out with a long bony finger, from a passing train, a strangely coloured pool...Steer in his little drawing-room, observing through closed windows the darkening skies above the Thames.

11

THE NEEDLE POINTS HOME

I have never been a really wholehearted lover of travel for its own sake, preferring as I get older and lazier to stay as long as I can in any one place where I am reasonably content in body and mind. Now that our European wanderings are memories to be taken out and looked at now and then as one takes out a book of old photographs on a wet day, I am free to confess that the process known as 'seeing the world' always left me glad to get home again to my own country. Australia was always just below the surface, waiting to break through at absurdly inappropriate moments. In a fogbound London bus, with a sudden nostalgic vision of Fulton's cows drinking from a raspberry vinegar pool at sunset, or a certain kind of north wind, travelling across the paddocks, curling and uncurling the grasses as it went, wave after wave on a brittle yellow sea. A frightening wind, bringing days heavy with the menace of bushfires in the Dandenongs, the garden wilting under a relentless sun. But they were *my* days, to be loved and endured in a way that the gentle green days of an English summer could never be mine. A relative, otherwise unremarkable, used to claim he could feel the pull of the North Pole through his bare feet as he lay in his bed, which he always had set at the correct angle for the magnetic north. My Father thought he was eccentric, but I always have a sneaking sympathy for Great-Uncle Tim because this is exactly the way I felt about Mulberry Hill—a pinpoint in time and space too small to be even marked on a professional map.

One of our happiest homecomings was the year we had made the journey all the way from Tilbury in an Australian cargo boat so heavily laden with explosives that we were not allowed to tie up like ordinary shipping at Port Melbourne Pier. We had to anchor like a plague ship far out in the Bay for fear of bumping against something solid and blowing up the whole thing, passengers and all. In the hold were some of Mr Haines' carefully packed glasses. In rough weather, the passengers were not allowed to dance on deck—we must have been a heavy-footed lot—for fear of dislodging the gelignite underneath. In spite of these minor drawbacks, it had been an uneventful, not to say deadly, voyage.

As we bumped through the Rip and into Port Phillip Bay after eight solid weeks at sea it began to rain. The low-lying Australian coastline with its flat white beaches and little red-roofed houses came and went under a light sea mist out of which the rusty stanchions of the Port Melbourne Pier presently emerged from a clamour of seagulls swooping amongst orange peel and newspaper on the grey choppy sea. Bobbing up and down in the open launch for the last time the few Australian passengers were childishly excited. 'Look! There's South Melbourne Beach! See the Baths!' Somewhere out of the mists an old-fashioned cable tram rumbled along a wide treeless road and Swallow and Ariell's biscuit factory rose up, hideous in a new coat of blue and yellow paint. The rest of the passengers, all English and bound for Sydney or Melbourne, had been up for hours waiting for this first sight of Australia—Land of SUNSHINE and OPPORTUNITY: They were goggle-eyed and rather solemn, as well they might be. For many of them this wet Australian morning was the most significant of their lives. Little Mr Waghorne said, 'Coo! but it's as chilly as London! Should have brought my mac on shore.' None of the migrants had been prepared for Australia being bitterly cold. The accent at Australia House had been all on sunshine. It was Mr Waghorne who particularly wanted to see our 'Tree geranium. They tell me it grows to thirty feet in height in Australia.' There were so many other disappointments in store for the little Cockney that I hadn't the heart to disillusion him. Most of the pleasant hopeful people appeared to have only the vaguest idea of what they were coming to. This of course was long before the days of mass migration—they came not as a last desperate measure but in a spirit of high adventure. Was little Mr Waghorne happily 'assimilated', sucked into the Australian sunshine along with his cheap fibre suitcase, white panama hat, brown shoes and wad of English bank notes? And Miss Gunter in her neat black dress who had asked us: 'This Australian bush we hear so much about—would there be any trees at all? or just bushes?' We never saw any of them again.

It had stopped raining as we drove through Frankston late that afternoon—the beach was deserted, the little seaside town was repeating its usual six o'clock week-day programme. Outside the ugly little brown railway station—since immortalized by Hollywood's *On the Beach*—a chicken farmer friend was loading a tip truck with children and groceries, and Commander Thompson, just arrived from Melbourne on the 5.5 train, was walking briskly down the asphalt ramp with a despatch case under his arm. At the Italian fruit shop opposite, Mr Sanatolia was unhooking a long iron pole from the un-glassed shop front to which were attached big juicy pineapples at a shilling each, while his boy put up the heavy wooden shutters preparatory to closing down for the night. The go-ahead fish and chips shop was still open, ablaze with the latest in mauve Neon lights, but everything else was shut. In summer when visitors stay up half the night on the beaches everyone stayed open—rules and regulations were elastic—and under the pines in the main street people in cars and pony traps stopped at a little whitewashed shop for lemonade and ice-creams on their way home. On the quiet Baxter road lights were coming up in the few houses tucked away in the scrub, where people were sitting down to the evening meal—chops tea tomato sauce scones tinned fruit and jam. No electric light, a few crystal wireless sets. There were practically no weekend houses with permanently-waved ladies sitting on their porches, cocktails in hand. As soon as you left the Post Office corner in Frankston it was country—real country

251

with trees, and birds asleep in them under the quiet night sky. We passed nobody on the road except on the last hill, so slowly that no actual movement was visible to the naked eye, a heavy dray, with Alec Vince fast asleep on the floor, the reins lying over his lap. The Horse who knew its way home blindfold, was probably asleep too.

It was just light enough, as we climbed over our little hill to see the white calico banner stretched above our gate. On it was written in scarlet geraniums and ivy leaves: WELCOME HOME FROM THE BAXTER STATE SCHOOL. It seemed only the other day that Daryl had asked: 'Would you mind very much, Puss, having a state school at our front gate?...' Before leaving for England, we had consulted the Frankston agent about the possibility of letting Mulberry Hill while we were away. He shook his head. 'What about the school next door? Don't the kids make a lot of noise?' To be truthful, they did, sometimes. The busy life hum from the other side of the fence that I had come to love as I did the neat Breughel-like glimpses of the school grounds through the screening trees, the children thick as ants leap-frogging, playing cricket, hopscotch, tops or marbles according to the season, collecting pine cones, sawing wood for the school fires, fighting chasing or drawn up in military formation to salute the Union Jack at the gate.

From time to time on our travels I had posted back to the children a few coloured postcards which the enterprising young schoolmaster had pinned to the school boards, with appropriate captions neatly printed underneath. When he asked me to slip down one morning and give them an informal travel talk I didn't like to refuse although

252

I knew only too well the misery of enforced listening to other people's travels. As soon as I had taken up my stand beside the board of postcards, pointer in hand, every eye in the room had swivelled round in an unwinking stare—the eyes of thirty-five lighthouses dutifully focused on those wretched postcards which they had been looking at every day for most of the year. I had never spoken in public before—not even to children. My mouth went dry and every word I had thought of as I walked across the paddocks dropped out of my head. There were two little girls about three rows from the front with tightly plaited hair and buck teeth, a redhead in a pink jumper, two or three quite big boys at the back. Those lighthouse eyes were still waiting... Suddenly I wasn't nervous at all—I knew exactly how it felt to be ten years old squeezed into a ginger desk in strap shoes and socks that had never gone more than five miles from home. There was nothing to worry about. Anything I was going to tell these children about the Pyramids and Vesuvius and St Paul's Cathedral was absolutely red-hot news. Even those big boys at the back and the sixteen year old sewing teacher in high heeled shoes. I plunged in and hardly drew breath for an hour. Towards the end when quite a lot of the audience had joined in the talk a boy asked, 'What did Vesuvius look like?' I told him to have a look at Mount Eliza on the way home and imagine it with a bushfire and a lot of smoke coming out of a hole on top which was the way I remembered it as we sailed past. I told them that in Egypt the boys wore red felt hats like flower pots upside down and I showed them the fez I had bought in Cairo and the packet of Lux soap flakes with instructions in Arabic lettering. I said everyone used Lux like we did all over the world on washing day, though it wasn't always on a Monday, and this great thought somehow made the whole wide world much smaller and cosier and more real not only for my wonderful little audience but for me. It wasn't in the least like the travel talk I had meant to give or the teacher expected but I think we all enjoyed ourselves. Nowadays when the children of Baxter could have seen the Coronation in Westminster Abbey or a hurricane in Florida, simply by twiddling a knob in their own homes, they probably have a much better knowledge of geography and world affairs in general. I understand that *The Inchcape Rock* is as popular as ever as a school recitation which seems a hopeful sign that Progress has not got completely out of hand. All the same, I suspect that some of the magic has gone out of foreign lands when anyone can go *Round the World in Eighty Days*, in colour, for half a crown.

There had been no more Protest Meetings for several years and no more chair throwing by infuriated parents. The Depression was lifting and with the new prosperity most of the parents had some kind of transport. The problem of the infant marathon walkers was no longer so acute but there was another problem of pressing urgency in the state of the little ginger schoolhouse itself, where the scholars were still condemned to spend a horrifying percentage of their waking hours, alternately sweating or freezing at the anti-quated desks, pockmarked with savage penknife thrusts and defiant daubs of red and black ink. There were not enough windows of course—no school in Australia was properly ventilated at the time ours was built at Baxter—not even the exclusive so-called 'Public' School, where the boys and girls were ruining their eyesight at great expense to their parents in precisely the same stagnant twilight as at the Baxter State School. In winter the one and only classroom was packed like a sardine tin, including the damp fishy smell, with rows of steaming children—the whole school reeked of wet woollen clothing disinfectant eucalyptus ink and blackboard chalk. In summer some of the classes exhausted by the stuffy heat overflowed into a brushwood shelter shed outside where there was more oxygen and more flies. When the summer winds blew from the north the pervading school smell was of hot feet perspiration and dust, and sometimes the aromatic scent of eucalyptus blown on the smoke of a forest fire in the hills. Although the screen of wattle and gum that Daryl had planted when we first came to Mulberry Hill had more or less blotted out the shabby little ginger monstrosity from our private view, it remained an eyesore on the quiet country road.

At last there came a day when the Education Department advised the teacher they were about to repaint the Baxter State School—the same old drab ensemble of stone grey and ginger brown inflicted on every government school in Victoria. Now or never was the time for action! After consultation with the contemporary-minded young teacher, Daryl wrote to the Director of Education offering to choose the school colours, inside and out, to his own taste at his own expense, on condition that the department supplied the labour. To the Director's undying credit and our amazement, this unusual request was granted with the added comment that he would be interested to see what sort of job an artist would make of painting a school. The first thing to do was to paint the whole of the exterior white, with a darkish green trim on roof windows and doors. Daryl had never been impressed by the official argument that 'white shows the dirt', pointing out that nothing could be more depressing than dirty peeling brown. He also stressed the practical point of white being easily matched up by any local tradesman when it began to fade. Inside to the delight of the scholars the dingy walls burst into light primrose yellow, the desks and cupboards a bright china blue. Egged on by teacher we scrapped the works of art thumbtacked to the unlined walls—including the current Prime Minister and a saucer-eyed kitten (both in bow ties)—replacing them with some large gaily coloured posters from the London Underground and an original flowerpiece from the studio at Mulberry Hill. The Education Department was generous in its praise of the transformation. The school never resumed its ginger coat and remained thereafter in sparkling whiteness. For years passers-by on the country road would stop and stare at the unusual spectacle of a state school that looked positively gay.

There was always a horse or two grazing in the school paddock. I like to see them cropping the grass under the open sky where by a miracle of divine creation sheep horses and cattle fit in perfectly with the landscape. I am always thankful that horses are not born blue like the Franz Marc horses that were once the rage in Europe. Nearly all horses are snobs and ours at Mulberry Hill were no exception. There were usually two for us to ride and a farm horse who did all the work about the place and was despised by the other two. Unless the work horse had a vile temper that made the others hang back, it was always the odd man out in the stable routine. Who gets the first bite at the fresh hay, the first nibble at the new grass by the dam, the first drink at the water trough after a hot day? Not poor hard working Whitey, or Browny, or old Rosie, the light draught who used to be driven in a baker's cart, her willing neck dark with sweat from the heavy collar, her furred ankles thick with grass seeds...Handsome thoroughbred Pompey, of course! or N—r, a bossy little ex-polo pony used to being ridden by the gentry and getting the best of everything.

It is one thing to enjoy looking at a nice friendly horse and feeding it handfuls of hay—quite another to actually climb onto its back and ride it. In the course of time I did learn to ride after a fashion and the school children had got used to seeing our little cavalcade passing the schoolhouse. Generally a dog fore and aft, with Daryl on a prancing steed and me trotting along several yards behind like Sancho Panza on his mule. Unless I happened to be mounted on Ginger—the strongest and most terrifying horse I ever had. Tall raw-boned Ginger whom I came in the end to love, who looked like one of those heavy merry-go-round horses with his great crested neck, Roman nose, flaring red nostrils and long yellow teeth. Ginger when he really got going would have pulled my arms out of their sockets rather than slacken his long swinging stride. The only obstacle that could pull him up was a pig—even a pig in the distance, like the pig in the open crate at the Baxter railway station which we were galloping past on the soft going one afternoon. Daryl had already spotted the pig and I could hear his frantic voice behind me, 'Pull him up! For God's sake, pull him up!' I couldn't, of course, and the next thing I knew I was lying flat on my back looking up at a triangle of sky between Ginger's hind legs. He could have flattened me out like a pancake but he was a sensible horse and stood perfectly still. My main trouble out riding was having practically no control over my mount. If the horse ahead decided to gallop, plunge into the scrub or jump a running creek, mine did exactly the same. Poor Daryl, himself a natural horseman of long experience, had wasted hours of patient tuition on a pupil who could never get used to having four unpredictable legs underneath instead of her own two. Even so, I look back with pleasure at our early morning rides, especially in spring when the bush tracks, slanted across with pale pre-breakfast sunlight, were soft and springy under the horses' hoofs, the still dewy branches of wattle and eucalypts brushing their flanks. Wrens and robins fluttered in and out of the sparkling dew-spangled scrub and sometimes a rabbit or a wallaby hopped across the track, making the horses jump out of their skins. Strange to say I hardly ever fell off. Our friend Alosha, a dancer with de Basil's Russian Ballet, had his first experience of horse riding at Mulberry Hill. He was not in the least nervous and after a preliminary bone-shaking jog trot round the school paddock, went off alone down the sandy road where the horse becoming bored with its unconventional rider had broken into a wild gallop and brought Alosha thundering home to the stable yard like Mazeppa pursued by the wolves. When Daryl asked, 'Well, Alosha, how do you like riding?' he said to our amazement: 'I like well the gall*op*, but I like not the half-going!'

A favourite early morning sport invented by Daryl was racing the mail train from Baxter to Langwarrin station. The course lay along the soft-edged bush road skirting the railway line. He had discovered after several near-misses that we had a sporting chance of catching the 8.5 train with our letters if we turned out of the gate at Mulberry Hill at the exact moment when the steam engine left the Baxter station with an earsplitting whistle and began to climb our little hill. The passengers at this early hour were mostly sailors from the Naval Base at Flinders or High School boys and girls bound for Frankston. Very few commuters to the city in those days, and as the man on the big bay horse came into view flying along beside the train the windows were lined with heads and waving hands. Following behind as best as I could—Ginger of course always wanted to be in at the death—I could see the stoker shovelling on coals at the Government's expense and the flash of his white teeth in the firelit cab as the train gathered speed for its final spurt of several hundred yards. The crew of the train entered wholeheartedly into the spirit of the race and after a specially close finish with Pompey belting down the whole length of the gravelled country platform—no gates or railings—the rider leaning over sideways to pass the packet of mail into the outstretched hand of the guard, the passengers would break into a spontaneous cheer. Many years later we were told by a regular passenger on the 8.5 that betting on the event was heavy. At Christmas an amnesty was declared and we arrived on the platform by car in good time with a cargo of bottled beer.

Daryl's life as a practising painter in those diligent country years was a well balanced mixture of two kinds of hard work, indoors and out. There was little time for play in the accepted sense and I can't remember a golf club tennis racquet or pack of cards at Mulberry Hill. An occasional jaunt to Melbourne, a few friends for dinner, a day at the beach and now and then a gymkhana were the highlights of our sporting and social activities.

Although Dick Westy did a lot of the outside work about the place, there were always seasonal jobs like burning off or bringing in the hay in which the whole household lent a hand. A job we both enjoyed was getting in the supply of winter firewood for the house. The working day might begin on a fine autumn morning soon after it was light with a drive in the spring cart through the bush. While Dick and the Boss chopped away in a clearing, I would collect bark and branches for the breakfast fire and when the cart was loaded high with logs all three of us sat down to bacon and eggs, crisp and frizzling in the iron frying pan, smoky toast and billy tea. In a haze of wood smoke, the patient horse stood swishing away the flies, and wrens and yellow robins busied themselves scavenging for grubs and scurrying beetles amongst the shavings of the freshly cut wood. Even now, the smell of bacon frying over an open fire brings back those early morning picnics with the ring of the axe echoing through the bright sparkling silence of the bush, the slow jogging drive home with two of us riding beside the cart, the last spurt uphill in the dam paddock already drying out under the mounting sun, and the grand finale of stacking the logs in the woodshed followed by Mrs Westy's hot scones and morning tea in the kitchen. After which Daryl would retire to the studio to spend the rest of the day painting.

The other day, on the wall of a strange house, I came upon a long forgotten Baxter Bunch. And just as Alice passed through the frame of her looking glass into her private timeless world, so did I find myself back in the garden at Mulberry Hill, knee deep amongst the phlox and petunias in a flower bed that smelled like an enormous bouquet waiting to be gathered under the morning sun.

A portrait painter can be selective only within certain well-defined physiological limits since every human face has two eyes a nose and mouth in varying degrees of beauty and character. Whereas the painter of flowers has an almost limitless botanical choice, from the thousand-petalled daisy lifting its flat disc to the sun to the vertical white kid sheath of the arum lily!

There were certain flowers that Daryl never grew tired of painting at Mulberry Hill: fuchsias and daisies, lilies and lilac, phlox and petunias, to mention only a favourite few, while others remained on a sort of unofficial blacklist which included (to the dismay of rose-loving friends) that much admired but unpaintable flower. And there were a hundred little flowery odds and ends—for us who could never remember their names, anonymous: exquisite fillers-in of a more substantial mixed bunch, that gave detail of grace and gaiety to the whole—tall meadow grasses that ran riot amongst the flowers in spring, tiny buds, fragile clusters of almost invisible trembling bells...

The traditional Dutch flower painters who knew exactly what they were doing, liked striped tulips, large single poppies and now and then a polyanthus complete with meticulous detail of dew-drop, dragon-fly or bee. Every individual painter

261

has his favourites but there are a few flowers that seem to have been classed as unpaintable, at least in Europe, notably that drawing room beauty, the shaggy poodle-headed chrysanthemum. English bluebells, hyacinths and violets are more or less ignored by the academician while even the heather-conscious Scotch boggle at painting that furry purple flower except as a distant background to Highland cattle. Only a few Australians have successfully tackled wattle blossom, The daffodil, an exquisite single bloom pictorially suspect *en masse*, has been sung by generations of English poets including Wordsworth (it nearly gave him a heart attack) nor did Tennyson and Gertrude Stein disdain the rose.

In the studio at Mulberry Hill we discovered that cut flowers have an astonishing range of free movement, turning their heads, slipping in and out of water, drooping, straightening, flinging themselves clean out of the container. Buds open and shut while you wait, or drop off, leaves uncurl. Certain flowers placed in the same vase with incompatibles will keel over and die, while the gentle lily, well known to painters for its persistence in following the light, can wreck a carefully arranged bunch overnight, unless it is stored in a darkened room. The most paintable bunch was often one that hadn't been 'arranged' at all—just a mixed lot of summer flowers hastily picked before breakfast and crammed into a kitchen jug: 'Don't touch it Puss! It's just right like that!' Other days the most painstakingly selected shapes and colours simply wouldn't come and I would be called in as assistant arranger. It was a tricky assignment, as I never knew just what was in the artist's mind—if the finished job was to be dark and richly textured (like the honeysuckle that went to the Riviera) or thin pale and flat. And especially if the flowers themselves were to be painted loosely or tightly. There are so many ways of painting and all of them right. Hoping for enlightenment I would ask 'Is that white camellia the highlight?'

'Heavens. No! It's only an accent!'

'And what about that yellow thing at the back?'

'Oh that...actually I had something greenish in mind...'

I take off my green overall and pin it up behind the skeleton bunch. Approved. The pale pink daisies I can see as a Marc Chagall nosegay charmingly suspended in mid-air, are scornfully tossed out. By the time the camellia (muted in deep shadow) and some white lilac are in place, the two Christmas lilies are facing the door instead of the window. It is as bad as getting the horses lined up at Flemington Racecourse. And, with the floor strewn like a battlefield with dead and dying flowers, cardboard, pieces of coloured silk, the clothes horse from the laundry, the screen from the drawing room, various pots vases scissors and pins, we start all over again. This time, without any more fuss, the whole thing comes beautifully right of itself in a few minutes and the artist is ready to begin painting.

Once settled down at the easel his patience was inexhaustible. Sometimes he would spend a whole day painting and re-painting a single lily bud. On those days silence flowed out of the closed studio like a visible thing, so that Mrs Westy and I unconsciously lowered our voices in the kitchen. At last when the daylight began to fade we would hear the scrape of a chair, the slam of the studio door as he went striding out to the stable yard where Pompey stood waiting, copper coloured in the last glowing light. And throwing a long expert leg across that creature of infinite understanding, he would go trotting off over the school paddock past the dam and into the scrub towards the Langwarrin Camp where the long shadows lay like water on the parched grass and at this quiet hour wallabies and birds crept out to drink at the secret pool. So did my artist rid himself of the evil humours of a working day.

In Europe he had learned a great deal about painting: his own and other people's. He was the first Australian to become a member of the historic Royal Watercolour Society and some of his work was finding its way into private collections and the South Kensington Museum. Harold Wright of Colnaghi's had clients awaiting his next one-man show in Bond Street, and *Punch*, not yet drained of the red blood of the original àBeckett founder, had actually approached him to undertake the traditional weekly Horse Drawing (robust bucolic humour of yokels and gentry, horses and hounds) that had been served up to the Squire at his breakfast table for over fifty years by such fine draughtsmen as Phil May and Raven Hill. Then, too, there was talk of further commissions for the painting of Irish and English horses. One way and another it had become a practical possibility for us to settle indefinitely in London, which seemed to offer boundless opportunities in so many fields. In Australia, he knew, he would miss the stimulating friendships and personal contacts of which I have written in another chapter. And for a painter, there would always be a sense of Australia's isolation from the great European galleries, reached from London in a few hours.

Daryl had always striven and would go on striving to be a good painter. Beyond this I think he had little personal ambition and such worldly plums as came his way were seldom of his own seeking. He knew now that the things he most wanted to paint were in his own country—the lonely men of the outback, Australian cattle and horses, the desolate plains where he had spent much of his youth. Sitting out on the porch on fine starry nights at Mulberry Hill, we could watch the Southern Cross traced in diamonds against the deep indigo sky of the Australian night that is like no other deep blue night in the world. Gradually it fell away towards the south, over the dark mass of the orchard. These were our stars...Long ago, when it was suggested that Daryl should try for the directorship of a provincial English gallery, Tonks had told him: 'Don't touch it, my boy! Go back and keep your brains for your own country. It may need them.'

1 2

THROUGH THE COURTYARD DOOR

The house had been painted pink with white trimmings and green shutters. The lemon scented gum threw an afternoon shadow across the sundial and the children passing underneath on their way home from school. The mulberry tree had grown so big that Russell Grimwade had cunningly tied the heaviest branches together with supporting chains. Even so, people coming in and out of the courtyard in the mulberry season were liable to be spattered with the purple juice of the dropping fruit.

Of all the friends who walked through the little green door in the courtyard, none was more eagerly awaited, more joyously met, than Lionel. It was an occasion for a serious session beforehand in the cellar, when my brother-in-law was expected on one of his rare visits from Sydney. Lionel who knew the finer points of vintage port old brown sherry and the French and German wines he had learned to love in Europe could be as eloquent on a cup of coffee as a magnum of champagne, and I sometimes suspected he found the ruby glow of the glasses, the conversation and candlelight more important than the wine. Faced with the practical necessity of taking a mouthful of chicken or a sip of claret and thereby interrupting the flow of talk at the dinner table it was often easier simply to go on talking. ('You know Joe, conversation today is a lost art') when eventually a desperate female hand would snatch away his plate, substituting cheese for untouched chicken, port or brandy for scarcely tasted wine. Relaxed and happy at a dinner party, I have seen him skip at least three courses blissfully unawares. At Cruden Farm one day, lunching with Keith and Elisabeth Murdoch, the host suddenly turned on Lionel, who was entertaining a delighted audience at his end of the long table, before a plate of untouched strawberries and cream. 'Lionel, you have picked up that strawberry nine times already and put it down again. I have been counting. Do you want Edith to take them away?' The parlourmaid giggled shyly, Lionel gave her one of his sweetest smiles, lifted the strawberry to his mouth for the tenth time and went on talking.

With Lionel in the house there was never any question of organised entertainment. As a guest, he provided his own and everyone else's. From the moment he stepped out of the train at Baxter he was on the ball, stopping for a word or two with the stationmaster, patting the dog, waving to old Mr Fulton cutting his hedges by the roadside. He was interested in everything, indoors and out, and no detail was too small to be observed and registered, so that twenty years later the way a certain dog wagged its tail or our Rhode Island rooster stood up to crow was still card-indexed in that amazing storehouse of visual memories.

One wet Saturday afternoon, he arrived at Baxter by train and Daryl met him at the station with the jinker in a deluge of spring rain. In macintosh and jaunty black beret, swinging a string bag containing pyjamas and a couple of Spanish paperback classics which he had been reading in the train, a woollen muffler tossed around his throat, he burst steaming and dripping into the sitting-room, where the Who-Dunit sisters Margot and Neville were sitting by the fire. I hadn't seen him since a recent illness and as he stood in the open doorway simultaneously skinning himself out of a dripping coat, unwinding the muffler from his neck, throwing the string bag to the floor and clasping me in a warm embrace, he went straight to the matter in hand. 'My God, the adhesions old girl!…the purging…You know, this business of stitches is the devil…' Then turning gallantly to the astonished sisters: 'Oh excuse me! Of course—delighted to meet you, Mrs Neville, and you too, Miss Margot. You write? The French…Superb artist Flaubert…*Madame Bovary*…greatest masterpiece of all time. Have you ever had your appendix removed, Miss Goyder?'

Still dripping and steaming, he moved one step nearer the fire while the howling gale blew in from the courtyard through the open door. 'A fire! Splendid! Thank you, dear. Yes, I'm low, very low. Tell you later what I suffered in Sydney. My God, those adhesions!' I had been trying to steer him to a seat by the fire, but he was sidetracked by the Wilson Steer watercolour on the other side of the room.

'I envy you that, old girl. Nobody like Steer for a free flowing wash!'

I had almost manoeuvred him into a comfortable chair by the fire when he put an urgent hand on my shoulder. 'All very well to talk about Cézanne.' (Nobody at the moment was further from my thoughts.) 'Old Turner was the Daddy of them all!' He kissed his hand to Turner who immediately seemed to have joined the party and to be standing beside us at the tea table. Meanwhile Daryl, who had unharnessed the horse and put the jinker away had joined us, ravenous for Mrs Westy's hot scones. 'Joe, aren't you going to get out of those wet clothes? You're soaking!' But Lionel held up this time by the Tonks drawing had forgotten all about the adhesions and was just getting into his stride. 'Did you say tea?...Splendid! I was just saying to these girls...'

'For Heaven's sake, Joe, let's have some tea. We've got all night to talk and I've got a damn good Burgundy for dinner.'

Lionel was looking better every minute. In spite of various minor physical ills throughout his long life, he was blessed with the magnificent Lindsay constitution. A meeting between these two brothers was a mutual tonic. For Lionel, especially, the right kind of talk revived him mentally and physically as water revives a drooping plant, so that he would reluctantly finish a really late session with the clear skin and bright eyes of youth. He hated to go to bed before midnight and would wake up lively as a cricket and ready to take up last night's conversation exactly where it had left off. I remember bringing him an early cup of tea when he was still fast asleep, flushed and rosy as a child,

269

but he immediately opened an alert blue eye. 'Thank you, no sugar…as we were saying old girl, the French are without sentimentality…What time shall I get up? Not yet? Then please hand me that book over there.' It was a Chinese dictionary. He must have been over seventy at the time. He had been studying Chinese during a protracted convalescence and had proudly told us that after two years he had 'just mastered the numerals'. The rare combination of exuberant vitality and unlimited patience was a characteristic of all the Joes.

There are many fine scholars in the world but few who could talk as Lionel talked, holding his audience spellbound under the sheer magic of the spoken word. To quote his lifelong friend and admirer R. G. Menzies: 'Lionel Lindsay is a master of divine and disorderly conversation.' And that, I think, is how those of us who loved him best will always remember him.

Nobody was more appreciative of good company than Menzies, who as Australia's Prime Minister must have talked, gossiped and dined with some of the best company in the world. A snatched hour at the artist's home in Wahroonga was a happy escape now and then from the pressure of mundane affairs. For Menzies of the diamond-hard legal mind, whose consuming passions were politics football and the law, art had always held a strange fascination, as it did for Sir Frederick Jordan, Chief Justice of New South Wales, another of Lionel's close friends.

Some years before Mr Menzies had stepped into the blaze of world publicity that illuminates his every action today, he and his wife had called in on us at Mulberry Hill.

The natural sweet-faced girl who later became Dame Pattie, launched ships and cut ribbons on bridges, performed her endless public duties with the same unaffected gaiety and grace with which she had squatted that day with Bob and the children for tea on our studio floor. They had been on a family picnic to the beach and the rather shabby black car was piled with children and dogs. From the studio window I could see Papa walking up the path from the sundial leading a little girl by the hand. A somewhat portly figure even then, and firm of tread. It was common knowledge amongst his contemporaries that seventeen year old Bob Menzies had confided to his partner at a Melbourne dance: 'Some day I'm going to be Prime Minister of Australia.'

Two other old friends destined like the Menzies to make news in the world's headlines, jointly and in their own right, were Dick and Maie (now Lord and Lady) Casey. Soon after their marriage in England they had returned to Australia and came down to see us at Mulberry Hill. Dick at the time was an ardent admirer of Stanley (later Lord) Bruce, then living in a large white-elephant of a house set down rather inconsequently amongst the tea-tree scrub at Langwarrin. Maie, an expert rider since childhood, was always glad to get a mount in the country. While Dick was enjoying long cosy chats with Bruce about Tariff Reform and the price of tin, Daryl had lent her a high-spirited little mare on which she arrived one afternoon at Mulberry Hill wearing flannel slacks, a neat little navy blue jacket with brass buttons and a large shady straw hat to protect her flawless complexion from the Australian sun. How pretty she was! The calm flowerlike face that could break so easily into slightly ribald laughter, set in a cloud of dusky hair. Like Bob Menzies—perhaps one of the few attributes they shared outside political life—Dick never looked really countrified even in old clothes. I remember him in those days at the wheel of a powerful car. A few years later the Caseys took to the air like ducks to water, expertly piloting their own plane. It was their natural element. They adored speed for its own sake and even the domestic tempo of their everyday lives seemed to progress at a quicker rate than other people's. They moved fast, ate and talked fast, and gave an impression of living at high tension even on holiday at Barwon Heads when the afternoon siesta at the seaside guest house was often shattered by the crack of rifle fire as the tireless Caseys blazed away at a target in a nearby field. In our sitting-room at Baxter one day, Dick, then at the cross roads of his personal career, rich, intelligent, bent on harnessing his dynamic energy to something really worthwhile, had said to Daryl: 'You know those linocut things Maie is always talking about? They rather interest me. Quite seriously, I'm thinking of taking them up myself.' Soon afterwards he took up not linocuts but politics and a career of selfless service that left him little leisure for anything but the job on hand.

Maie, ever since I had first met her at one of those exclusively female Melbourne parties that both of us hated, always had a full social background. A unique power of concentration and boundless enthusiasm enabled her no matter where she found herself—an art students' camp at Mount Macedon or Government House in Bengal— to write paint and draw. Before either of us was married we had shared a studio in Bourke Street somewhere near Spencer Street Station—not a party-giving studio but a big dusty room—it never entered our heads to dust it—where in frenzied bursts of amateur energy we really worked away at our drawing. We even wrote a book together about a ballet dancer called Anna, for which Maie had drawn a spirited portrait of the heroine in red blue and yellow chalks. We were uninhibited by knowing practically nothing about ballet (although Maie had once been in Vienna) which gave us scope for a colourful background of throbbing romance. When we got bored with the illustrations for *Anna* or painstakingly drawing Miss Minty—a professional model who only consented to sit if the poses were not what she called 'rude'—we would take our 'Greyhounds' (packets of cheap coloured chalks) and go off somewhere by tram to sketch out of doors. It must have been about this time that Dick and Daryl made their respective appearances. Both came now and then to the studio but visitors were not much encouraged—we were more interested in *Anna*. Poor Dick must have felt heartily sick of *Anna* who was liable to get a new lease of life whenever her creators got together over the next ten years. At Mulberry Hill one year we made an entirely new version—still colourful, still throbbing with passion but not quite so many adjectives!

We had the house to ourselves and somebody in the kitchen to get us a meal when we felt hungry. We wrote as usual on the floor, in front of a large fire. When Daryl came home, he found us in the drawing-room with a note pinned to the non-ticking Sèvres clock on the mantelpiece: Twenty past four. He told Dick afterwards: 'Those two are crazy! They put a notice on the clock and when they think it's an hour, or half an hour later, they put up another!' Crazy or not, for people without trains to catch or appointments to keep, our system worked very well. Besides there were always the bees, in permanent residence over the side door, whose planned comings and goings are more reliable than any clock; only you must, of course, understand bee language to make full use of their talents. Daryl and I had got quite used over the years to their zooming around the porch, but our visitors were not always immune and an elderly Englishman, a relation of Hamilton Russell's, who had come to tea one Sunday, was stung, to our shame and sorrow, on his shining pink scalp. I had just removed the almost invisible tiny black sting and was about to throw it away when he laid a restraining hand on mine: 'No, please! Allow me to put it in my pocketbook as a memento of a delightful afternoon in the Australian country.' Nobody at Mulberry Hill had ever reacted to a bee sting with such disarming courtesy.

Old Hammie himself, now more absent-minded than ever, turned up at Baxter now and then, still driving his own car. To travel as a passenger with Hammie at the wheel called for exceptional gifts of patience and physical bravery, Hammie being not only a fast but thoroughly bad driver. If the old man were in one of his silent moods with the sad blue eyes fixed on some far distant horizon, he would sail all unconscious past frustrated traffic cops and street lights. Once when he was driving Daryl on the Sandringham Road, the passenger ventured to bring the driver down to earth with a question concerning a mutual friend in England. There was no reply and the nerve-racking progress continued for another eight miles by the speedometer before it came, precise and tactful: 'As far as I know, my boy, he was transferred to the London Hospital.' It was impossible to assess just where Hammie's vagueness left off and the clear vision that had solved so many surgical problems took over. Perhaps because of Daryl's family background, we seem always to have numbered the medical profession amongst our friends. Another distinguished Melbourne surgeon, Dr Julian Smith, would like Hammie appear at our door now and then when the spirit moved him. (Hammie, expected to lunch one Sunday at Mulberry Hill, had appeared, long after the roast beef had been put away in despair, urbane and charming at four o'clock.) Dr Julian Smith, with his dark clothes, his big round spectacles and rakish soft felt hat, and the wiry little vandyke beard which he had a trick of pulling into his mouth and chewing at the ends, was something of an eccentric and a well-known figure in Melbourne's social life. Nobody could be more charming to the ladies at a party, unless he happened to be bored or thinking of something more interesting—his next operation at the Mercy Hospital or a new gadget for his camera. As an amateur photographer of professional skill and status, he was inclined to take the art of photography rather too seriously for a painter's liking, so that when Daryl at last reluctantly consented to sit for his portrait I sensed trouble ahead. The pernickety little doctor would never condescend to waste time on a hit-or-miss job, and as usual that day everything had been thought out long beforehand, with the victim dressed up in a rather embarrassingly special attire. After sitting as directed for half an hour or so on a high stool with a handkerchief carefully knotted about his neck, Daryl had lost patience and begun wandering about the studio when the photographer, still busy with lights and curtains, had flown into one of his nervous tantrums. Turning to me (by a miracle I had been allowed to be present at the taking), he said: 'I don't know how you put up with that man! He's impossible!' However we were used to such little outbursts and presently the actual photography got under way under a crossfire of mutterings, curses sighs groans cries of encouragement and despair, in all of which the model was a belligerent protagonist. I don't think any of us were much surprised when the resulting proofs were far from the doctor's best work. In all things temperamental, he must have been a difficult man to cater for in the home, even for his highly capable wife, who once told me that her husband insisted on being served at lunch in East Melbourne with a choice of sixteen different dishes of stewed fruit—presumably uncrunchable. He had once prefaced an invitation to Daryl to lunch with: 'Do you like toast? Then don't expect it for lunch because I can't stand the sound of people crunching the stuff!' Arriving unexpectedly one day with Mrs Smith and the children he found us at tea with nothing to eat but crumpets, which he declined almost with relish! 'I *hate* crumpets...' I mention these trifling eccentricities because they gave Dr Julian his unique flavour. Behind the rather petulant façade he was a good clever and kindly man, mourned by thousands of friends and patients when he died.

For several years during the thirties Daryl was a member

of the T-Square Club—a lively group of architects and a sprinkling of painters who met together to talk drink and dine, but mostly to talk. One can imagine Melbourne's ornate State Theatre coming under fire, discussion of Annear's latest Neo-Georgian mansion or Bob Hamilton's Elizabethan shopping centre in Toorak. At every dinner an individual member would be asked to speak on a special topic. They were some of the best minds of the day, and I hope some record has been preserved of their uncensored commentaries on the growing city of Melbourne in the thirties.

An informal T-Square dinner was held one year in the studio at Mulberry Hill, with the guests sitting on wooden forms borrowed from the Baxter school, at long trestle tables lit by two hanging kerosene lamps. The simple country food, washed down by plenty of fresh air laughter burgundy and beer, was acclaimed as a change from the more sophisticated urban menus of the club. Mrs Westy produced cold roast beef—was ever beef so tender as those big juicy sirloins of Jim Hearne's?—our own potatoes baked in their jackets, our own green salads home-made pickles and our 'potage de la maison', a speciality of Mulberry Hill. On the floor behind the diners were placed zinc-lined wash tubs full of ice and bottles—none of your niggling ice-cubes—but big chunks of ice brought all the way from Chelsea. There was still no electricity in Baxter although, like the removal of the Baxter School, it was expected 'any time now'. The peak of the evening's entertainment was reached when Harold Herbert rose to speak but lost his footing and fell over backwards into the ice tub behind him. He was rescued by John Longstaff, whom I had watched from an upstairs window arriving in his well-cut dress clothes, looking like a high-ranking ambassador bound for an official reception. A carefully preserved waistline, social poise and a natural Edwardian charm, made him a distinguished figure in any company. No women were allowed at the T-Square dinners, and near midnight when the sounds of revelry were wafted through the open windows below, I stole downstairs to see for myself, through the pantry keyhole, how the feast was progressing. My curiosity was rewarded at the foot of the staircase by tripping over what appeared to be a large faintly groaning parcel wrapped in a rug—an unfortunate guest who had passed out in the garden earlier in the evening, advised by Daryl to lie down in the privacy of the cool dark hall until the party was over. As far as I know there were no other casualties although when the last cars turned into the drive a few early rising magpies joined in the goodnights at the courtyard door.

A diner-out of the older generation who sometimes attended the T-Square dinners—whether as a member or not I don't know—was Blamire Young, then at the height of his popularity as a watercolourist. Blamire's romantic watercolours were so watery that the rich reds and blues, purples and greens, that he loved seemed to be literally dripping from the coarse grained paper, like honey from a piece of bread: an effect quite arbitrarily achieved by the artist tipping the paper this way and that before the paint had actually sunk in. In this way he often brought off the decorative colour notes eagerly sought by Australian collectors bored with too much pseudo-impressionism or the realistic tonal school of the so-called Meldrumites.

Blamire spent a week-end with us at Mulberry Hill—a soft-voiced amiable citizen of the world with a pretty wit and nice taste in wines. He dressed well after his individual fashion and was one of the last of Melbourne's spat-wearing fraternity, which included Russell Grimwade and Stanley Bruce. He liked our dining-room by candlelight and said of one of Daryl's more formal flower paintings: 'Of course, my dear Daryl, this is a true *dining-room picture*', a phrase I have always treasured. Like my Mother and her Professor, he preferred his scenery from the fireside and hardly stepped out into the spring sunshine of the courtyard during the weekend. He enjoyed a day out at the races and I daresay some of the ladies who doted on his ethereal watercolours would have been surprised to see him, as I did, looking rather like an expurgated edition of Maurice Chevalier, debonair in hard straw hat and yellow gloves, operating a highly complicated betting system of doubles and trebles at Caulfield. Still more surprised would they have been to learn that he had started off his career as a brilliant mathematician at Cambridge. He was a voracious reader and had written a scholarly book on the cartoons of Goya. At Baxter I galloped that week-end through Joyce's *Ulysses*, which our guest had somehow got hold of before it was banned in Australia. Painting was only one of a variety of interests. He was something of a dilettante: enjoying the graces of life, savouring old china, copper warming pans and Maeterlinck's *Blue Bird*. In short he belonged spiritually and mentally to another age. His was a minor artistic talent and if the critics took it too seriously as a major contribution to Australian art, the artist, surely, cannot be held responsible!

An important painter and old friend of much the same vintage as Blamire, who lived to a very great age and produced an incredible number of paintings sketches and drawings, was Rupert Bunny. For Bunny, the natural beauty of sea and sky, mountain and plain, a woman's rosy flesh gleaming through a muslin dress, held an almost painful joy. A shy sensitive creature was Rupert with his quick endearing smile, and gentle diffident manner, always in a stiff white collar—a barricade of starched linen between his shyness and the outside world. I had shaken hands with him once, as a little girl, when he had brought his elegant French wife to lunch with my Mother at St Kilda. For the greater part of his painting life however he had lived and worked out of Australia in France, a country which he passionately loved. It was not surprising that he was more widely recognised in France than in his own country, when he returned there to settle down for the rest of his life. Actually he had little personal vanity beyond a deep pride in his calling. He was convinced that artists were the salt of the earth, and with him art was everything. He lived very simply and was perfectly satisfied so long as he could remain independent and free to go on painting. When his first one-man exhibition in Melbourne after his return failed to attract the practical support of the public, he would ask, not in anger but with the naïve bewilderment of a child: 'What do they *want*? What *do* they want?' He was greatly heartened by the efforts of Daryl, George Bell and a group of other Victorian painters who actively sought his public recognition, in the Press and elsewhere. Like so many painters of prodigious output, he was hopelessly lacking in self-criticism and in the various studios which he occupied in old age could be found brilliant sketches and studies in oils, chalks and watercolours rolled up in corners or walked over on the floor. Others which in the opinion of painter friends were in no way comparable in quality were carefully framed. Although he did now and again go to a party or dine with relatives or friends, we liked best to entertain him alone, when he would talk to us freely about painting and painters, or perhaps with his great friend Basil Burdett who had a special sympathy and understanding of Bunny's work. Basil, who later became the art critic for the Melbourne *Herald*, was often with us at Mulberry Hill. He had a good deal more of what is commonly called 'artistic temperament' than most practising painters. An unexpected meeting with a loved friend, a Bach piano recital, the modest purchase of a drawing for his collection, a new ballet, could carry him away on a fifth dimensional wave of pure joy, for hours afterwards a shining-eyed changeling living and breathing in a new element. A trifling mishap could send him just as quickly to the lower depths. He suffered, too, from a chronic double-barrelled nostalgia for both sides of the world that kept him restlessly on the move. We never knew when we would find him sunk in one of his fits of yearning for England Italy or his adored Spain. One day when we were lunching gaily in the courtyard with unaccustomed festivity of chicken strawberries and white wine our guest suddenly put down his glass and with a woebegone glance at the blue Australian sky through the leaves of the pear tree over our heads almost groaned: 'Oh if *only* we were in Barcelona!'

Certain people were closely woven into the texture of our lives at Mulberry Hill, appearing and reappearing at varying intervals: sometimes the threads were sombre, sometimes gay, but somehow completing and embellishing the main design. Such were the Murdochs. When we first came to live at Baxter, Keith, still a bachelor and living mainly at his house in town, had just bought Cruden Farm a few miles away from us, at Langwarrin. Even, then, he must have had the urge for a domestic base. The tradition of family life in his background was strong. The son of a Presbyterian minister of moderate means and a large family, young Keith had made an immediate mark in the newspaper world. His was in some ways the typical success story. Nothing could hold him back in his chosen career. In no time he was making money and could afford to indulge a growing taste for the best of everything in the way of furniture glass old silver, cars horses and wines. In this apparently effortless gravitation towards ultimate connoisseurship, he was probably influenced to some extent by his friendship with Nellie Melba, who for her part no doubt enjoyed advising the impressionable, rather shy, ambitious young man obviously with the world before him, criticising his latest purchase and casting a shrewd eye over the prices. Keith had brought Melba to tea at Mulberry Hill one day, and she had taken one of her spontaneous likings for the simple country house. 'Tell me, you two, if ever you want to sell! This is just the sort of place I'd like to retire to some day!' In her exuberant way, she ran about on her high heels looking at everything. She adored tiny frivolous pieces, as I did, and later gave me, from her collection at Coombe Cottage, an exquisite little Sèvres box.

Cruden Farm was not a bachelor dwelling for long. It was soon infused with life and laughter by Keith's young wife Elisabeth and a brood of enchanting children. With Keith's horizons ever-widening, the original one-storied dwelling was only a stepping stone, and Desbrowe Annear was called in to transform it with a Georgian portico and big open fireplaces into a commodious country house in the American Colonial style. Handsome stone stables with cast iron fittings from the demolished Crotonhurst stables of our mutual friend Bill Langdon, gave character to the grounds, newly laid out with sunken garden, tennis courts and rockeries, and planted with an avenue of white-stemmed eucalypts leading to the front gate. Although the Murdochs lived most of the year at Heathfield—a splendid boom-time mansion in Toorak, where they did their formal entertaining—it was at Cruden Farm that the whole family had their fullest flowering. At the farm we watched the children growing up, Helen and Rupert learning to fish and ride and swim, Anne and Janet getting through chickenpox and measles. Sometimes we joined them at a gymkhana or a picnic at Point Leo, then a wild almost deserted beach; when Keith, lying full length on the yellow sand, tipped his hat over his eyes, forgot the *Herald* office and for those few glorious sun-drenched hours became the family man. If only he had lived in the eighteenth century—a period in which he would have been very much at home—what a splendid subject he would have made for a conversation piece by Joseph Highmore: 'The Murdoch Family at their Country Seat', with Keith in a Georgian arm-chair dandling the latest infant on an elegant silken knee.

The Murdochs out riding on Sunday mornings made an unforgettable spectacle—a sort of medieval cavalcade of children, servants, outriders, horses and dogs—along the rough tree-lined roads of Baxter and Langwarrin. At the head of the gay motley procession rides Keith, mounted on a massive charger, an upright rather heavily-built figure immaculate in English tweed and riding, boots; proud and happy, as well he might be, in the company of his lively affectionate brood, enjoying the sights and scents of the bush tracks, the anticipation of an excellent midday dinner with claret and roast beef at Cruden Farm. Beside him rides Elisabeth, slim and fearless, sometimes on a half-wild racehorse liable at any moment to bolt the last few miles to the home stables. Friends and children rode animals of varying quality according to their skill and experience— 'Auntie Marie', game to the last hair of her head, would ride anything on four legs, shaggy ponies begged or borrowed for extra children, stock horses spelling from a drought-stricken station, a quiet hack or two reserved for timid house guests. Sometimes Daryl would join the procession at our cross-roads, perhaps on Pompey or Mickey the flighty Arab brought up on the treeless northern plains, who would dance halfway across the sunflecked track at the mere shadow of a leaf. Amongst the riders could occasionally be seen poor Basil Burdett, who hating and fearing all horses, jogged his unhappy way on a solid little old pony, with his long legs almost touching the ground, and once (in a macintosh cape and black beret) looking remarkably like the Friar from Chaucer's *Canterbury Tales*. And lastly, alert and loving in the rear, 'Kimpo' the adored English governess, on horseback with the younger children or driving the pony cart, with little tow-headed Rupert bouncing up and down on Joy Boy the miniature Shetland, a present from Godfather Daryl, attached by a leading rope to the tail board.

Keith will not ride our quiet country lanes again but the pattern continues, with other happy children and other Joy Boys, equally cunning, belaboured and beloved.

Another summer was slipping away. Friends came and went through the courtyard door, the mulberries ripened and fell in purple stains on the grass, Mrs Westy baked her usual sponge cake for Daryl's birthday. The garden was full of Christmas lilies and one morning I picked them all—far more than I could ever arrange in the house or Daryl hope to paint. It didn't matter: there would always be flowers at Mulberry Hill.

Nothing told us there would be no more lilies to pick for a long long time, that my flower garden would become a wilderness of weeds, that the house would soon be standing empty and silent, the shutters closed on cool empty rooms. Our time without clocks was passing...had already passed...Summer ended abruptly with the Present spilling over into the Past almost overnight. The Future had crept upon us unawares and we set out to live it under the batswing shadow of the Government Clock.

Text Classics

textclassics.com.au